he spends 2 entire chapters (2+3) on absence of a 'criterion of demarcation' in EEOC guidelines

Q: can a law be justified w/o being morally justified?
A. p. 41

Pickering's examples bear out his analysis (& mine): aim seems to be to outlaw anything that might be upsetting to a woman - even a look.
Problem of infinite regress.

Only chap 3 has a "Conclusion": others don't

To Professor Patai,
with respect for her
work in this area,
[illegible]

The Law of Sexual Harassment

The Law of Sexual Harassment

A Critique

Mane Hajdin

SUP

Selinsgrove: Susquehanna University Press
London: Associated University Presses

Associated University Presses
440 Forsgate Drive
Cranbury, NJ 08512

Associated University Presses
16 Barter Street
London WC1A 2AH, England

Associated University Presses
P.O. Box 338, Port Credit
Mississauga, Ontario
Canada L5G 4L8

The paper used in this publication meets the requirements of the American National Standard for Permanence of Paper for Printed Library Materials Z39.48-1984.

Library of Congress Cataloging-in-Publication Data

Hajdin, Mane.
The law of sexual harassment : a critique / Mane Hajdin.
p. cm.
Includes bibliographical references and indexes.
ISBN 1-57591-058-6 (alk. paper)
1. Sexual harassment—Law and legislation—United States. 2. Sex discrimination in employment—Law and legislation—United States. 3. Sex discrimination in education—Law and legislation—United States. I. Title.
KF3467 .H34 2002
344.7301'4133—dc21 2002020834

PRINTED IN THE UNITED STATES OF AMERICA

Contents

Acknowledgments 7

1. Sexual Harassment and Other Problems 11
2. The Demarcation Problem 42
3. Demarcation and Reasonableness 72
4. How Much Is Too Much? 102
5. Sexual Harassment and Freedom of Speech 131
6. A Tale of Two Levels 154
7. Sexual Harassment and Discrimination 172
8. Alternatives 213

Notes 225
Bibliography 255
General Index 263
Index of Cases Cited 267

Acknowledgments

Some of the research on which this book is based was conducted while I was a visiting scholar at the Center for the Study of Law and Society of the University of California, Berkeley, on leave from the Department of Philosophy of the University of Waikato. I am grateful to both institutions for making that research possible.

This book incorporates the material that appeared in volume 25 of the *Journal of Social Philosophy*, under the title "Sexual Harassment in the Law: The Demarcation Problem," and in volume 28 of the same journal, under the title "Sexual Harassment and Negligence." That material is reprinted by permission of *Journal of Social Philosophy*.

The Law of Sexual Harassment

1
Sexual Harassment and Other Problems

The Law and the Public

Since its appearance on the scene in the mid-seventies, there has been continuous strengthening of the law about sexual harassment. Until the nineties, the creation and strengthening of the sexual harassment law were largely unopposed. There was no genuine public debate about the law that would be comparable to the debates that accompany any changes or proposed changes in the law about, say, abortion, or affirmative action, or pornography, or gun control.

Whatever one's opinion about sexual harassment, one should be puzzled by this lack of public debate. One would not normally expect a body of law on such subject matter to get so firmly entrenched with such ease. After all, the law about sexual harassment affects (or attempts to affect) the day-to-day lives of almost all of us, in an area that most of us are very sensitive about, that of our sexuality. It would therefore seem reasonable to expect its strengthening to have been surrounded by a public debate at least as vigorous as the public debates about abortion or pornography.

It was only in 1991, after the rules about sexual harassment had been a well-established part of the U.S. legal system for some time, that some kind of public debate about it was triggered by the scandal that surrounded the appointment of Clarence Thomas to the Supreme Court. Since then, we have seen a few more bursts of public debate about sexual harassment, notably at the time when the movie *Disclosure,* based on Michael Crichton's novel of the same title, was released, and at various points in Paula Jones' pursuit of her sexual harassment claim against President Clinton. But although there were moments in the nineties when the debate about sexual harassment was vigorous, it has never been as articulate and as structured as the debates on comparable issues of public policy.

One partial, but only partial, explanation of why there was very little public debate about sexual harassment at the time when the crucial developments in the law about it were taking place is that the law is largely a creation of the judiciary. The law about sexual harassment was not created through a debate and vote in the Congress. It is normally the consideration of a proposed new law by a legislative body that gives the principal impetus to the public debate about the underlying issues, but no such impetus was available when the sexual harassment law came into being. The law about sexual harassment sneaked into existence quietly on 20 April 1976 in a decision of the federal district court for the District of Columbia.[1] The decision was, technically, merely an application of a statute that the Congress did vote on some twelve years earlier, but the content of the decision was probably beyond the wildest speculation of the people who voted for that statute. There is thus a clear intuitive sense in which the decision amounted to creation of a new law. But, despite the decision's novelty, only a handful of people could have appreciated its potential significance at the time when it was rendered.

Another aspect of the law that may help to explain why much of its development was accompanied by relatively little public debate is that the development was very gradual. Numerous judicial decisions about sexual harassment have been rendered since 1976, and the current shape of the law is a cumulative effect of these decisions. As more and more decisions appeared, the law became more and more elaborate and the range of conduct covered by it kept getting wider. These developments were, however, made in many small steps: there was no one judicial decision about sexual harassment that was, on its own, obviously revolutionary in the way in which, for example, the famous judicial decisions about abortion or affirmative action were. Because of that, there was, until the Thomas/Hill scandal, no specific event that would have provided an occasion for public debate.

A related aspect of the federal law about sexual harassment is that the Supreme Court was, until recently, not very active in shaping it. It took the development of the sexual harassment law ten years to reach the Court. In 1986, the Court made one decision that, by and large, endorsed the developments that had taken place in the appellate and district courts up to that point.[2] After that, the Court again became silent on the topic until 1993. It was, in fact, only in 1998 that the Court started playing a more active role in shaping the sexual harassment law. That the Supreme Court was, until recently, relatively uninvolved in the development of the law about sexual harassment, again implies that there was a shortage of decisions that would have focused public attention on the law.

One of the many disturbing things that the Thomas/Hill scandal revealed was that many Americans were, up to that point, simply not aware of what the law about sexual harassment really was. Many people voiced their opinion about the issue of sexual harassment for the first time in October 1991, simply because it was then that they became, for the first time, aware of what was involved. This ignorance can partially be explained by the aspects of the law's development that were described above, but that doesn't seem to be a fully satisfactory explanation.

What makes that ignorance specially puzzling is that it is one of the features of the law about sexual harassment that it makes it advisable for employers to provide their employees with "training" about sexual harassment. Many employers faithfully tried to do that, and a whole industry sprang into existence to assist their efforts. Dedicated professionals organized "training" programs about sexual harassment; videos about it were produced and screened as part of such programs; posters, leaflets, and brochures about it were printed and widely disseminated. Almost every employed American was exposed to some form of such "training," many of them several times. One wonders how these carefully designed programs, which were well in place by 1991, could have been so unsuccessful, that so many people began to understand the law about sexual harassment only after the Thomas/Hill scandal broke out.

Part of the explanation is probably that the media coverage of sexual harassment at the time of the scandal was genuine journalism, while the "training" about it to which one gets exposed in connection with one's employment is, after all, something that is imposed "from above," and thus has a certain air of artificiality about it, no matter how skillfully designed it might be. Many people sense that, and that leads them to switch their attention off.

A more important part of the explanation, however, has to do with some features of sexual harassment itself. The conduct that is currently labeled "sexual harassment" overlaps with many kinds of conduct that most people had regarded as wrong before they heard the phrase "sexual harassment" for the first time. Sexual harassment often involves adultery, promiscuity, gross insensitivity, abuse of institutional power, and so forth—kinds of conduct that most people have always thought of as wrong. When one is, within a "training" program, presented with an example of sexual harassment which is, at the same time, also an instance of, say, promiscuity, there is a natural tendency to assimilate the point of the example to one's well-established, relatively uncontroversial views about promiscuity. One may thus easily fail to notice the controversial implications of what the example is supposed to show about sexual harassment. As a result of this mechanism, many people who were exposed to "training" programs about sexual harassment in the eighties may have had an impression that these programs were not really telling them anything new.

This overlap between sexual harassment and various kinds of conduct that are widely regarded as wrong (on grounds independent of their being sexual harassment) is probably the main reason why, even in the nineties when the public began to understand better what the law involved, the debate about it has not had the same intensity as the debates about, say, abortion or affirmative action. Abortion is something that one can be for or against (i.e., one can think that abortion is morally neutral and thus ought to be readily available or that it is profoundly wrong and ought to be outlawed). Similarly one can be for affirmative action (one can think that it is required by justice and thus ought to be supported) or against it (one can think that it is unfair and thus ought to be abolished as soon as possible). On the other hand, it is unlikely that anybody would be *for* sexual harassment; that is, that anybody would seriously think that sexual harassment is, in general, something that ought to be supported and encouraged. Many instances of what is classified as sexual harassment are wrong, and practically nobody would deny that. If one wants to start a discussion about sexual harassment, one needs to ask questions that are more subtle than "Are you for or against it?" In order to come to grips with the morality of sexual harassment we need to separate different possible grounds of the wrongness of the conduct in question and determine which one is the real ground. We need to ask questions such as "Is this conduct wrong *in virtue of* being sexual harassment, or is it wrong *in virtue of* being promiscuous?" Such questions do not easily lend themselves to popular debate.

As a result, the issues about sexual harassment are unlikely to capture as much public attention as the issues that can be cast in the simple for-and-against format. The opposition between the two main parties to, for example, the abortion debate is so sharp that it is impossible to misunderstand what the issue is, while sexual harassment overlaps with so many other morally relevant matters that it is difficult to keep the debate about it focused.

While the general public is nowadays better informed about the sexual harassment law than it was ten years ago, many important facets of the law are still not widely understood. Even people who are intellectually sophisticated and otherwise well informed often turn out to be unclear about, for example, the role of employers in the operation of the law, or the significance of the connection that the law makes between sexual harassment and sex discrimination. This lack of clarity is, of course, a hindrance to profitable debate about whether the law is morally justified. When specific examples of morally problematic applications of the law are presented, people often seem to be uncertain whether they should think of them as merely instances of overzealousness or sloppiness in applying a law that is basically sound, or as indications that something is wrong with the law itself.

This book attempts to stimulate the public debate about sexual harassment and to contribute to making that debate somewhat clearer. The question that the book tries to answer is whether the law about sexual harassment is morally justified. The answer that the book offers to that question is "No." The body of the book is an argument for that answer.

If the argument of this book is sound, then the law about sexual harassment cannot be repaired just by changing this or that detail; what the argument tries to show is that the law is fundamentally flawed.

In the course of developing the argument, various specific aspects of the law will be considered and various subordinate moral issues will be dealt with. The book tries to consider as many as possible of the aspects of the sexual harassment law that could be reasonably regarded as relevant to its overall moral justification. It does not, however, attempt to say everything that can be said about the law on sexual harassment: it does not attempt to deal with the many facets of the law that, interesting as they might be, don't seem to have a bearing on whether the law is, on the whole, morally justified.

The book is written for the general educated audience and does not presuppose that its readers belong to any particular academic discipline. Specialized jargon is either avoided or, when unavoidable, explained. It also does not presuppose any previous familiarity with the law on sexual harassment that would go beyond the vague general knowledge that any casual reader of newspapers is likely to have. The aspects of the law that are relevant to the argument will be presented and explained as the argument progresses.

The Scope of the Book

This book is principally about the law regarding sexual harassment in employment and in the education of adults. ("The education of adults" is here meant to include most college-level education and not only "adult education.") Legal prohibitions of sexual harassment have been extended to a number of other institutional settings, such as the education of children and the provision of housing and professional services. This book does not purport to reach any definite conclusion about sexual harassment in the settings other than those of employment and the education of adults. Some of the arguments I make may turn out to be applicable to these other settings as well, but not all of them are. Sexual harassment in these other settings raises a number of special issues that I will not discuss. However, given that the prohibitions of sexual harassment in employment and the education of adults are generally perceived as the core of the law, an argument that shows them to be unjustified casts a shadow over the law about sexual harassment in other settings, even if it doesn't apply to it directly.

Because the law about sexual harassment in employment has had a longer history, and is more developed than the law about it in education, most of the specific legal provisions referred to in the text will concern employment. Moreover, writing every sentence in this book so that it explicitly covers both employment and education would have made the text exceedingly cumbersome, and most of my discussion will, therefore, be worded as a discussion of sexual harassment in employment, with explicit references to education appearing only occasionally. But although the discussion will be so worded, the argumentative points made will generally be intended to apply to the education of adults as well. I trust that my readers will have no problem seeing how what I say about employers, employees, workplaces, promotions, and so on, can be transposed to colleges, students, campuses, grading and so on.

A legal prohibition of sexual harassment first appeared within the federal law of the United States. Later on, some states within the United States created their own sexual harassment laws, and some foreign jurisdictions did the same. All developed English-speaking countries now have sexual harassment laws of some kind. These laws are, by and large, modeled after the federal U.S. law on the topic.

Given that it is within the federal U.S. law that the law about sexual harassment has its most elaborate form, most of the examples in the discussion that follows will be from the federal U.S. cases, and references to other jurisdictions will be made only occasionally. However, given that the laws about sexual harassment in other English-speaking jurisdictions are generally modeled after the federal U.S. law, most of the arguments of this book apply to them as well.

It should be mentioned here that some jurisdictions outside the English-speaking world, such as France and Israel, have introduced into their legal systems terms that are direct translations of "sexual harassment." Despite the terminology, these laws may operate very differently from the sexual harassment laws of the English-speaking countries, and the arguments of this book generally do not apply to them.

The Concept of Sexual Harassment

"Sexual harassment" is a technical term of the law. The phrase "sexual harassment" should, therefore, throughout this book, be understood to stand for whatever is covered by the sexual harassment law.

Some philosophers have attempted to analyze the concept of sexual harassment as something that is independent of the law.[3] I believe that these attempts are misguided. The phrase "sexual harassment" has no established history of use in the everyday language that would be independent of its use in law-related contexts. Nor does it have an established history of use in any other kind of context that would not be law-related. The concept of sexual harassment was invented as a part of an attempt to prompt the creation of the law about sexual harassment. After that attempt had turned out to be successful, the phrase "sexual harassment" acquired a relatively established meaning within the law. It is only after the phrase had developed roots within the law that it began appearing in everyday contexts. The phrase is nowadays often used in everyday conversations, but its everyday use is dependent on its use in legal contexts: the everyday concept of sexual harassment is simply a watered-down version of the legal concept. It cannot be anything else, because the phrase lacks an independent history of everyday use that would have given it a law-independent meaning. There is no concept of sexual harassment that is unrelated to the law. One may, of course, introduce such a concept by stipulation,[4] but that is likely to breed confusion, and is, in any event, unhelpful in trying to reach a moral judgment about the actually existing law regarding sexual harassment.

Some of the authors I criticized in the preceding paragraph would respond by saying that their accounts of sexual harassment are stipulative but not arbitrarily stipulative: the stipulations capture something morally significant.[5] Moreover, these authors could say that, although their accounts are independent of what the current law about sexual harassment says, they are not entirely law-independent: they could serve as staring points for creating a new, morally better, law in this area. That new law would prohibit "sexual harassment" in the sense stipulated by these authors, rather than sexual harassment, in the current sense of that phrase.

While I, of course, think that it is very important to discuss what laws about sexual conduct would be morally desirable, I do not think that the clarity of that discussion is enhanced by inventing new senses for the phrase "sexual harassment." That phrase is already, so to speak, *taken* by the existing law. Any discussion that we might have about these matters will be clearer if we stick to using "sexual harassment" in the sense it has in the current law, which is its only established sense, and use other terms for other concepts. Moreover (and this is an independent criticism), I think that it is misguided for philosophers to discuss these matters in a vacuum, as if the current law about sexual harassment did not exist.[6] The law does exist, and before we even start thinking about what might replace it, we first have to understand it, and to show what, if anything, is wrong with it.

Trying to analyze the concept of sexual harassment independently of the law is like trying to analyze the concept of manslaughter or the concept of an individual retirement arrangement independently of the law. "Manslaughter" and "individual retirement arrangement" are terms that simply have no established uses that would be independent of the law. While they may be used in everyday conversations, their meanings in such contexts are dependent on their meanings in the law. The question "What does the phrase 'individual retirement arrangement' really mean, apart from what the law says it means?" cannot be answered, because it embodies a mistaken presupposition that the phrase means something apart from the law. If we cut the concept of an individual retirement arrangement from its legal roots, there will be no concept left. The same is true of the concept of sexual harassment.

Moreover, if one wanted to argue that the current tax treatment of retirement savings ought to be changed, it would surely be confusing to formulate that criticism by saying that the phrase "individual retirement arrangement" really means something different from what the law says it means. It is equally confusing to formulate a moral criticism of the sexual harassment law as an account of what the phrase "sexual harassment" really means.

It is true that the words "sexual" and "harassment" have everyday meanings, but the meaning of 'sexual harassment" is not a simple combination of the meanings of its component words. Because the phrase "sexual harassment" is a technical term, it has to be considered as an indivisible whole. A person unfamiliar with the phrase "sexual harassment" cannot find out its meaning by consulting separate dictionary definitions of the words "sexual" and "harassment,"[7] just as a person unfamiliar with the phrase "individual retirement arrangement" cannot discover its meaning by consulting separate dictionary definitions of "individual," "retirement," and "arrangement." One's trying to find out the meanings of such phrases in this way would likely lead to significant misunderstandings.

Some psychologists have tried to discover what has been referred to as the "empirical definitions"[8] of sexual harassment, by conducting studies in which they asked their subjects whether this or that is or is not sexual harassment. These attempts are as misguided as the philosophical attempts at analyzing the concept of sexual harassment as something independent of the law. Because the phrase "sexual harassment" has no established history of use that would be independent of the law, asking ordinary people how they would use the phrase cannot reveal any profound truth about what sexual harassment really is.[9] The only thing that such studies can reveal is how well or poorly people are informed about the sexual harassment law. This is analogous to the fact that asking ordinary people whether they would call this or that an "individual retirement arrangement" cannot reveal any profound truth about individual retirement arrangements; it can only reveal how well or poorly people are informed about the relevant law. (Asking ordinary people whether this or that is sexual harassment, is different from asking them whether it is morally objectionable; the latter question may well elicit interesting insights.)

The general idea as to what the concept of sexual harassment applies to, that all my readers are bound to have acquired through even casual exposure to the news reports on the topic, will be sufficient for following the arguments of this chapter. A careful analysis and detailed criticism of the concept of sexual harassment will be undertaken in chapters 2 and 3.

DISENTANGLING THE ISSUES

As I have argued, the public debate about sexual harassment has been significantly hampered by the fact that sexual harassment overlaps with various other kinds of conduct that are wrong on independent grounds. If one does not put special effort into keeping distinct issues separate in one's thinking, one's attitude toward sexual harassment will tend to merge with one's attitude toward the practices with which it often (but not always, and certainly not necessarily) overlaps. The first step in trying to think about sexual harassment clearly is therefore to disentangle the issue as to whether the sexual harassment law is morally justified from other moral issues with which it is likely to be confused. The rest of this chapter will be devoted to such disentangling: in the sections that follow I will discuss various considerations that may, at first sight, seem to morally justify the law about sexual harassment, and I will show that they do not really justify it. (However, I will not in this chapter discuss the considerations that are used to justify the law about sexual harassment *within* the legal system, those of discrimination—that will be done in chapter 7.)

LEGAL MORALISM

An act of sexual harassment is often an attempt to establish a sexual relationship that would be adulterous. It is also often the case that an act of sexual harassment is an attempt to add yet another relatively brief and not too emotional sexual relationship to a long list of similar "conquests" that the harasser's promiscuous life already contains (or, in some cases, to a long list of such "conquests" that the harasser wishes his life to contain).

The fact that a certain act involves (actual or attempted) adultery and/or promiscuity tends to loom large in one's perception of that act. If a friend confides to you that her boss has made a pass at her, chances are that among the first questions you are going to ask are "Is he married?" and "Does he know that you are [not] married?" The answers that your friend gives to these questions will significantly determine the tone and the direction of the rest of the conversation. Whether the boss in question is known to have made passes at other women he works with is a question that is also likely to come up early in the conversation.

While most people readily assume that adultery and promiscuity are morally wrong, spelling out what precisely makes them wrong is not an easy task, and there is plenty of room for disagreement about the precise ground and extent of their wrongness.[10] Getting into a discussion of these matters is, however, not necessary here: I shall assume, for the sake of argument, that adultery and promiscuity are, in general, morally wrong.

What people disagree about much more is whether the moral wrongness of adultery and promiscuity is, in itself, a sufficient reason for a legal prohibition of the conduct. The view that all such immoral conduct ought to be legally prohibited just because it is immoral is known as legal moralism, and it is a highly controversial view. If one thinks that the adulterous and promiscuous character of much sexual harassment provides moral support for the law about sexual harassment, one presupposes that controversial view.

While the theoreticians who support the sexual harassment law in its present form, or advocate its strengthening, tend to explicitly dissociate themselves from traditional legal moralism,[11] the thinking of the general public about the law is often semiconsciously influenced by moralist ideas. Many people perceive the law as prohibiting conduct, such as adultery and promiscuity, that is wrong anyway,[12] and think of the wrongness of adultery, promiscuity, and so forth as a sufficient reason for not opposing the law. Such thinking presupposes legal moralism, even if the people in question do not express an allegiance to that outlook in so many words. Bringing this line of thinking to the surface and responding to it is important, because the relative lack of opposition to the law probably owes much to it.

Moreover, careful reading of the literature about sexual harassment shows that its authors sometimes do rely on the wrongness of adultery and promiscuity in defending prohibitions of sexual harassment. One well-known empirical researcher of sexual harassment, for example, observes that "[m]ost of the sex at work . . . does not grow out of a person's interest in establishing a long-term relationship with another employee,"[13] and a highly influential book on sexual harassment in higher education announces that "faculty Casanovas usually forget to inform the woman that she is only one in a long procession."[14] An empirical study about sexual harassment may point out that a large percentage of sexual harassers are married.[15] Such observations are presented as a part of the reason for prohibiting sexual harassment. A certain amount of moralism is thus implied, not only in the thinking of ordinary people on this topic, but in the literature about it as well.

The association between sexual harassment and the kinds of sexual conduct that most people have always regarded as wrong also plays a role in the activities of various consultants who, on behalf of employers, provide "training" about sexual harassment. They often recommend, for example, that, in order not to be guilty of sexual harassment, one not do or say at the workplace anything that one would not do or say in front of one's spouse.[16] As most people would not do or say in front of their spouses anything that indicates adulterous interest in another person, such advice encourages people to think of the wrongness of sexual harassment as closely related to the wrongness of adulterous conduct.

That the consultants would operate in this way is not surprising: the success of the "training" programs they design is usually judged by their consequences and not by the intellectual integrity of their content. Their aim is typically to maximize compliance with the prohibition of sexual harassment while, at the same time, minimizing any rebelliousness against it. Their aim is not to promote clear thinking about sexual harassment, but to pacify. Presenting the prohibition of sexual harassment as an enforcement of the traditional sexual morality helps in accomplishing that aim.

Because of all this it is important to understand that legal moralism is, in fact, incapable of supporting the sexual harassment law in anything like its present form. Most people nowadays reject legal moralism, or would reject it if they reflected on the matter. In other words, most people do not think that the immorality of a particular form of conduct (especially of sexual conduct) is, in itself, a reason for prohibiting the conduct. Thus, most people think that adulterous and promiscuous conduct, although immoral, ought not to be illegal. Colloquially put, they think that it is none of the business of the state whether competent adults engage in such immorality. As a result of the prevalence of such opinions, the laws against adultery and other forms of sex outside marriage have been steadily disappearing.[17] In the jurisdictions in which they still remain "on the books,"[18] they are practically never enforced.

If one morally endorses these trends, then one cannot consistently think that adulterous and promiscuous character of much of sexual harassment constitutes a justification for the laws about sexual harassment. If one rejects legal moralism, one cannot consistently accept any arguments in favor of the sexual harassment law that depend on legal moralism. In other words, if moralism is itself unjustified, as most people seem to think, than it cannot provide a sound basis for anything, including the law about sexual harassment. Those who reject legal moralism are rationally committed to the view that any reasons for supporting the law must be independent of the adulterous and promiscuous character of the conduct in question.

What I have just said is, as the reader has probably noticed, conditional: it merely says that *if* one rejects moralism, then one also has to reject the arguments about sexual harassment that are based on it. I have not offered any argument against legal moralism. What if one belongs to the minority (a significant minority, to be sure) that accepts legal moralism? Can't one then, without inconsistency, defend the sexual harassment law on the ground that sexual harassment involves adultery and promiscuity?

The answer is, again, "No." If one is a legal moralist, and if one thus believes that adulterous and promiscuous character of some conduct is a reason for prohibiting it, then one ought to support the laws that prohibit adultery and promiscuity *as such*. The law about sexual harassment does not do that: it prohibits conduct that merely overlaps with adultery and promiscuity. One can think of cases of sexual harassment that are neither adulterous nor promiscuous, nor immoral in any other way that traditional sexual morality would recognize. Clumsily executed, but well intended, attempts at courtship, that was meant to be neither adulterous not promiscuous, may, for example, constitute sexual harassment. On the other hand, much adultery and promiscuity takes place outside employment, education, and similar settings and is thus outside the reach of the sexual harassment law. A consistent legal moralist should be as keen to see that conduct outlawed as he is to see outlawed adultery and promiscuity within employment, education, and other settings to which the sexual harassment law applies. The sexual harassment law thus fails to accomplish the aims of legal moralism. The laws that would accomplish these aims would be very different laws, that would prohibit adultery and promiscuity *as such*. The conclusion that legal moralism does not provide a reason for supporting the law about sexual harassment is thus warranted, regardless of whether legal moralism is itself an acceptable position.

Of course, a committed legal moralist may say that, ideally, he would, indeed, like to see legal prohibitions of all adulterous and promiscuous conduct enacted or revived, and enforced, but that he realizes that, in the culture we live in, it is unlikely that this goal would be achieved. He can thus say that, although the sexual harassment law falls short of the goal of moralism, he welcomes it as something that satisfies at least a part of the goal. In saying this, the moralist would, however, be endorsing the law by way of a political compromise; he would not be endorsing it as genuinely justified. The moralist's (or anybody else's) willingness to endorse a law by way of a compromise does not answer the question of whether there is a coherent justification of the law.

It should be noted that although the promiscuous character of sexual conduct does not figure in the legal definition of sexual harassment (and is not logically related to what does figure in it), it nevertheless plays a role in the law in a roundabout way. The courts often treat the evidence about the alleged harasser's overall behavior and attitudes in sexual matters, such as the fact that the alleged harasser had affairs with people other than the alleged victim or "described himself as a life-long 'womanizer,' "[19] as relevant to determining whether the specific alleged instances of sexual harassment did, in fact, occur. (As is well known, this feature of the law played a crucial role in the events that led to the impeachment proceedings against President Clinton.)[20] Thus, from the viewpoint of the law, although your being casual about sex does not make you a harasser, it makes it easier to prove that you are one.

SEXUAL HARASSMENT AND JOB DESCRIPTIONS

It is sometimes suggested that prohibitions of sexual harassment are morally justified because exposure to such conduct is not a part of one's job. A French-Canadian book about sexual harassment is thus entitled *It's not a part of the job.*[21] What is presumably meant by such claims is that exposure to what is nowadays characterized as sexual harassment is not included in one's official job description, and that one should therefore not be exposed to it while at work.

While it is undoubtedly true that sexual harassment is never included in one's job description, that does not prove that prohibitions of such conduct are morally justified. Listening to one's colleagues opinions about the last weekend's baseball game or to their comments about the weather is also not included in one's job description. Yet, most people think that there is nothing wrong with such conduct, and it is unlikely that anyone would seriously support laws against it. People in certain occupations, such as hairdressers and bartenders, often find themselves engaged in detailed conversations with their customers, sometimes on topics that are quite personal and completely unrelated to the activity at hand. The job of a hairdresser is presumably to cut and style the customers' hair, and the job of a bartender is to mix and serve drinks, and yet it is not only tolerated, but widely expected that they would listen to their customers' ramblings on topics ranging from their vacation plans to conflicts with the in-laws. The official descriptions of these jobs are unlikely to mention such conversations, and yet it would generally be thought undesirable for the law to prohibit them. Thus, the fact that something is not a part of the job does not seem to constitute a reason for prohibiting it. Whatever reasons there might be for prohibiting sexual harassment, they must be based on something other than the fact that sexual harassment is not a part of the victim's job.

Moreover, if the reason for prohibiting sexual harassment were the simple fact that it is not a part of the job, then it would follow that the reason could be removed by simply making sexual harassment a part of the job. One could write it into the description of the job of, say, a secretary that she will listen to her boss's sexual jokes, accept physical contact with him, and so forth.[22] Surely, those who support the current laws about sexual harassment do not think these laws would become unnecessary if the job descriptions of the potential victims were to be rewritten in this way. Quite the contrary: they probably think that rewriting the job descriptions in this way would make things worse rather than better, and that it would make the sexual harassment laws that much more needed.[23] But that, again, shows that the reason for the existence of these laws is not that sexual harassment is not a part of the job.

A related argument is sometimes made that the prohibitions of sexual harassment are justified because sexual harassment reduces productivity. If people, while at work, direct their energy at sexually harassing others or at fending off the sexual harassment to which they are exposed, then they have that much less energy to devote to the work they are paid for, and that is, presumably, undesirable. There are three responses that can be made to that argument.[24] The first is that it, again, does not justify focusing on sexual harassment. Numerous other kinds of conduct at work, such as inane conversations on nonsexual topics, can be as distracting and interfere with productivity as much as sexual harassment. A colleague who insists on frequently telling me nonsexual jokes (which are beyond the reach of the sexual harassment law) can interfere with my concentration as much as a colleague who tells me off-color jokes (to which the prohibition of sexual harassment may apply). Considerations of productivity therefore do not justify the specificity of the prohibition of sexual harassment: they do not justify treating sexual harassment differently from other distracting conduct at work. The problem of sexual harassment is thus distinct from the problems of less-than-maximal productivity.

The second response to this line of argument is to point out that the currently prevailing opinion is that there are moral limits on how much the individual freedoms of workers may be limited in the pursuit of higher productivity. It is nowadays generally thought that it is immoral to treat workers as if they were nothing but cogwheels of some machinery. The sweatshops of the early industrial era, in which the workers were made productive by highly restrictive rules that were rigidly enforced, have largely disappeared in the developed countries. When we hear that such working conditions still exist in some parts of the world, we are generally appalled. What this entails about the issue at hand is that the fact that the prohibition of sexual harassment may increase productivity cannot on its own morally justify the prohibition. Even if the argument based on this fact were otherwise unproblematic, it would still not be *sufficient* to show that the prohibition is justified: it would need to be supplemented by a further argument showing what it is about sexual harassment that makes it legitimate to restrict it in the name of productivity.

The productivity-based argument is, however, problematic in other ways as well. The third response to it, and that is the crucial one, is that the considerations of productivity can, at most, show that it would be morally permissible if individual employers, on the basis of their own business judgments, prohibited sexual harassment within their businesses. But the law against sexual harassment is something entirely different: it is a *law,* that is, a creation of the state. The state, by that law, does not merely permit employers to prohibit sexual harassment within their businesses if they so choose: it requires them to do so. Sexual harassment is not prohibited because the employers have seen it fit to prohibit it for reasons of their own; it is prohibited because the state has made it prohibited. A prohibition created by the state cannot be justified by the considerations of productivity. It is not a proper role of the state to force businesses to be maximally productive. It is generally thought, at least in the Western political tradition, that the state should leave business owners free, within certain constraints, to follow their own judgments as to how to maintain or increase the productivity of their businesses. In fact, for much of the twentieth century, the governments of the Western world have assumed that businesses already have more than enough zeal to increase productivity, and have regarded it as their role to protect the workers from the excesses of that zeal. Trying to justify the *law* about sexual harassment by the considerations of productivity is, therefore, incompatible with the views about the proper role of the state that are generally accepted in the Western world.

Yet another one in the same family of arguments that may seem, at first glance, to justify the law against sexual harassment is that treating people, especially women, in sexually harassing ways involves treating them as sexual beings, which, in turn, involves treating them as if they were not capable workers, committed to doing their job. That argument is defective, because it is unclear why treating people as sexual beings would typically involve treating them as if they were not capable and committed workers. The argument hinges on the assumption, which is rarely made fully explicit, that it is somehow psychologically impossible to be aware of someone's sexuality *and* that person's other attributes, at the same time. There is no reason to believe that this assumption is true. Most people, of both sexes, as they reflect on their own lives, will probably discover that their appreciation of a person's sexuality does not magically make them forget the person's other qualities.[25] Treating someone as a sexual being can perfectly well coexist with treating the person as a capable and committed worker.

The implausibility of the assumption that the two cannot coexist becomes even more obvious if we reflect on the fact that there is no sharp boundary between the qualities that, in many occupations, make one a good worker and the qualities that make one erotically attractive. Good workers may, for example, be expected to be able to get along with their coworkers easily, to maintain a "professional appearance," and to exude confidence in their dealings with customers. But the personal charm that makes one get along with coworkers easily may be the very same charm that contributes to one's appeal as a potential romantic partner. What is generally regarded as a good "professional appearance," for a woman, is also an appearance that subtly accentuates her sexuality (although the present-day employers are very careful never to say so explicitly). The confidence that enables one to make an irresistible sales pitch to a potential customer is often the very same confidence that also makes one erotically attractive.

Abuse of Institutional Power

The activities that are classifiable as sexual harassment often involve abuse of institutional power. In other words, they involve the harasser's diverting the institutional power that has been conferred on him for a specific purpose to a different, sexual purpose. For example, a supervisor who uses his power to fire his subordinates so as to penalize those who do not comply with his sexual requests is using the power for a purpose other than the one for which it has been conferred on him. It can thus be said that he is abusing the power. Similarly, a professor who uses his power to grade students so as to penalize those who have rejected his sexual advances is thereby abusing that power; that is, using it for a purpose different from the one for which it has been conferred on him.

That such abuse of power is morally wrong is probably uncontroversial. There are, however, at least two reasons why its wrongness does not justify the law against sexual harassment. The first reason is similar to the ones that have already been invoked above: while sexual harassment does indeed overlap with the abuse of institutional power, it merely overlaps with it. Many acts of sexual harassment take place between people who simply have no institutional power over each other, and consequently cannot abuse it. Moreover, power can be abused in all manner of ways that have nothing to do with sex: it can, for example, be abused for the sake of financial gain, or out of sheer spite. If the abuse of power is what one is concerned about, then one should be supporting the rules that are aimed at *it*, rather than the rules that are aimed at something that merely overlaps with it, such as sexual harassment.

The second reason is that every prohibition of abuse of power is, as a matter of logic, bound to be redundant. Something can be identified as an abuse of a particular power only relative to a set of rules that spell out what the proper use of that power is. That means that, if we are able to say that something is an abuse of power, then it must be that it already is a violation of some rule; that is, it must be that it is something prohibited. If it hadn't been a violation of any rule, then we wouldn't have been able to identify it as an abuse of power. Creating a rule that prohibits some conduct that has been found to involve abuse of power would thus amount to prohibiting something that is already prohibited, and doing so would be redundant.

For example, when we say that a professor who uses grades to penalize the students who reject his sexual advances is abusing his power, we imply that there are rules that say that professors ought to assign grades on the basis of something else. There indeed are such rules: they say, roughly, that grades ought to be assigned so as to reflect the quality of the student's work. But then, these rules imply that professors are prohibited from assigning grades in ways that do not reflect the quality of students' work. This, in turn, implies that they are prohibited from assigning them so as to penalize those who reject their sexual advances. The conduct in question is thus already prohibited by the general rules about the practice of grading, and no further rule, such as the rules about sexual harassment, is needed to make it prohibited. It follows from the very concept of abuse of power that this will be so in every other case of abuse of power. The wrongness of abuse of power, consequently, does not justify the law about sexual harassment. The concern about abuse of power and the concern about sexual harassment are distinct concerns.

The argument that I have just made is not meant to rule out the possibility that sexual harassment may be an aggravating factor in some instances of abuse of power. It is thus not meant to rule out the possibility that it may be justified to have rules that allow for treating sexually harassing abuses of power (already prohibited by other rules) differently from other abuses of power. However, even if one believes that the sexually harassing character of some case of abuse of power makes it worse than other cases of abuse of power, one still has to acknowledge that the wrongness of sexual harassment is distinct from the wrongness of abuse of power. This is because an aggravating factor is, by definition, something distinct from the underlying wrong that it aggravates. As a consequence of that conceptual truth, one cannot account for the wrongness of an aggravating factor (i.e., one cannot explain why it is an aggravating factor) by merely pointing out that the underlying wrong is, indeed, a wrong. Thus, one cannot explain why sexual harassment would be an aggravating factor in abuses of power merely by pointing out that all abuses of power are wrong. That the two problems may be intertwined does not entail that they are not distinct.

It should perhaps be made explicit that what I have said about abuse of power in this section covers not only the cases such as those in which a supervisor fires someone for noncompliance with his sexual requests or in which a professor assigns a bad grade for similar reasons, but also the cases in which people in such positions threaten to do so. Someone's threat to abuse his power is, typically, itself an abuse of power. As such it is typically already prohibited by the norms that specify the proper uses of that power. This is because the powers to fire, re-hire, promote, grade, and so forth are typically intended to provide incentives and disincentives; the beliefs that the people subject to these powers have about how the powers will be exercised are, consequently, as important as their actual exercise (if not more important). For example, the norms of the practice of college grading typically impose on professors not only an obligation to actually assign the grades in ways that reflect the quality of the students' work, but also an obligation to avoid anything that would imply that the grades may be assigned on some other basis. This is because the whole institution of grading would lose its point if students did not, by and large, believe that grades are assigned so as to reflect the quality of their work.

It is interesting to note here a further difference between abuse of power and sexual harassment. So far as abuse of power is concerned, a supervisor who threatens a subordinate with demotion if the subordinate does not comply with his sexual requests, and a supervisor who offers to reward a subordinate with promotion if the subordinate complies with his sexual requests, are exactly on a par. Both supervisors are quite obviously abusing their powers, and both misdeeds undermine, in very similar ways, the incentives and disincentives that the practices of promoting and demoting are supposed to provide to the subordinates.

On the other hand, so far as sexual harassment is concerned, the two cases are not *obviously* on a par. This is because thinking about such incidents in terms of sexual harassment focuses on the individual exposed to the conduct in a way in which thinking about them in terms of abuse of power does not. In the case of the person threatened with demotion, it is quite clear that the person's position has been made worse than it would have been otherwise, and that the person deserves to be compensated for that unjustified worsening.

If anybody is a victim of sexual harassment, this person surely is. On the other hand, the position of the person who has been offered a promotion in exchange for sexual favors does not seem to have been obviously worsened. The person can either accept the offer and thus obtain the benefit of promotion, or reject it, in which case everything would seem to remain as it would have been otherwise. In neither case is there any definite worsening of the person's situation. It is not obvious that there is anything that the person would deserve to be compensated for. These considerations make it problematic why this person should be regarded as a victim of sexual harassment, while they are completely irrelevant when one thinks about the matter in terms of abuse of power, because the notion of abuse of power does not require a readily identifiable victim in the way in which the notion of sexual harassment does.

Arguments can be made that show that the above reasoning about such offers oversimplifies the matter, and that they can, in fact, worsen the subordinate's position. First, it can be said that, for many people, such offers are in themselves detestable and being exposed to them is humiliating and traumatic. The mere experience of having to respond to such an offer can thus, in many cases, worsen one's position, even if the offer is rejected and no further consequences follow. Second, it can be argued that, in this context, offers are not really separable from threats. When a supervisor offers a promotion to a subordinate in exchange for sex, the subordinate may quite reasonably think that, if the supervisor has no qualms about abusing his power to reward sexual compliance, then the supervisor is unlikely to have qualms about using that power to penalize sexual noncompliance. The subordinate may thus easily perceive something like a threat in the offing, although what has been made explicit is merely an offer.[26]

However, even if these arguments are accepted as showing why some such offers should be covered by the notion of sexual harassment, they do not quite seem to show that the offers are as bad as threats, so far as sexual harassment is concerned. Moreover, it is noteworthy that these arguments need to be made: how such offers fit under the notion of sexual harassment is not immediately obvious. This is a difference between sexual harassment and abuse of power: when such offers are considered as instances of abuse of power, they are obviously on a par with the threats.

CONFLICTS OF INTERESTS

A matter related to abuses of power is that of conflicts of interests. When we say that one ought to avoid conflicts of interests, what we mean is, roughly, that one ought to avoid situations in which one may be tempted to abuse one's institutional power, and perhaps also situations in which one may be reasonably perceived by others as tempted to abuse that power. The prohibition of sexual harassment often converges in its effects with the norms against conflicts of interests. Nevertheless, the convergence between the two is only very rough, and the moral concerns that underlie them cannot be the same.

First, many cases of sexual harassment (e.g., crude sexual jokes between coworkers at the same level of institutional hierarchy) have nothing to do with any conflicts of interests and, of course, many problematic conflicts of interests have nothing to do with sex. Second, among the sexual relationships that give rise to the concerns about conflicts of interests, the nonharassing ones cause the concerns that are at least as serious as the concerns due to the harassing ones (if not more serious). A fully reciprocated, harmonious, happy, long-term romantic relationship between a supervisor and a subordinate may create much stronger temptations for the supervisor to abuse his institutional power than most kinds of sexual harassment. Third, even when the prohibitions of sexual harassment and of conflicts of interests converge in their operation, they differ in that thinking about a particular incident as a case of sexual harassment, as has been pointed out in the preceding section, focuses on specific, readily identifiable, direct victims, while thinking about it in terms of conflicts of interests need not. It is a feature of the concept of sexual harassment that one cannot meaningfully say that something was a case of sexual harassment unless one can identify its direct victim, while no specific victims need to be identified in order to say that there exists a conflict of interests. (This follows from the fact that concerns about conflicts of interests are derivations from the concerns about abuse of power.)

It may also be worthwhile to say, although that is not essential to my argument, that, in thinking about what may or may not be justified by the concerns regarding conflicts of interests, one should be careful not to exaggerate the dangers that these conflicts pose. Conflicts of interests are not wrong in themselves, but only insofar as they may lead to abuses of power. In determining whether rules against conflicts of interests are justified in a particular setting, one should thus always ask how likely it is that these conflicts would, in fact, lead to the abuses of power. Conflicts of interests are essentially temptations, and how worrisome a temptation is depends on how likely it is that it will be succumbed to. The likelihood varies from one institutional setting to another: it depends on the history and traditions of the institution, its aims and organization, and the typical background and character of those who work in it. In at least some settings, the professionalism and integrity of the people involved, or their dedication to the aims of the institution, may be such that they can be relied upon to resist any temptations to abuse their power that they may face. In such settings, the rules against conflicts of interests may well be unjustified. They may also be unjustified in the settings in which actual abuses of power can be easily detected and remedied. As any other rules that are aimed at something that is not wrong in itself but may lead to wrongful results, they seem justified only when these wrongful results cannot be easily dealt with on their own.

ROMANTIC INFELICITIES

Many people, when they think of sexual harassment, tend to visualize a male middle-aged executive, physically unattractive, but worldly-wise and relatively successful in his career, pursuing his young and attractive, but also shy and inexperienced, female secretary.[27] Many of these people also think that romantic relationships between middle-aged, worldly-wise men, and women who are just beginning their adult lives, are undesirable, even if they do not involve adultery, promiscuity, abuse of institutional power, or anything similar. One can reasonably think, for example, that the backgrounds of such two people are bound to be so vastly different that it is simply impossible for them to develop the kind of mutual understanding that is necessary for the closeness and intimacy that characterize fulfilling romantic relationships. One could thus argue that, even if both parties enter into such a relationship with the best of intentions, they will sooner or later face their insurmountable incompatibility and the relationship will reach its bitter end, probably accompanied by a fair amount of suffering. Most of that suffering is likely to befall the younger party, who can be quite seriously traumatized by the experience. It is thus best, one could conclude, if such relationships are never even attempted.

This reasoning can be developed further. One can say that it is understandable that the younger party to such a liaison is, because of her lack of experience, unaware of just how hopeless these relationships are. A worldly-wise man should, however, know where such relationships lead, and therefore has the responsibility to resist whatever temptation youthfulness might present for him. He should never, ever, make sexual advances toward his secretary.

The reasoning that has just been outlined colors many people's attitudes toward sexual harassment. When they hear that a middle-aged executive is accused of sexual harassment because of the sexual advances he has made to his young secretary, they may think "He should know better than to go around chasing someone who is less than half his age. It's so disgusting. After all, he could be her father."

Several comments need to be made against the line of thought I have just presented. First, the empirical basis of that line of thought is quite speculative. Whether it is really impossible for people of vastly disparate ages and backgrounds to have genuinely fulfilling romantic relationships is debatable. Some people insist that they have experienced them. Second, although such relationships may be many people's stereotype of sexual harassment, much sexual harassment is not like that at all, in that it involves interaction between people of similar ages, backgrounds, and so forth. Third, middle-aged, worldly-wise men sometimes make sexual and romantic advances to young and inexperienced women outside the institutional settings to which the sexual harassment law applies. Whatever might be wrong with that, nobody seriously thinks that there should be laws against it. (I am assuming that the women, although young, are adults; i.e., that they are above the "age of consent.") But if one thinks that whatever may be problematic about such interactions is not a sufficient ground for making them illegal outside employment, education, and similar settings, then it is not clear how it could be a sufficient ground for making them illegal within such settings. (Remember that the abuses of institutional power are not under discussion in this section—they were already discussed in an earlier one.)

The responsibility that the older party has for ensuring that such relationships are not even attempted can be boosted by pointing out that the younger party may, because of her inexperience, be confused by the advances, and consequently uncertain how to respond to them. She may be disinclined to accept them, but not quite know how to decline them. Moreover, the difference in social status can make it quite awkward and difficult for her to be assertive in declining them. That is sometimes expressed by saying that the older person in such interaction has "power" over the younger one. While this use of the word "power" is generally legitimate, it is, in this context, dangerous, because it breeds confusion between such informal social power and the institutional power of the kind discussed above.

While this informal social power is certainly something that thoughtful people ought to be aware of, its existence does not really provide support for the law about sexual harassment. Older, charismatic, worldly-wise people have that kind of power over young, inexperienced ones, not only within employment, education, and similar settings, but also outside them. Nobody thinks that this power provides a reason for prohibiting the older people from making sexual advances to the younger ones outside such settings. Therefore, nobody should think that it provides the reason for prohibiting it within such settings. (Remember, the informal social power is the very same power in both settings; what differs between them is the institutional power, which is not under discussion here.)

The argument made in the preceding paragraph also shows that the power that men, according to certain feminist theories, generally have over women in the societies we live in, cannot, on its own, justify the legal prohibition of sexual harassment. If these theories are true, then the power in question permeates all interaction between men and women, and certainly all sexual interaction between them. Invocations of that power consequently cannot, on their own, justify the specificity of the prohibition of sexual harassment.

Some people will respond to the argument I have just made by claiming that my separation between the informal social power and institutional power is artificial. That argument will be taken up in the next section.

What I want to do in the remainder of this section is deal with a more general version of the problem I have discussed above. Many instances of sexual harassment do cause suffering. At first sight, that looks like an excellent reason for prohibiting sexual harassment. Surely, one may think, suffering is bad and the prevention of suffering is good.

The literature on sexual harassment often embodies this line of thought. One article on sexual harassment, for example, presents the following list of "consequences [which] may be experienced by student victims" of sexual harassment:

- general depression, as manifested by changes in eating and sleeping patterns, and vague complaints of aches and pains that prevent the student from attending class or completing work;
- undefined dissatisfaction with college, major, or particular course;
- sense of powerlessness, helplessness, and vulnerability;
- loss of academic self-confidence and decline in academic performance;

- feelings of isolation from other students;
- changes in attitudes or behaviors regarding sexual relationships;
- irritability with family and friends;
- fear and anxiety;
- inability to concentrate;
- alcohol and drug dependency.[28]

Such data are all presented in the literature in a way that suggests that they provide an irrefutable argument for the prohibition of sexual harassment. At first sight, they indeed seem to do so. However, upon reflection, it turns out that they do not.

What is missing in the line of thought that relies on these facts is comparison between the sufferings caused by sexual harassment and the sufferings caused by romantic infelicities in other settings. Jilted lovers often turn obnoxious and make one's life difficult in ways that may cause "inability to concentrate" and "irritability with family and friends." An unfulfilling liaison with a bitter ending can easily lead to "general depression" and "undefined dissatisfaction" with one's circumstances. Being pursued by someone who at first feigns genuine emotion, but then turns out to be a cold manipulator, may engender a "sense of powerlessness, helplessness, and vulnerability" and lead to "changes in attitudes or behaviors regarding sexual relationships." Tension and irritability are also often caused by a rejected would-be lover who doesn't accept the rejection graciously. All this is true both when the conduct in question can be characterized as sexual harassment and when it cannot be so characterized. In particular, it is true both within employment and education (where the prohibition of sexual harassment applies) *and outside* such settings (where it does not). The recitations of the harmful consequences of sexual harassment, such as the ones quoted above, thus do not prove anything definite about sexual harassment as such, because they are all too similar to what can be said about the possible consequences of romantic infelicities in general. This similarity, together with the fact that nobody thinks that it is the proper role of the state to generally prevent the sufferings caused by romantic infelicities, implies that the sufferings caused by sexual harassment do not provide the ground for the legal prohibition of sexual harassment. (It should perhaps be emphasized that this argument does not reflect a lack of sympathy for these sufferings, but only respect for consistency, together with an appreciation of the bluntness of the state power as an instrument for solving human problems.)

It may be useful to make the argument I have just made more vivid by considering an example. A book on sexual harassment presents at considerable length the case of a woman whose first sexual experience was with her professor, and who was seriously traumatized by it. Here are the woman's own words, as quoted in the book:

> The only thing I remember now is finding myself in his apartment and seeing dirty dishes on the table. I thought, "So this is it," and I'm sure that everything that happened I wanted to happen. Only it wasn't the way I thought it would be at all. He didn't talk much. I guess I wanted him to say he loved me or something. Remember I was pretty young. All I remember is that it hurt and there was blood and I was embarrassed because I didn't know what to do about the sheet.
>
> . . . And you know, even after all this time, I don't remember anything that hurt worse.[29]

The authors of the book in which this testimony appears obviously think that it contributes to their main point: that sexual harassment is a serious problem, which needs to be controlled by formal mechanisms. But does it really do that?

The testimony certainly elicits sympathy. It is easy to understand how the woman could have been traumatized by the experience. But what *exactly* is it that made the experience traumatic? On the basis of the above quotation, it seems to be a combination of factors such as the man's not having made any effort to make the experience enjoyable for the woman, his complete lack of interest in the emotional significance that this event had for her, his having made it obvious that he didn't really love her, and his apparent lack of concern about her physical pain. These are all bad things, and it is easy to agree that the man behaved very badly. But, if one reflects carefully on the factors that made the man's conduct bad, one will notice that they are all completely unrelated to the fact that the man was a professor and that the woman was his student. The experience would have been similarly traumatic for the woman even if the man had not been her professor, as long as he displayed the same kind of insensitivity. This example therefore doesn't prove anything about sexual harassment or about relationships between professors and students. The example is misleading as an illustration of sexual harassment, because one essential feature of the concept of sexual harassment, the institutional nexus, plays no role in our emotional reaction to, and the moral judgment about, the example. What the example does aptly illustrate is a far more general phenomenon of insensitivity in sexual matters.

FEAR

In the above discussion, I insisted on separating the moral concerns related to abuses of institutional power from the concerns related to the effects of informal social power. I then argued that neither of the two can provide a justification for the law about sexual harassment. Some people may respond that my separation of the two kinds of power has allowed something important to slip through the cracks. There is, they can say, a kind of phenomena that does not fit neatly into either of these two categories, but rather falls somewhere between them, and that is quite relevant to the issue of the moral justification of the law against sexual harassment.

Consider a supervisor who makes sexual advances to a subordinate. Suppose that the advances are quite insistent, but that the supervisor at no point makes the slightest threat that the subordinate will be demoted, fired, or subjected to any other reprisals if she declines. The subordinate is, however, apprehensive that, if she declines, the reprisals may nevertheless come. In feeling that apprehension, she need not be assuming that the supervisor is, at the time of making that advances, consciously planning the possibility of such retaliation; her worry can be that he may just spontaneously become vengeful after his advances are rejected. She is acutely aware of how many ways there are in which the supervisor can make her life difficult if he so chooses: the supervisor can assign her less desirable work, indefinitely delay the payrise she has been hoping for, demote her, fire her. She knows that the supervisor has considerable discretion in making his decisions about such matters, and that, if he claims, for example, that she is being demoted because of poor performance, she has no real way of proving that this is a pretext. Having all that in mind, she feels that she is under considerable pressure to go along with his advances, although she has no genuine desire to do so.

Given that no threat has been made, this kind of a scenario does not in itself constitute an abuse of institutional power. On the other hand, the power that keeps the woman from declining the advance is not merely informal social power. The institutional power plays a role in a case like this, in spite of the fact that the power is not abused. What the subordinate fears in such a case is a *possible*, but not threatened, abuse of power.

The cases of this kind are morally problematic, and unlike the ones we have been considering so far, they do not readily fit under any well-established "heading" in our moral thinking. Focusing on these cases may thus seem to have a better chance of providing a justification for the law against sexual harassment than the considerations that have been discussed so far.

Nevertheless, no definite justification of the sexual harassment law can emerge from our reflecting on cases like these. First, even when such cases are combined with the cases of abuse of institutional power, they do not cover all of sexual harassment. Much sexual harassment takes place between coworkers at the same level of institutional hierarchy, and the above account of what may make a supervisor's sexual advances to a subordinate problematic cannot be applied to them.

Second, it is not clear why the mere fact that the subordinates feel the fear should be accepted as a reason for the prohibition. Surely, it should be relevant whether the fear in question is reasonable. That will sometimes be the case, but not always. The mere fact that the supervisors have the power that makes it *possible* for them to inflict undesirable consequences on the subordinates who refuse to go along is not sufficient to make the fear of these consequences reasonable.

In order to see that a mere possibility of harm is not enough to make the fear of that harm reasonable consider that, whenever I interact with a man who is physically stronger than I am, it is *possible* that the man would beat me up. We would think it eminently unreasonable if I were to experience the fear of being beaten up every time I talked to a physically stronger man. Some physically strong men may, indeed, not only find such fear on my part unreasonable, but also feel insulted by it. As a reasonable person, I am expected to distinguish the encounters with strong men in which my being beaten up is a *mere* possibility from those in which there is a significant probability that the difference in physical strength would be abused. Analogously, a reasonable subordinate should be expected to distinguish between the interactions with supervisors in which the possibility of retaliation is a *mere* possibility from the cases in which it is more than a mere possibility. Distinguishing between the two will hinge on such things as the available information about the supervisor's character and professionalism. Once the account we are considering is limited to the cases in which the subordinate's fear of retaliation is reasonable, we see that it covers only a relatively narrow subset of all the cases that are classifiable as sexual harassment.

Third, that account cannot explain why the sexual harassment law applies only to *sexual* harassment. The features that make us concerned about the cases of the kind we are considering here often appear in nonsexual interaction. Suppose that a supervisor keeps inviting his subordinate to play golf with him on weekends. (Assume that they are both of the same sex and known to be heterosexual, so that there is clearly no amorous overtone to the invitations.) The supervisor does not intend any harm by these invitations, but he is quite insistent. The subordinate fears that if he declines the invitations too often, the supervisor may become annoyed with him, and that this annoyance may influence the supervisor's decisions about work-assignments, payrises, promotions, contract renewals, and so forth. Out of that fear, the subordinate often goes along and plays golf with his supervisor on weekends, in spite of the fact that he would much rather be doing something else. Although the subordinate's participation in the golf sessions is, on the face of it, voluntary, we can easily imagine that he feels really violated by this incursion in what little free time he has. If the subordinate's fear of adverse consequences were a good reason for a legal prohibition in the sex-related cases, then it should be a good reason for a legal prohibition in the golf-related cases, because the two kinds of case are exactly parallel. Indeed, if such fear provides a good ground for a legal prohibition, then one should be supporting a prohibition of all interaction between supervisors and subordinates that is not strictly a part of the job. Such a prohibition would be something very different from the law about sexual harassment.

Sexual Harassment as a Patchwork

Some readers may be reacting to the arguments of the preceding sections in the following way: "Okay," they could say, "we agree that none of the considerations discussed in the preceding sections can *on its own* justify the law about sexual harassment. But why can't we say that the wrongness of promiscuity provides the justification for prohibiting *some* cases of sexual harassment, while the wrongness of abusing institutional power provides the justification for prohibiting some other cases, and so forth? Why can't we say that the law is justified by a combination of all these considerations?"

The answer is that we expect the way in which our legal system operates to, by and large, reflect the underlying moral justifications. We expect the legal classifications of human conduct to, by and large, mirror their moral justifications.

Of course, we know that a legal system cannot do so perfectly. The law sometimes needs to make sharp boundaries where the corresponding boundaries in the supporting moral justifications are fuzzy, and it may sometimes need to prohibit conduct that is not wrong in itself but merely in some way related to genuine moral wrongs. Many states, for example, used to have the rule that an act cannot constitute murder unless the death occurs within a year and a day after the act, even though that precise length of time has no moral significance. The belief that the recreational use of narcotics is morally wrong can lead to the legal prohibition of the possession of narcotics, even though nobody thinks that the possession is wrong in itself.

But whenever a law thus departs from the moral considerations that support it, we expect the departure itself to be justified in some way. Such departures may, for example, be justified by the need to avoid excessive difficulties in adjudication, to make the results of the law predictable, or to make its enforcement manageable. For example, when a death occurred a long time after the event that allegedly caused it, it used to be extremely difficult to establish whether the act really caused the death or not; in order to avoid these difficulties it was useful to have the year-and-a-day rule about homicides. It can also be argued that a prohibition of the recreational use of narcotics would be very difficult to enforce, and that the only manageable way of curtailing such use is to prohibit their possession, which is, of course, closely connected with use.

In general, we do not want our laws to be structured and to operate in a haphazard manner, even if the results of that operation *happen to coincide* with what is morally justified. We would certainly think that something is wrong with a code of laws that has one legal category which jumbles together rapes and pickpocketing that occur on Tuesdays, and then another, entirely separate legal category that groups together the acts of rape and embezzlement committed on Wednesdays, and yet another one, which combines murders and thefts on cloudy days, and so forth. We would think that such a code of laws would be subject to serious criticism even though the acts it prohibits (rapes, pickpocketing, and so forth) are indeed morally wrong. What makes rape wrong is entirely different from what makes pickpocketing wrong, and we expect that difference to be reflected in the legal system. We would thus think that a law that jumbles together rape and pickpocketing is, in the absence of some special explanation, defective. On the other hand, it makes no difference to the moral wrongness of a rape whether it takes place on a Tuesday or a Wednesday: in the absence of some special explanation, we would thus find a law that draws the distinction between the two problematic.

That many of the acts that the law about sexual harassment prohibits are morally wrong in some way or other (some are adulterous, some involve an abuse of power, and so forth) is thus not enough to make the law justified. If the concept of sexual harassment is merely a patchwork, then the law against it is not justified, even if most of the "patches" are taken from something that is morally wrong. A convincing justification of the law about sexual harassment would have to account for the unity of sexual harassment: it would have to explain why the various kinds of conduct that the law prohibits have been brought together within the same legal category. In the absence of such an explanation, the prohibition of sexual harassment doesn't look any better than a prohibition of rapes and pickpocketing on Tuesdays.

It is important to understand here that the reason why we expect legal classifications of human conduct to mirror their moral justifications is not simply that such orderliness is pleasing to theoreticians. The expectation itself has moral underpinnings. It is a part of the political traditions which inform the liberal state, that everything the state does to its citizens needs to be justified. It is also a part of these traditions that the justifications need to be open to public scrutiny. Laws that arbitrarily jumble together disparate kinds of conduct or arbitrarily separate the kinds of conduct that are similar, elude public scrutiny of their moral justifications, and are, for that very reason, morally problematic. When a law is structured in a haphazard way, it is very difficult to be sure that it won't cause injustice somewhere, even if it is granted that many of its results clearly coincide with what is morally right.

Let me, at the end of this chapter, make it clear that the conclusion reached so far is relatively modest. It is that several kinds of considerations that may, at first sight, seem to provide a moral justification for the law about sexual harassment do not, in fact, provide it. I have examined these considerations at the very beginning of the book because experience suggests that they tend to confuse people's thinking about sexual harassment. Setting them aside at the very beginning of a discussion about sexual harassment can thus help to keep the rest of the discussion clear and focused. In the next chapter I will begin to criticize the law more directly: I will begin to develop an argument that will show that the law is, in fact, morally unjustified.

2
The Demarcation Problem

The Need for a Demarcation

In order to be morally justified, the law about sexual harassment would need to be able to provide a workable criterion of demarcation between sexual harassment and those forms of sexual interaction between people who work together that do not constitute sexual harassment. Moreover, it would need to provide the criterion in a way that does not leave the latter class empty or almost empty. In other words, if the prohibition of sexual harassment is to be morally justified, it would need to be a prohibition of only some, and not all sexual interaction between people who work together. If the law, upon investigation, turns out to amount to a prohibition of all sexual interaction between people who work together, it will follow that the law is unjustified.

In saying that the law ought to provide the criterion of demarcation in order to be justified, I do not mean that the demarcation ought to be sharp. It is well known that practically all legal concepts (just like everyday concepts) have fuzzy edges. Around almost every legal concept there is bound to be a gray area (what theoreticians like to call "penumbra") to which the concept neither indisputably applies nor indisputably fails to apply. All this is taken for granted here. The requirement that the law provide a workable criterion of demarcation should be interpreted as allowing that the demarcation be as fuzzy as similar legal demarcations usually are.

It is also important to note that the requirement does not say anything specific as to *what* kinds of sexual interaction in employment should be left outside the scope of the prohibition of sexual harassment; it merely says that *some* should.

Most people would, I believe, readily endorse the requirement that I have just formulated. The people who support the law generally do so in the belief that the law prohibits only some, and not all, conduct of a sexual nature in the workplace. Many people who are now not opposed to the law would become opposed to it, if they discovered that the law does not provide the demarcation, and that it amounts to a prohibition of all conduct of a sexual nature, within employment settings.

I will devote this chapter and the following one to investigating whether the law satisfies this requirement. However, before I proceed with that investigation, it may be worthwhile, for the sake of completeness, to spell out the reasons for the requirement. These reasons are probably obvious to quite a few of my readers, but the literature on the topic shows that spelling them out is not entirely redundant.

An Overall Ban on Sexual Activity?

Some people believe that all sexual interaction between those who work together is undesirable. Some among them think that such sexual activity is so undesirable that a prohibition of all of it should be welcomed.[1] People who hold such a position, may be tempted to reject the requirement for the justifiability of the sexual harassment law that I have formulated in the preceding section: they could claim that there is no need for the demarcation between sexual harassment and other forms of sexual interaction. If it turns out that the sexual harassment law amounts to a prohibition of all sexual interaction within employment, they could say, so much the better.

This line of thinking may not be very popular, but it still needs to be responded to. There are two responses to be made to it. The first is that, if one really believes that a prohibition of all sexual activity in the workplace is desirable, then one should fight for enactment and enforcement of rules that formulate that prohibition straightforwardly, clearly and unambiguously. The rules against sexual harassment do not do so. Although they may, upon investigation, turn out to prohibit all sexual interaction in the workplace, they, on the face of it, seem to prohibit only some of it. One should generally not support a law that accomplishes in a confused and confusing way something that could be accomplished straightforwardly (no matter how strongly one believes that what the law accomplishes is desirable). The belief that it would be desirable to prohibit all sexual interaction within employment, therefore, cannot provide a reason for supporting the sexual harassment law.

The second, more substantive, response to the line of thinking outlined above is that it would be morally wrong to prohibit all sexual interaction in employment settings.

OFFICE ROMANCES

The most obviously problematic consequence of such a prohibition is that it would prohibit a great deal of worthwhile interaction of a sexual nature from actually taking place. This point is not affected by the disagreements that people might have about what counts as "worthwhile" in this context. Whatever your criterion for worthwhile interaction of a sexual nature, chances are that this prohibition would prohibit a considerable amount of interaction that satisfies the criterion. Given that personal relationships that have a sexual component are, for most of us, among the most important sources of happiness and fulfillment in our lives, this counts very strongly against such a prohibition. It is difficult to see how that could ever be outweighed by the administrative convenience of having a general, and thus easy to apply, prohibition, and the administrative convenience seems to be the only advantage that the overall prohibition would have over a narrower, more carefully focused, prohibition.

A defender of the overall prohibition could, however, still respond that its bad consequences are not nearly as bad as the preceding paragraph makes them appear. For each of us, the number of potential sexual and romantic partners among the people who work at the same place is bound to be very small in comparison with the total number of such potential partners in the world at large. Therefore, it could be argued, the prohibition of sexual interaction with the people one works with would result only in a very small reduction of one's overall chances of achieving happiness, fulfillment, and so forth through relationships that have a sexual component. A defender of the prohibition could says that when the bad consequences of the prohibition are viewed that way, they turn out to be only minor, and that it is therefore not at all obvious that they cannot be outweighed by the considerations of administrative convenience.

Given that this response has a great deal of initial plausibility, it is important to spell out what exactly is at stake here. Where one works is in general related to what kind of a person one is. One normally chooses one's occupation and through that choice one normally manifests some important aspects of one's personality. Moreover, after one has been pursuing a certain career for some time, one often finds that one's preferences, interests, outlooks, and lifestyle have been importantly influenced by that career in many ways that go well beyond the boundaries of the job itself. As a consequence of all this, and of the history of shared experiences, one tends to have a lot in common with the people one works with. If one's interest in sexual interaction is directed primarily at such interaction within more elaborate personal relationships, which include genuine communication, deep understanding, shared interests, and so forth, in addition to their sexual component, then one is likely to value the opportunities for sexual interaction with the people one works with far more than the opportunities for such interaction with the people at large. The prohibition we are considering is thus likely to have a rather significant impact on such a person, even though the number of that person's potential partners that the prohibition covers may be small. (It is interesting to note in passing that the prohibition would have very little impact on those who are interested in purely sexual liaisons, because they can easily shift their pursuits away from their place of work.)

At this point, the reader will realize the significance of my stipulating, at the beginning of this book, that my discussion will be only about sexual harassment in employment and in the education of adults. The remarks that I have just made about the special value of the opportunities for romantic and sexual interaction with the people one works with can be readily extended to the education of adults (what one chooses to study or teach is importantly related to the kind of a person one is), but it is all too obvious that they cannot be extended to, say, the education of children.

It is important to note here that what has been said in this section does not depend on one's acceptance of any particular, controversial, moral theory. Different moral theories differ in why they regard personal relationships with a sexual component as desirable (some will say that that's simply because of the amount of happiness they generate, others will say that that's because they are an essential component of a well-rounded human life, or because of their importance to self-realization, and so forth), but practically all contemporary moral theories will agree that at least some such relationships are desirable. What has been said above also does not depend on one's acceptance of a particularly permissive outlook on sexual matters: even those who endorse a relatively restrictive sexual morality are likely to think that there are *some* relationships with a sexual component, notably marriage, that are desirable, and that it is important that people have opportunities to find the right partners for these relationships.

The fact that an overall ban on sexual activity within a workplace would significantly reduce people's opportunities for worthwhile interaction of a sexual nature is the main reason against it. An additional reason is that many people would, because of the importance they attach to romantic and sexual pursuits, have a strong temptation to disobey such a prohibition. Coupled with the fact that many of the violations of such a prohibition would be difficult to detect, this entails that the prohibition would be widely disobeyed, usually with impunity. This in itself constitutes a reason against the prohibition, because of the well-known general arguments against having rules that are generally violated with impunity. Such a rule is likely to diminish general respect for the system of rules of which it is a part. Moreover, such a rule invites selective enforcement. In other words, whenever there is such a rule, then any one out of the many people who have violated it is liable to be persecuted for illegitimate reasons (e.g., because someone harbors grudges against him) under the guise of being prosecuted under the rule.

The arguments of this section show that a prohibition of all sexual interaction between people who work at the same place would be morally unjustified. From this it follows that, if the law about sexual harassment amounts to such a prohibition, then it is morally unjustified. In other words, if the law about sexual harassment is to avoid the force of the argument of this section, then it would have to be possible to distinguish between sexual harassment and those forms of sexual interaction between people who work together that do not constitute sexual harassment, and to do so in a way that does not leave the latter class empty or nearly empty.

The arguments made in this section can be applied both to an overall ban on sexual activity within a particular workplace that an employer creates on its own,[2] and to an overall ban on sexual activity at all workplaces, that would be created by the state. The argument, however, has a special force in the latter case. When a particular employer enacts such a ban on its own, the undesirability of the ban is tempered by the fact that those who find it specially burdensome can seek employment elsewhere. If the ban were to apply throughout the jurisdiction, then, for most people, it would be very difficult to avoid it. Moreover, the political traditions of Western societies impose constraints on the state that are not imposed on private employers. If the state reduces its citizens' chances of reaching happiness and fulfillment, that is (in the absence of some very powerful further argument) at odds with the proper role of the state, and thus a ground for great concern. It is even arguable that, within the United States, a government-imposed ban on all sexual activity within employment would be constitutionally suspect, as "dating is a type of association which must be protected by the first amendment's freedom of association."[3]

Having said this, let me repeat that this book is primarily about the *law* about sexual harassment (and not about possible regulations that private institutions would choose to create for reasons of their own). If that law turns out to be incapable of providing demarcation between sexual harassment and other kinds of sexual interaction between people who work together, then the law will end up amounting to a government-imposed prohibition of all sexual interaction between people who work together. Being government-imposed makes it subject to the arguments of this section in their fullest force.

OFFICE AND TABOO

Many of the authors writing about sexual harassment[4] quote with approval a popular article that Margaret Mead published shortly before her death in 1978, according to which the society should establish a taboo, akin to the incest taboo, "that says clearly and unequivocally, 'You don't make passes at or sleep with the people you work with.' "[5] The arguments made in the preceding section already provide sufficient reasons for disagreeing with Mead's claim, but given that it is so often quoted, it may be worthwhile to make some additional comments about it.

The first thing to notice is that a taboo is by definition something that has a long history, something that is a part of the society's traditions. The existence of a taboo in the present or in the near future thus necessarily involves the past. Given that it is impossible for us to create something in the past, it is impossible for us to create *any* taboos in the near future. There is thus something odd about *proposing* that a taboo be created (Mead's article is entitled "A Proposal"):[6] to propose that a society introduce the taboo against sexual relationships between people who work together makes as little sense as it would to propose that we build a 300-year-old house.

There are admittedly no logical obstacles to our doing things that will result in there being such a taboo in some distant future, several generations from now. However, the contingent obstacles to our having any significant influence over such a distant future are far too obvious.

The point that I have just made can be regarded as purely terminological. It is possible to respond to it by saying that "taboo" is perhaps a wrong word to use here, but that we should nevertheless go ahead and create something like a taboo against sexual interaction between people who work together. My preceding point is, however, related to the following point which is definitely not terminological. A typical taboo, such as the incest taboo, is a prohibition that is very deeply internalized by the overwhelming majority of those to whom it applies. This being so is largely a spontaneous outcome of its long history. It is difficult to see what kind of deliberately undertaken action could ever produce comparable results. It seems that only an Orwellian society could hope to come even close to ensuring that almost all of its citizens internalize a prohibition that is not a genuine taboo as deeply as if it were a taboo.

A further relevant dissimilarity between the incest taboo and any prohibition of sexual relationships between people who work together that society might attempt to create is this. In most cases the relationship to which the incest taboo applies cannot be dissolved. One's siblings, for example, always remain one's siblings. One thus knows with certainty that the individuals who are one's siblings will always remain covered by the incest taboo. One cannot even think of any circumstances in which sexual relationships with them would cease to be prohibited by the taboo. This, as matter of psychological fact, makes it relatively easy for everyone to develop, toward each individual covered by the incest taboo, a disposition that very firmly precludes any sexual relationship from even being considered. The relationship of employment, on the other hand is, at least within the Western culture, regarded as something that can be dissolved fairly easily. One typically changes employers many times in one's lifetime, and even if one chooses to work for the same employer for a long period of time, chances are that other people will be joining and quitting that employer throughout that period. For each of us, the membership of the class of people who work at the same place, therefore, keeps changing almost continuously.[7] As a consequence of this, the operation of any possible prohibition of sexual relationships between people who work together would be psychologically very different from the operation of the incest taboo. Even if I endorsed such a prohibition and did my best to abstain from attempts at sexual interaction with some person I work with, I could still not regard that person as someone with whom I shall *never* be allowed to have a sexual relationship. Chances are that at some point in the future, or maybe even tomorrow, one of us will quit or be fired and the prohibition will then cease to apply. My awareness of that fact would make it psychologically impossible to develop toward such a person the firmly nonsexual disposition of the kind that one normally develops toward persons covered by the incest taboo.

Consent

Before we embark on the investigation as to whether the law provides a criterion of demarcation between sexual harassment and other kinds of sexual interaction between people who work together, which (as we have seen in the preceding sections of this chapter) it needs in order to be morally justified, it will be instructive to look at the way the problem of demarcation is treated in some nonlegal writings about sexual harassment. The authors of such writings are typically confident that the demarcation can be made, and they sometimes make their own attempts at formulating the criterion of demarcation. These attempts often differ from what actually appears in the law, without their authors being aware of the differences.

One widely quoted book on sexual harassment, for example, raises the question of demarcation by acknowledging that

> Sexual give-and-take—the friendly verbal interaction between colleagues, the acknowledged attraction between coworkers, the accepted physical gesturing of male and female—is a healthy behavior in which individuals of various ages and stations choose to engage.
>
> . . . The humor and affection in sexual give-and-take may be a way to reduce sexual tensions. It may relieve the monotony of routine work. It may even be preliminary courtship, a kind of testing before proceeding with a more serious relationship.[8]

and offers the following as the solution:

> "Choice" is the critical concept. . . . Whatever the intent, sexual give-and-take is based on mutual *consent* of equals. This is obviously not the case in sexual harassment.[9]

Relying on the word "consent" to mark the boundary between sexual harassment and other forms of sexual interaction between people who work together appears natural both because of the widespread usc of the phrase "consenting adults" in connection with other sex-related matters and because the word "consent" usually marks the boundary between rape and sexual intercourse that is not rape, and analogies between sexual harassment and rape readily suggest themselves. Another popular book on the topic thus says that

> Sexual harassment is not synonymous with all sexual activity any more than rape is synonymous with intercourse.[10]

and an article in a law review similarly declares

> From a feminist perspective, love and sexual harassment are as different as love and rape.[11]

The actual law explicitly[12] rejects the presence of consent as the criterion of demarcation, but the idea that the presence of consent *could* be the criterion is nevertheless a tempting one. It is therefore worthwhile to devote this section to investigating whether the notion of consent would be capable of playing the same role in the case of sexual harassment that it plays in the case of rape. Showing, within this section, why it is incapable of playing that role will facilitate our discussion of the actual law, in the sections that follow.

People, in general, have no difficulty understanding the requirement that one should seek the consent of one's intended partner before engaging in sexual intercourse. It is notorious that cases occasionally arise in which one's general understanding of that requirement may be difficult to apply, but such cases are exceptional. In the overwhelming majority of cases, people know how to go about complying with this requirement, and find it relatively easy to pursue their sexual interests without violating it. Rapists typically rape not because they find the requirement unintelligible or impossible to satisfy, but because they simply choose to disregard it.

There is also no deep difficulty about understanding how the requirement of consent applies not only to sexual intercourse itself, but also to many other forms of physical contact aimed at sexual satisfaction. Both the criminal and the civil law have always required consent for such activities, even in the absence of any law about sexual harassment.

The law about sexual harassment, however, does not apply only to activities of this kind, but also to acts such as "requests for sexual favors" and "sexual advances." Those who think about sexual harassment in terms of consent seem to believe that this is simply an *extension* of the range of activities to which the requirement of consent applies and that the requirement can still be understood by analogy with the requirement of consent for sexual intercourse.

This is not so. The analogy breaks down because requests for sexual favors and sexual advances *are* precisely the acts of seeking consent for sexual interaction. To say that one should seek consent for these acts is to say that one should seek consent for seeking consent for sexual interaction. Thinking about sexual harassment in this way thus introduces *iterated* requirements of consent, which is something that is absent from the straightforward requirement of consent that is embodied in the law about rape, assault, and so on.

This is not in itself an argument against looking at sexual harassment in terms of consent. *Sometimes* it makes perfect sense to say that one should not even seek consent for something unless one is in the appropriate relationship with the person whose consent one intends to seek, and that one can be in such a relationship only as a result of having sought and obtained consent to be in it. In the matter at hand, for example, it makes sense to say that one should never straightforwardly ask for someone's consent to sexual intercourse, unless that person has already consented to be in a certain kind of personal relationship in which consent for sexual intercourse may be sought. Whatever one might think about the wisdom of making this into a legal rule, one cannot claim that the fact that this rule involves iterated requirements of consent in any way impairs its intelligibility, or that it would make it unduly difficult to comply with it. In fact, most people have always followed some such rule as a matter of social convention anyway.

One could easily think of other examples, in which there are three, four, and perhaps many more iterated requirements of consent, and in which that still does not cause any serious problem. There is, however, a serious problem when we have *infinitely* many iterated requirements of consent, and this is precisely what we end up having if we think about sexual harassment in terms of consent. An act of seeking consent for sexual interaction of any kind can always be aptly described as a sexual advance itself, and this is what generates the infinite regress. If there were a requirement that one seek consent for every sexual advance one intends to make, then one could comply with that requirement only by making another, prior, sexual advance. But given that the requirement applies to all advances, it applies to that prior advance too: in order to legitimize it, one has to make another, still earlier sexual advance. The requirement, however, applies to *it* as well, therefore etc. *ad infinitum.*

The requirement that one seek consent prior to engaging in sexual intercourse and the requirement that one seek consent prior to engaging in any form of behavior that is currently within the scope of the sexual harassment law are therefore radically different: while the former is relatively easy to comply with, the latter would be not just difficult but in principle impossible to comply with. What I have just said is, of course, slightly exaggerated, because there would in fact be one (but only one) way of complying with the requirement, and that would be never to engage in *any* form of sexual interaction with the people one works with.

Every relationship of sexual nature, as a matter of logic, begins with a first step, and that first step is, again as a matter of logic, bound to be nonconsensual. To prohibit all nonconsensual sexual interaction is thus to prohibit the first step of every relationship of sexual nature, and to prohibit the first step of something is to prohibit the whole of it. The prohibition of all nonconsensual sexual interaction would therefore amount to a prohibition of *all* sexual interaction.

In assessing the impact of this discussion, it is important to realize that many of the types of acts that are routinely listed as examples of sexual harassment are precisely the types of acts that are, within our culture, often used to seek *initial* consent for further sexual interaction. Staring at someone is, for example, often a way of trying to establish eye contact, and eye contact is often sought because it communicates consent to further interaction. Sexual jokes or comments on someone's physical appearance are often made precisely in order to enable one to see whether the person to whom they are addressed will respond to them in a way that will signal consent to further interaction of that kind or not.

An argument similar to the one made in this section can be used to dismiss the recommendation made by Mary Radford that the criterion of demarcation in the sexual harassment law should be whether the conduct in question "was actively solicited or freely consented to."[13] The argument made above applies straightforwardly to the part of her criterion that invokes free consent, so the only part that requires special comment is the one about active solicitation. (That part is incidentally reminiscent of the purported criterion of demarcation that appeared in the early "Policy Statement and Definition on Sexual Harassment" for federal employees,[14] which made it crucial whether the conduct was unsolicited; the comment that follows applies to it as well.)

Saying that someone's sexual advances do not constitute sexual harassment if they have been "actively solicited" by the other person does not bring us any closer to solving the demarcation problem, because it seems obvious that active solicitation of someone's sexual advances is itself a sexual advance, and the question thus immediately arises as to whether that active solicitation done by the other person constitutes sexual harassment or not. If two people, A and B, took Radford's proposed criterion seriously, the result would be that A would be waiting for B to actively solicit A's sexual advances, and B would be waiting for A to actively solicit B's active solicitation of sexual advances, and that no sexual advances would ever be made, because each party would be waiting for the other one to make the first move.

The active solicitation part of Radford's criterion effectively gives us the rule "Don't be the one to make the first step in interactions of a sexual nature." But if everyone is under the rule that prohibits the first steps of such interactions, then we in fact have a wholesale prohibition of sexual interaction, because it is, as a matter of logic, impossible to make a second, third, or any further step in such interaction without someone making the first one.

Unwelcomeness

Having disposed of the suggestion that the term "consent" could play a role in providing the criterion of demarcation, we should now examine whether the criteria that the law actually uses fare any better. According to the Supreme Court, "[t]he gravamen of any sexual harassment claim is that the alleged sexual advances were 'unwelcome.' "[15]

The term "unwelcome" comes from the well-known Guidelines on Sexual Harassment,[16] promulgated by the federal Equal Employment Opportunity Commission (EEOC), where it is used in a way that appears to provide a criterion of demarcation. These guidelines are widely quoted, and nonlegal writings on sexual harassment often leave the impression that the Guidelines are *the* law on sexual harassment in the United States,[17] although strictly speaking they do not have the force of the law on their own but only because and insofar as the courts have chosen to endorse them, which is something they were not obliged to do. Like other EEOC interpretations of civil rights legislation, they are "entitled to deference by the courts only insofar as the underlying reasoning is convincing,"[18] but although "not controlling upon the courts by reason of their authority, [they] do constitute a body of experience and informed judgement to which courts and litigants may properly resort for guidance."[19]

Although the Guidelines are an interpretation of a *federal* statute, their wording has influenced the state law as well: some state legislatures have enacted statutes about sexual harassment in which the term "unwelcome" plays the same or similar role as in the federal Guidelines.[20] The formulation has also had influence outside the United States: the term *unwelcome*, for example, plays a similar role in the section on sexual harassment of the New Zealand Employment Relations Act.[21] In the Guidelines the word "unwelcome" appears in the context of "unwelcome sexual advances, requests for sexual favors, and other verbal or physical conduct of sexual nature" in a way that leaves it ambiguous whether the word "unwelcome" was intended to qualify only "sexual advances" or the phrases that follow after it as well. This ambiguity, however, does not affect my argument, which concentrates on sexual advances.

Now we can all probably think of clear-cut cases of unwelcome sexual advances and clear-cut cases of welcome sexual advances, and it therefore seems unquestionable that the word "unwelcome" marks a genuine distinction here. This, however, is not enough, because if the rules about sexual harassment are to be legitimate legal rules, they have to be capable not only of being applied by various observers after the fact, but also of playing a role in guiding potential harassers before they act.

In order to comply with a rule that prohibits unwelcome sexual advances, one has to find out, of each sexual advance that one considers making, whether it would be unwelcome or not. Given that people's preferences in sexual matters tend to vary greatly from one individual to another, and that they usually don't advertise them, readily available information about a given person typically does not provide sufficient ground for concluding whether that person would, under the given circumstances, welcome a sexual advance from such-and-such other person or not. Broad generalizations, such as the generalization that a married person is less likely to welcome an advance than an unmarried one, are far too broad to entail anything useful about individual cases. This means that, in a typical case, the only way to find out whether the sexual advance one is contemplating would be welcome is to ask whether it would be welcome.[22] But asking whether something would be welcome is very similar to seeking consent for it. Therefore, although the consent-based and welcomeness-based demarcation may look different from the viewpoint of an after-the-fact observer, they are very similar from the viewpoint of a person who is trying to comply with the prohibition of sexual harassment. This similarity makes welcomeness-based attempt at the demarcation liable to the argument that was used in the preceding section.

Asking whether a sexual advance would be welcome need not, of course, take the form of a straightforward verbal inquiry: our culture provides numerous nonverbal and roundabout verbal ways of accomplishing the same purpose. But in whatever way it may be carried out, it remains true that this prior inquiry itself constitutes a sexual advance. The prohibition of unwelcome sexual advances therefore applies to it as well: the only way to comply is to find out whether it would be unwelcome, and one can find that out only if one undertakes another, still earlier, inquiry, which inquiry, in turn, is going to constitute yet another sexual advance, and so on. The same infinite regress gets generated again.

Someone may try to respond to this argument by claiming that an *inquiry* as to whether *X* would be (un)welcome is, in general, *less likely* to be unwelcome than *X* itself. On that basis, one could argue that the likelihood of unwelcomeness keeps diminishing as we follow the regress, and that after a certain *finite* number of steps it becomes so low as not to create any practical difficulty. Therefore, he could claim, for most ends and purposes, the regress need not be regarded as infinite, after all.

This counterargument is, however, mistaken: the likelihood of unwelcomeness does *not* diminish along the regress. An inquiry as to whether *X* would be unwelcome, other things being equal, has *exactly* the same likelihood of being unwelcome as *X* itself. This is because whenever *X* itself would be unwelcome, an inquiry as to whether *X* would be (un)welcome is bound to be unwelcome too. If I would not welcome *X*, then I have no reason whatsoever to welcome an inquiry about it (viewed as such) and at least some reasons not to welcome it, namely that answering it requires expenditure of my time and energy (not to mention that it might be disruptive).

If I would not welcome owning a new vacuum cleaner, for example, then I would not welcome a visit from a vacuum cleaner salesman either. There is nothing that I can gain from such a visit, and there is something I am bound to lose if the salesman knocks on my door: I have to stop doing whatever I am doing at the moment, go to the door, open it, and then explain that I am not interested in vacuum cleaners. The loss of my time and energy may be relatively minor, but a loss it nevertheless is.

The same reasons entail that, if I would not welcome membership in the Jehovah's Witnesses, then I would not welcome a visit from a proselytizing Jehovah's Witness; and that, if I would not welcome a certain form of sexual interaction with someone, then I would not welcome a sexual advance aimed at that interaction either.

For some values of *X*, I may have further reasons for not welcoming any inquiries as to whether *X* would be welcome, but we do not need to discuss these, because the reason based on expenditure of time and energy is sufficient to establish the connection between the unwelcomeness of *X* and the unwelcomeness of inquiries about it, for all values of *X*. We therefore have to conclude that the word "unwelcome" does generate the same kind of infinite regress as the word "consent."

The above reasoning is of course concerned with inquiries as to whether *X* would be (un)welcome only *as such*: an inquiry that is unwelcome as such may well turn out to be welcome because of some special circumstances. A visit of a vacuum cleaner salesman may provide a welcome break for someone who has been grading first-year essays for hours, but such examples do not refute the general point that is made above.

To make this point still clearer, I should emphasize that the "logic" of the word "unwelcome" is different from that of some other words for negative attitudes, such as "repugnant" and "outrageous." The appeal that the above objection to my infinite regress argument may have, at first sight, is probably due to not appreciating that difference.

From the fact that I would find *X* repugnant it does not, in general, follow that I would find an inquiry about it repugnant. This is because the *intensity* of my negative attitude toward the inquiry is often lower than the intensity of my negative attitude toward *X*, and it is thus possible that it would fall below the threshold for application of the word "repugnant." The crucial difference between "repugnant" and "unwelcome" is that "repugnant" is not simply a word for a negative attitude, but a word for a negative attitude above a certain threshold of intensity, while the meaning of "unwelcome" does not involve the intensity of the attitude. As long as the attitude *is* negative, rather than positive, the word "unwelcome" is appropriate, no matter how low the intensity of that negative attitude might be. It is quite possible that, as we follow the regress that my argument presents, the intensity of the negative attitude is diminishing, but the likelihood of the applicability of the word "unwelcome" to describe that attitude is not thereby diminishing, because the meaning of that word is indifferent to intensity. If one attempted to create such a regress with the word "repugnant," the intensity-threshold that is built into the meaning of *that* word could prevent the regress from becoming infinite, but there is no such threshold to stop the regress with the word "unwelcome."

The word "unwanted," which is sometimes[23] also used in characterizations of sexual harassment, is in the same category as "unwelcome": the above infinite regress could have been created with that word as well.

OFFENSIVENESS

The argument that I have just presented shows that the word "unwelcome" is incapable of playing any useful role in providing the criterion of demarcation. This still does not constitute a complete argument against the present law, because the law, following the EEOC Guidelines, does not treat the unwelcomeness of a sexual advance as a sufficient condition for its being an instance of sexual harassment: the criterion of unwelcomeness is supposed to work together with a number of other criteria.

Let us therefore examine more closely the part of the Guidelines that purports to provide the criterion of demarcation. Its actual wording is:

> Unwelcome sexual advances, requests for sexual favors, and other verbal or physical conduct of a sexual nature constitute sexual harassment when (1) submission to such conduct is made either explicitly or implicitly a term or condition of an individual's employment, (2) submission to or rejection of such conduct by an individual is used as the basis for employment decisions affecting such individual, or (3) such conduct has the purpose or effect of unreasonably interfering with an individual's work performance or creating an intimidating, hostile, or offensive working environment.

As can be seen, this formulation has the structure of a complex disjunction. The rate of incidence and the intuitive moral gravity of the behavior described varies considerably from one disjunct to another. Because of its complexity, one cannot tell whether this formulation is capable of providing the criterion of demarcation just by glancing at it.

However, for my purposes, it might not be necessary to examine all the elements of the formulation. In order to see why this is so, consider a simpler but structurally similar purported criterion of demarcation which says "X or Y constitutes sexual harassment." Suppose that upon analysis it turns out that X cannot be demarcated from other forms of sexual interaction. In such a case we would be entitled to conclude that the purported criterion as a whole is defective, without investigating Y at all. If there is no form of sexual interaction for which we can confidently say that it is *not* X, then there is no form of sexual interaction for which we can confidently say that it is not X-or-Y. This is so whatever Y is and however well it might be possible to separate *it* from other forms of sexual interaction. In other words, something that purports to be a disjunctively structured criterion of demarcation is only as good as its most problematic disjunct. In order to prove that a disjunctively structured criterion of demarcation is defective, it is thus enough to show that one of its disjuncts "leaks."

This pattern of reasoning is valid regardless of how simple or complex the relevant disjunctive structure is. We can therefore use it in criticizing the above quoted part of the Guidelines. We can concentrate on the disjunct(s) in it that strike us as demarcation-wise weakest and examine them, setting aside the rest of the disjunction. If we succeed in proving that there is no workable criterion of demarcation between the conduct covered by *one* disjunct that purports to spell out *a* sufficient condition for sexual harassment and sexual interaction that does not constitute sexual harassment, we shall have succeeded in proving that the Guidelines, as a whole, do not provide the criterion of demarcation we are looking for.

Let us therefore first analyze the quoted part of the Guidelines with the view to extracting from it the disjunct that, so far as the demarcation is concerned, appears to be the most problematic one.

The conduct that is characterized by (1) and (2) taken together is usually referred to as *quid pro quo* harassment while the conduct characterized by (3) is known as the *hostile environment* harassment. Hostile environment sexual harassment has also been referred to as *sexual annoyance*[24] and in the nonlegal literature a great deal of it is referred to as *gender harassment.* The hostile environment harassment seems more problematic than the quid pro quo, so far as the demarcation is concerned, and we should therefore concentrate on it, setting aside the quid pro quo: that there are forms of sexual interaction that do not constitute quid pro quo harassment seems fairly obvious.

It is, by the way, interesting to note that although the wording of the Guidelines presents these two as distinct classes of harassment, a moment's thought will show that the class of phenomena that satisfies (1) and (2) can, for most ends and purposes, be regarded as included in the class of phenomena that satisfies (3).[25] Behavior that involves quid pro quo harassment but fails to constitute hostile environment harassment is logically possible, or so it could be argued, but it is difficult to see how it could ever be significant. The presence of (1) and (2) in the quoted wording is thus largely redundant, and it is not immediately obvious why they have been included. Perhaps the point of formulating (1) and (2) as distinct conditions has been not so much to include an additional class of phenomena, but rather to allow for different legal treatment of quid pro quo harassment from the conduct that is *merely* hostile environment harassment. Thus the relationship of (3) to (1) and (2) could be regarded as akin to that of a "lesser included offense." A less charitable explanation is that (1) and (2) were included simply to make the Guidelines more palatable: their absence would have made the problems associated with what is now (3) far more obvious. Or perhaps the inclusion of (1) and (2) did not have any definite point at all, but was simply an accidental remnant of some earlier stage in the drafting of the Guidelines.

In 1989, the Supreme Court of Canada, in commenting on the U.S. distinction between quid pro quo and hostile environment harassment, characterized it as something that "may have been important to illustrate forcefully the range of behaviour that constitutes harassment at a time before sexual harassment was widely viewed as actionable," but failed to explain how singling out the least controversial form of harassment could have accomplished that purpose.[26] It went on to reject (for the purposes of Canadian law) the distinction as something for which "there is no longer any need."[27] Nine years later, the U.S. Supreme Court declared the distinction as of "limited utility."[28]

Whatever the reason for distinguishing these two forms of harassment might have been, hostile environment harassment is more likely to create demarcation problems than quid pro quo, and our argument about demarcation should therefore concentrate on it. In analyzing its characterization in the Guidelines, we find the disjunction "purpose or effect." It seems that here we can safely concentrate on "effect." It is again unclear why we have the distinction in the first place, because most of the conduct that has the purpose of creating an intimidating, hostile, or offensive working environment will also succeed in having that effect. Conduct that has that purpose but fails to produce the effect is admittedly possible, but unlikely to be very significant. The "effect" is the important disjunct in the "purpose or effect" disjunction because it covers almost everything significant that is covered by "purpose" plus much more, and it is that "more" that is likely to cause problems so far as demarcation is concerned.

The phrase "requests for sexual favors" seems to pick out a species of sexual advances and is therefore also redundant so far as the demarcation is concerned. Between "verbal" and "physical conduct" it is obviously "verbal" that is more likely to cause problems, and from "intimidating," "hostile," and "offensive" I propose to concentrate on "offensive." We are thus left with the following:

> unwelcome sexual advances or other verbal conduct of a sexual nature which has the effect of creating an offensive working environment.

According to the EEOC Guidelines, it is a sufficient reason for regarding something as sexual harassment that it can be characterized in this way.

Suppose one wishes to avoid engaging in this kind of conduct. How does one go about that?

Given that we have already seen that the word "unwelcome" is not doing any useful job here, the only thing that remains to be done is to try to predict whether the conduct that one is contemplating will actually have the effect of "creating an offensive working environment" for the person (or persons) in question.

Before I start examining how one might go about that I should perhaps mention that in deciding to discuss the notion of unwelcomeness first (in the preceding section) and then separately (in this section) the notion of offensiveness, I have assumed that the notion of offensiveness is not contained in the notion of unwelcomeness, which is, I suspect, how most people would tend to understand these notions. In assuming that, I have set aside the rather peculiar position of the Eighth Circuit, according to which unwelcomeness entails offensiveness, or in the words of the court that "to find that the conduct was unwelcome but not offensive was internally inconsistent."[29] This position is peculiar not only because it is at odds with the ordinary meaning of these words, but also because it misinterprets the court's own earlier view that unwelcomeness means that "the employee did not solicit or invite it, and the employee regarded the conduct as undesirable *or* offensive"[30] (which is based on the Eleventh Circuit opinion in *Henson v. City of Dundee*[31]) as the view that it involves its being "uninvited *and* offensive."[32] However, even if one were to accept the new position of the Eighth Circuit that wouldn't significantly affect the outcome of my argument. In order to adapt the argument to that position one would only need to reword the preceding section as being about one aspect of the Eighth Circuit's notion of unwelcomeness and the present section would need to be treated as being about another aspect of that notion. The substance of the argument would, however, remain the same.

It should be noted that one's conduct may have the effect of creating an offensive working environment not only for the person to whom it is directed, but also on those who witness it, hear about it, or are otherwise exposed to its side effects.[33] Indeed it is possible for one's conduct to have such effect on these third parties, while being enjoyable to the person to whom it is directed. The prediction as to whether one's conduct will have the effect of creating an offensive working environment therefore needs to be made not only with respect to the person to whom it is to be directed, but also with respect to everyone who may come to be influenced by it. If the conduct is to be directed to A, but B, C, and D may come to know about it, then one needs to predict that with respect to each of them. That such third parties may have an actionable claim of sexual harassment even if the conduct is not at all offensive to the person to whom it is to be directed[34] is one of the many features of the sexual harassment law that are not appreciated by the general public. Even a respectable journalist was obviously unaware of it, when in reporting on a case of sexual harassment at the University of New Hampshire, he remarked with surprise that "the conclusion of the university apparently [was] that one can be harassed even when the harasser is talking to somebody else."[35]

Now, again, given that people tend to differ greatly in what they find offensive in sexual matters, a prediction as to whether something will create an offensive working environment for someone is often very difficult to make on the basis of the readily available information about the person. Even a book that strongly supports the current sexual harassment law readily acknowledges that "[w]hat is offensive to one person may be perfectly acceptable to another."[36]

For example, some married people, who have strict views about adultery, may be offended by *any* sexual advance directed at them, no matter how it is formulated, because they regard it as implying that they are immoral, while some other married people are longing for affairs. Yet, the two may be indistinguishable in terms of the general information that is likely to be available to those who work with them. The readers who are tempted to respond to this example by saying that the desires of those who are longing for extramarital affairs are somehow unworthy of being taken into consideration should return to the section on legal moralism in chapter 1.[37] Here we are taking the Guidelines and related court cases at face value, and taken at face value they do not constitute a mechanism for legally endorsing the ideal of marital faithfulness.

Or, to take another example, some people strongly believe that old-fashioned gallantry is inherently sexist, and may consequently be offended by sexual advances formulated in the style of old-fashioned gallantry. Others may find such advances intensely romantic or endearing. Some people believe that propriety requires that sexual advances always be made in a roundabout way, and will consequently be offended by any sexual advance that is direct, explicit, unambigous. Others may find the directness and explicitness refreshingly honest. Again, which such group a particular person belongs to may be far from obvious to those who work with the person. Readers can probably easily formulate numerous other examples of such differences.

The language of the quoted part of the Guidelines makes it irrelevant that the conduct at issue in a particular case could have been inoffensive and even pleasing if directed at somebody other than the plaintiff; the only thing that matters is whether the conduct *actually* has the required kind of effect on *the plaintiff*. The Commission of the European Communities has similarly declared that '[t]he essential characteristic of sexual harassment is . . . that it is for each individual to determine what behaviour is acceptable to them and what they regard as offensive."[38]

In many cases, the only way to arrive at a prediction as to whether certain conduct of a sexual nature will create offensive working environment for a specific person seems to be to ask the person. But to do that is to engage in "sexual advances or other verbal conduct" that may well turn out to contribute to creating "an offensive working environment." So we seem to have the regress again.

However, the argument I used above cannot be transposed here completely. This is because the word "offensive" seems to be, in the relevant respect, more similar to the word "repugnant" than to "unwelcome." The infinity of the regress may therefore be avoidable. It is indeed quite possible to make inquiries as to whether *X* is offensive in a way that will not be offensive even to those who find *X* itself offensive. For example, the question "Do you find it offensive if someone tells sexual jokes in your presence?" (asked in a serious tone of voice) is unlikely to be offensive even to those who find actual sexual jokes offensive.

Such cautious inquiries may indeed stop the infinite regress, but they give rise to another problem. They purchase their relative inoffensiveness at the price of imprecision. If I put to someone the above question about sexual jokes, that person may well answer "no" having in mind some mildly off-color jokes, and then nevertheless feel offended by a particularly gross joke that I proceed to tell. If the person is more thoughtful, the answer may end up being the true but unhelpful "it all depends on the joke." In order to get the information one needs one has to make one's inquiry more specific. But the more specific, precise, unambiguous, such an inquiry is, the more similar to its subject matter it becomes. This similarity entails increased likelihood of offensiveness. If one makes the inquiry about jokes more specific by asking "Do you find it offensive if, in your presence, people tell sexual jokes that contain the following features: . . . ?" one reduces the probability of misunderstanding, but also creates the risk that the listing of the features of sexual jokes that one has in mind will itself be offensive to one's interlocutor. Increase in the precision of such inquiries thus goes together with increase in the likelihood of their being offensive. The limiting case would be to ask something like "Do you find it offensive if, in your presence, people tell jokes like this one: ' . . .'?", which is bound to trigger the same reaction as if the joke had been straightforwardly told. (An average person in such a situation is unlikely to be impressed by philosophical arguments that this utterance does not really constitute telling the joke, because the text of the joke appears between quotation marks, and quotation marks radically change the character of what appears between them.)

If one is to be reasonably certain that one's preliminary inquiry as to whether one's contemplated course of behavior would be offensive, will not itself be offensive, one has to formulate it in vague general terms, which means that it becomes unlikely to accomplish its purpose. If one is to ensure that it does accomplish its purpose, one has to make it specific, unambiguous, precise, but in sexual matters such a specific, unambiguous, precise inquiry is almost as likely to cause offense as the behavior that it is about. Because of this dilemma, compliance with the requirement presented by the EEOC Guidelines is *impossible*, except by abstaining from *all* sexual advances and other verbal conduct of a sexual nature.[39]

It should be noted that this problem with the sexual harassment law is not simply a matter of its imposing what amounts to strict liability. What the sexual harassment law has in common with other instances of strict liability is that no precautions are sufficient to ensure that one won't "break" the law (short of completely abstaining from the whole general area of activity to which the law applies). However, the important difference is that, under an ordinary strict liability law, one is still *permitted* to take the precautions. One thus still has a considerable amount of control over whether one will run afoul of the law or not. Indeed, the purpose of having a strict liability law is usually to strongly encourage the taking of precautions. The sexual harassment law, on the other hand, in virtue of applying to sexual advances and verbal conduct, preempts all precautions that law-abiding citizens may make against violating it (short of abstaining from all sexual interaction with the people they work with).[40]

The arguments that I have presented so far in this chapter apply to the present sexual harassment law in virtue of the role that it assigns to the notions of unwelcomeness and offensiveness. In the case of *DeAngelis v. El Paso Municipal Police Officers Association*, Fifth Circuit has, however, used a criterion of sexual harassment that required the conduct in question to be "extremely insensitive."[41] On the face of it, it would seem that a criterion of what sexual harassment is that is centered around that concept could easily avoid the arguments that I have adduced here. We can, however, treat that decision as solving the problem of demarcation only if we are prepared to read it as promulgating a *new* criterion of what sexual harassment is, a criterion *different* from anything that can be found in the rest of the sexual harassment law in the United States. Such a reading would, however, put the decision in conflict with the Supreme Court's decisions in *Meritor Savings Bank v. Vinson*,[42] which seems to endorse the EEOC Guidelines. It would also be at odds with the fact that the Court of Appeals has itself presented this criterion as merely an interpretation of the existing body of law and not a change in it.

In dealing with the *DeAngelis* decision we thus have two options. One is to take the way the criterion is presented as decisive, and to treat it as simply a confusing and potentially misleading reformulation of the existing law, which does not really affect its substance. The other is to take the ordinary meaning of the term "extremely insensitive" as decisive, in which case we would have to treat the decision as an illegitimate attempt on the part of the Court of Appeals to surreptitiously overrule the Supreme Court. In any event, this decision is definitely not representative of the law as a whole, and it would thus be unwise for individual potential harassers to rely on it.

A DIGRESSION ON NONSEXUAL INTERACTION

While the fact that the prohibition of sexual harassment amounts to the prohibition of all sexual interaction between people who work together is, according to the argument of the first three sections in this chapter, sufficient to make it morally unjustified, I would like to point out that the unfortunate consequences of there being no demarcation extend into the realm of nonsexual interaction as well.

Many people believe, for various reasons, that their sexual relationships should not be openly and unambiguously sexual from the beginning.

They believe, rather, that a certain degree of friendship should be established between the two people involved before the sexual character of the relationship is brought into the open. A person who holds such a belief will, when sexually interested in someone, first undertake to establish the requisite degree of friendship. In its initial stages, such a relationship may be called "sexual" insofar as it is motivated by sexual interest, but is, in terms of overt behavior, indistinguishable from nonsexual friendship. During these initial stages, even the person who initiated the relationship need not be fully committed to its becoming an openly sexual relationship. The person may be open to *both* the possibility of its turning into an openly sexual relationship *and* the possibility of its turning into a clearly nonsexual friendship: the choice between the two can be left for a later stage.

For the purposes of this argument it is irrelevant whether the reasons for which people hold such views are good or bad: the only thing that is relevant is that quite a few people do hold them and act accordingly. Given that we all know that this approach to sexual relationships is widespread, we all interpret the behavior of others in the light of that knowledge. An act that otherwise has no visible sexual character, such as inviting someone for a drink, or simply engaging someone in a conversation that goes beyond the conventional "small talk," thus often gets, quite reasonably, interpreted as a sexual advance.

In fact, *any* act directed at establishing friendship with someone may be regarded as possibly a sexual advance, unless there is something about the situation that makes the existence of sexual interest unlikely (e.g., both people are of the same sex and known to be exclusively heterosexual). Attempts at establishing friendships are thus, at least within the contemporary Western culture, often indistinguishable from sexual advances. A prohibition of sexual advances between people who work together is therefore bound to discourage attempts at establishing friendships wherever sexual interest is *possible.* By discouraging these attempts at establishing friendships one, of course, discourages all the friendships that would have eventuated from the attempts, including the nonsexual friendships.[43]

It needs to be emphasized that the problem described here is *not* that certain sexual advances just *happen to be similar* to, and are thus difficult to distinguish from, attempts at establishing nonsexual friendships. These sexual advances are *deliberately made indistinguishable* from attempts at establishing nonsexual friendships. As a consequence, the two are not just difficult but *impossible* to distinguish. The problem is not just another one among many problems that are due to our power of discernment not being refined enough. There is thus no hope of our ever becoming able to distinguish them, no matter how carefully we think about the matter.

The Severe-or-Pervasive Test and the Two Levels

There is an important objection that can be raised against my argument so far. The Supreme Court has held that sexual harassment of the kind I have been considering is actionable only if it is "sufficiently *severe or pervasive* 'to alter the conditions of [the victim's] employment and create an abusive working environment.' "[44]

The final words are taken from the 1982 Eleventh Circuit decision in *Henson v. City of Dundee,*[45] although the actual test used there was only whether the harassment was sufficiently pervasive and that was treated as equivalent to whether it was "sufficiently severe *and* persistent,"[46] which appears to be a narrower test than the Supreme Court's "severe *or* pervasive." In 1990, in deciding *Andrews v. City of Philadelphia,* the Third Circuit used a similarly narrow test of whether the conduct in question was "pervasive and regular,"[47] thereby apparently disregarding the Supreme Court's severe-or-pervasive test, which by that time should have been controlling.[48] Such a lapse is perhaps understandable in the light of the fact that, when the courts find the severe-or-pervasive test to be satisfied, they typically do so on the basis of the pervasiveness of the conduct, or pervasiveness together with severity, rather than on the basis of severity alone. That a severe incident of harassment may give rise to an actionable claim even without pervasiveness is sometimes mentioned in passing,[49] but has only rarely been the basis of actual decisions.[50]

Whether the severe-or-pervasive test has spelled out the meaning of the EEOC Guidelines or introduced an element that is not in the Guidelines is debatable. The phrase "severe or pervasive" certainly does not appear in the actual wording of the Guidelines and it is thus possible to argue, as was done by Wendy Pollack, that in putting forward the test the Supreme "Court ignores the EEOC Guidelines entirely" and replaces them with something "more formidable."[51] On the other hand it could be argued that the severe-or-pervasive test is in harmony with the Guidelines, because, although the Guidelines don't say anything about severity or pervasiveness, they do speak of "creating an intimidating, hostile, or offensive working *environment.*" It is difficult to see how, say, offensive conduct that is neither severe nor pervasive could ever succeed in creating anything that could be called offensive *environment.* It could thus be argued that the severe-or-pervasive test merely makes explicit what is, in the Guidelines, implicit in the word "environment."

In any event, it is clear that, except for severe incidents, a single act is not sufficient to give rise to liability: viable action has to be based on "incidents, comments, or conduct that occurred with some frequency."[52]

Someone may try to argue that, when this requirement is taken into account, the law about sexual harassment turns out to be much less absurd than my argument has made it appear.

In order to see why the severe-or-pervasive test does not, in fact, detract from the argument I have presented, we need to fully appreciate the implications of one important feature of the sexual harassment law that is often misunderstood by the general public. It is that the mechanism by means of which the harassment law is intended to prevent harassment has two levels.

Unlike, say, the criminal prohibitions of rape, assault, and similar acts, that directly require individual potential rapists, assaulters, and so on to abstain from such acts, the law about sexual harassment, in general, does *not* operate primarily through requiring individual potential harassers to abstain from harassment.

The law about sexual harassment is primarily addressed to employers: it requires *them* to *see to it* that there is no harassment in their businesses. In court cases under the sexual harassment law, it is typically the employer, rather than the alleged harasser, that appears as the defendant. The federal law on sexual harassment provides the option of naming the alleged harasser as a defendant only if that individual exercised a supervisory role over the plaintiff. Even then, the alleged harassers can, according to the widely,[53] but not universally,[54] accepted interpretation of the law, be sued only in their official capacities, and not in their individual capacities (and "official-capacity suits generally represent only another way of pleading an action against an entity of which an officer is an agent"[55]). The plaintiffs who have the option of naming the alleged harassers as defendants sometimes do use it, but even when they do, they will sue their employers as well. (One book of advice for people who perceive themselves as victims of sexual harassment says: "In filing claims, the rule of thumb is: sue everybody.")[56] In any event, we should not allow the availability of this option to obscure the fact that the plaintiffs can *always* sue their employers, and that the main operation of the sexual harassment law is *via* the employers rather than by being directly addressed to potential harassers.

Thus, so far as most people who might engage in acts of sexual harassment are concerned, the law does not say anything directly to them. The law nevertheless affects their lives, because it requires their employers to see to it that there is no harassment in their businesses and the employers normally comply with that requirement by enacting and enforcing various internal regulations of their businesses that require individual potential harassers to abstain from harassment.

Let us call the legal requirement that employers see to it that there is no sexual harassment in their businesses, together with the legal mechanisms for adjudicating the claims about alleged breaches of that requirement and imposing sanctions for the breaches, *the upper level of the operation of the sexual harassment law.* Let us, on the other hand, use the phrase *the lower level of the operation of the sexual harassment law* for the regulations that employers enact by way of complying with the requirements of the upper level, together with the mechanisms that they put in place for publicizing those regulations, adjudicating the claims about the alleged breaches of the regulations, and imposing sanctions for the breaches that occur.

At the upper level, EEOC and similar bodies provide something that may be regarded as preliminary adjudication, but ultimately adjudication at the upper level is in the hands of the courts of law. At the lower level, the adjudication is carried out by whatever person or body the employer designates for the purpose, and the proceedings in front of such an adjudicator follow whatever procedural rules the employer has enacted for such cases. At the upper level, sanctions are imposed by the court *on the employer*: the employer may, for instance, be required to provide reinstatement with back pay and monetary damages to the victim of harassment. At the lower level, if a breach of the regulations is found to have occurred, the employer will impose a sanction on the individual harasser: the harasser may, for instance, be demoted or fired.

There is a strict sense in which only what happens at the upper level constitutes the operation of the sexual harassment law. What happens at the lower level can, however, still be regarded as operation of the law, because it is required by the upper level. Presumably, the very purpose of the upper level is, in the long run, to ensure the existence of the lower level.

This two-level operation makes sexual harassment law importantly different from criminal prohibitions of rape, assault, and similar acts, which all operate on a single level.

When lawyers think of the sexual harassment law, they tend to think primarily of the upper level, because it is at that level that most of their professional involvement is. On the other hand, in the minds of the general public the two levels tend to be jumbled together. If, however, one wants to understand the operation of the sexual harassment law, one needs to keep in mind *both* the close connection between the two levels and their distinctness.

Now, the severe-or-pervasive test belongs to the upper level: it is a condition of employers' legal liability. Thus, if *A*'s harassment of *B* crosses the threshold of pervasiveness, then their employer becomes legally liable for having allowed this to happen. Until *A* crosses the threshold, *B* cannot win an upper-level case against the employer in a court of law, but *as soon as* the threshold is crossed, *B* has a winnable upper-level case against the employer. This means that the employer cannot afford to wait until the threshold is crossed. In order to avoid liability, the employer has to have in place lower-level mechanisms that will make it possible to interfere with *A*'s conduct *before* it gets to the threshold. In other words, the lower-level regulations have to make it possible to interfere with the conduct that *may lead to* the creation of "intimidating, hostile, or offensive working environment" before that conduct actually creates such environment. The lower-level regulations thus, if they are to enable the employer to avoid the upper-level liability, have to make internally actionable offensive conduct of a sexual nature even if that conduct is, on its own, neither severe nor pervasive.

Moreover, it's not just that employers can't afford to build the severe-or-pervasive test into the internal regulations of their businesses. In formulating their criteria of the kinds of conduct that are actionable as sexual harassment at the lower level, it would be irrational for employers to use anything that would be even close to the severe-or-pervasive test that is used at the upper level by the courts. From the viewpoint of employers, it is very important that there be a wide margin between the criteria of what is actionable at the upper level and the criteria of what is actionable at the lower level. There are several reasons for that.

First, the severe-or-pervasive test used at the upper level is rather imprecise. When looking at a case of somewhat offensive conduct of a sexual nature that recurred a few times but not very many times, it is difficult to be certain whether the relevant courts would regard it as pervasive enough to satisfy the severe-or-pervasive test or not. Employers who want to avoid the upper-level liability need to take into account this rather wide penumbra of uncertainty that surrounds the severe-or-pervasive test. They need to ensure that in the lower-level rules they cover not only the conduct that the courts are certain or likely to regard as harassment, but all conduct of which it is not certain that the courts will not regard it as harassment.

Second, no matter how efficient the mechanisms at the lower level are, they still need some time to deal with a case. During that period the conduct complained of may continue. There is thus a possibility that even if the conduct did not yet reach the (upper-level) threshold of pervasiveness at the time when the complaint was made, it will cross that threshold before the employer's adjudicators have had the time deal with the matter, and that the employer will thus incur liability. In order to make this possibility unlikely, an employer needs to make it possible for employees to make complaints even about conduct that is *well below* the threshold of pervasiveness set by the courts, so that, if the conduct continues while the complaint is being processed, it is still unlikely to reach the threshold before it is stopped by the imposition of some lower-level sanction on the harasser. The lower-level rules thus need to prohibit even conduct that is well below the upper-level threshold of pervasiveness.

Third, in formulating the lower-level requirements, employers want not only to ensure that they will in fact win any upper-level lawsuit that may be brought against them, but also to minimize the likelihood of being sued in the first place. This is because such lawsuits, especially in the United States, are likely to impose considerable costs even on the employers who eventually win them, in terms of working hours spent on preparing for the suit, attorney's fees, and possibly negative publicity. Employers thus have an incentive to ensure that it is immediately obvious to potential plaintiffs that they have no case, so that they are not at all tempted to sue. In order to achieve that obviousness, they may again need to proscribe at the lower level much more than is covered by the criteria that operate at the upper level.

From the viewpoint of employers, the difference between what is proscribed at the lower level and what is actionable at the upper level constitutes a margin of safety, and when the above three reasons are added together, it becomes apparent that the margin needs to be rather wide.[57]

Moreover, it should be noted that the above reasons that all pull employers in the direction of enacting lower level regulations that prohibit more than what counts as harassment at the upper level, are not counterbalanced by any significant reasons that would be pulling in the opposite direction. In the present climate, an employer is unlikely to be sued because its lower-level prohibitions of sexual harassment are excessive. (Some of the rare cases in which such suits have been initiated will be discussed elsewhere in this book.) Even if someone were to initiate such a suit, it is not likely that it would be successful.[58] Finally, even if such a suit were to be successful, chances are that it would result only in a declaratory judgment or an injunction against the enforcement of the lower-level regulations, and not in any other kind of sanction. From the viewpoint of employers, those relatively remote possibilities do very little to outweigh the very serious threat of upper-level sexual harassment suits, in which substantial damages are often awarded. Employers thus have a great deal to fear if they prohibit too little by their lower-level regulations, and very little to fear if they prohibit too much.

The upshot of the argument so far is that sexual harassment law results in employers' having every reason to make punishable (at the lower level) and to actually punish even conduct that is far from satisfying the severe-or-pervasive test that operates at the upper level. The argument so far suggests but does not conclusively prove that the most reasonable strategy for an employer who wants to avoid upper-level liability may be to prohibit at the lower level *all* offensive acts of a sexual nature. That employers have to prohibit all such acts, however, follows conclusively from the Fifth Circuit decision in *Waltman v. International Paper Co.*.[59] According to that decision it is not necessary that the threshold be crossed by the cumulative effect of the acts of one harasser or a group of harassers acting in concert. The threshold may, instead, be crossed by the cumulative effect on one person of the acts of different harassers who are acting independently of each other. Thus, if A_1 performs one and only one act that is offensive to *B*, and A_2 then independently performs another, but again only one, act that is offensive to *B*, and A_3 etc. . . . and A_n independently performs one act offensive to B, the threshold may be crossed and the employer liable. Given that A_1, A_2 and so on are *ex hypothesi* acting independently of each other, the employer can prevent this from occurring only if each individual act of A_1, A_2 and so on is prohibited by its regulations.[60]

The severe-or-pervasive test, used by the courts in deciding upper-level cases, thus doesn't percolate to the lower level. It is therefore largely irrelevant to individual potential harassers, whose conduct is governed by the lower-level regulations. From the viewpoint of individual potential harassers, the operation of sexual harassment law therefore, in spite of the severe-or-pervasive test, amounts to a prohibition of *all* offensive acts of a sexual nature. This prohibition is subject to my argument according to which it, in turn, amounts to a prohibition of all conduct of a sexual nature.

In this section I have been arguing that, given that the upper level is as it is, and assuming that employers are rational, certain things are bound to happen at the lower level. It may be worthwhile to point out at the end that what, according to my argument, is supposed to happen at the lower level is precisely what in fact does happen. Lower-level regulations typically do not incorporate anything like the severe-or-pervasive test, and sometimes explicitly state that "[s]exual harassment may be found in a single episode, as well as in persistent behavior."[61] And people do actually get punished at the lower level for single acts that are only somewhat offensive and that do not belong to a pervasive pattern of conduct. A senior vice president of the New York City Transit Authority has, for example, been demoted and had his salary cut for a single sexual joke, uttered over the phone.[62] A sergeant of the Los Angeles Police Department was put on a five-day suspension for a single joke, which appears to have been made in a clumsy attempt to encourage a junior female officer, and which was sexual only insofar as it metaphorically used the word "ovaries."[63]

3
Demarcation and Reasonableness

Reasonable Person

In the preceding chapter, I was treating the criterion of demarcation set out in the EEOC Guidelines as a *subjective* standard, which is what it, on its face, appears to be. On its face the criterion requires only that the conduct complained of in fact creates the offensive environment *for the person in question.* Courts, however, often make the standard partially objective by introducing into their deliberations the perspective of a *reasonable person*:

> To accord appropriate protection to both plaintiffs and defendants in a hostile and/or abusive work environment sexual harassment case, the trier of fact, when judging the totality of the circumstances impacting upon the asserted abusive and hostile environment placed in issue by the plaintiff's charges, must adopt the perspective of a reasonable person's reaction to a similar environment under essentially like or similar circumstances.[1]

It is again debatable whether in introducing the perspective of a reasonable person, the courts are bringing into their deliberations an element that is not in the Guidelines or providing an interpretation of the Guidelines. In the part of the Guidelines that purports to provide the criterion of demarcation the word "unreasonably" does occur, but only within one of the disjuncts ("unreasonably interfering with an individual's work performance"). Its occurrence there, on the normal reading of the relevant sentence, appears to have no bearing on the other disjuncts; in particular, it seems to have no bearing on the disjunct about offensive environment that my argument has focused on.

Lynn McLain has argued that "the word 'unreasonably' should be read to modify 'intimidating, hostile, or offensive' as well as 'interfering,' " despite the fact that such interpretation is not indicated by the grammatical structure of the sentence,[2] but such a reading doesn't seem to help the interpretation a great deal (nor does it fit the rest of what McLain says) because it is not entirely clear what would it mean to say that a certain environment is "unreasonably offensive": is there anything that is reasonably offensive?

A better way of establishing harmony between the wording of the Guidelines and the use of an objective standard in determining whether something constitutes sexual harassment is to argue that the meaning of the word "environment" requires that an objective standard be used. It can be said that, in virtue of the meaning of the word "environment," no offensive conduct can amount to an offensive *environment* unless it would be regarded as offensive by a reasonable person. This move is similar to the one that has been used above in an attempt to establish harmony between the wording of the Guidelines and the severe-or-pervasive test.

In any event, even if the objective standard is not implicit in the Guidelines, it still remains a fact that it is used by the courts and that it thus constitutes a part of the sexual harassment law. We should not forget that, as has been pointed out above, the Guidelines have no force of law on their own.

Similar objective standards can be found in the sexual harassment laws of other countries: the statutory definition of sexual harassment in South Australia, for example, requires that it be reasonable that the victim "should feel offended, humiliated or intimidated."[3]

It is, however, important to realize that there are several significantly different ways of bringing the perspective of a reasonable person into the criterion of sexual harassment, that haven't always been distinguished. One way of doing it is to require that, in order to count as sexual harassment, the relevant conduct not only be in fact unwelcome and offensive to the given person, but also

(1) conduct that a reasonable person in the position of the alleged victim *could* have found unwelcome and offensive.

This excludes the cases in which the plaintiff is paranoid, neurotic, or hypersensitive and in which the plaintiff's negative reaction to the conduct of the alleged harasser is a result of such unreasonableness.

To be sure, there may be some case where the negative reactions to behavior of sexual nature are clearly unreasonable. We can, for example, imagine a case where someone has an intense negative reaction to a casual sexual remark because of the belief that the remark is somehow a part of some elaborate world-wide conspiracy. It is probably worthwhile to formulate the rules about sexual harassment so as to keep such cases out, and insofar as (1) enables us to do that, bringing it into the criterion of sexual harassment should be regarded as salutary (although some radical commentators seem to regard even that as too much of a concession).[4] The modification, however, does very little to alleviate the concerns that were raised by my arguments, because the only cases that it is capable of excluding are such rare and bizarre cases.

The exclusion of such cases should probably be regarded as salutary, but given that they are bound to be rare anyway, it has only negligible impact on the arguments made in the preceding chapter. These arguments did not hinge on the possibility of plaintiff's *unreasonableness*; they were based on the claim that what will be unwelcome and offensive in sexual matters is often unpredictable simply because people *differ* greatly in that respect. That claim is not significantly affected by the exclusion of unreasonable people, because there are huge differences in that respect among reasonable people themselves. For example, some reasonable people find deeply offensive the same sexual jokes that some other reasonable people find highly entertaining. This is an empirical fact that would be difficult to deny.

Given that, for almost any conduct of sexual nature one can find some reasonable people that would be offended by it, and whose existence thus proves that a reasonable person *could* be offended by it, the prohibition of sexual harassment based on (1) still amounts to a prohibition of almost all conduct of a sexual nature.

The only way to get around that conclusion would be to argue, for example, that someone's being deeply offended by a mildly off-color joke in itself constitutes a proof of unreasonableness, even if the person passes all the usual tests of reasonableness. That strategy, however, misuses the word "reasonable" by putting into it more substantive content than it has traditionally had in legal contexts.

A very different way of bringing the perspective of a reasonable person into the criterion is to require that, in order to qualify as sexual harassment, the conduct complained of be

> **(2)** conduct that *any* reasonable person in the position of the alleged victim would have found unwelcome and offensive.

Now (2) quite obviously provides the demarcation as it excludes all cases in which the negative reaction of the victim would not have been shared by (other) reasonable people. However, (2) does not provide a useful interpretation of the law as it actually is. Taking (2) seriously would change the sexual harassment law beyond recognition, as very little of the behavior that is currently regarded as hostile environment sexual harassment would satisfy it. Deliberate insults of a sexual nature would, but it is difficult to see what else would: for almost any other form of conduct that is currently regarded as hostile environment harassment, one can find some reasonable people who are not offended by it. For example, in the petitioner's brief in *Harris v. Forklift Systems, Inc.*,[5] after the description of vulgar behavior that involved a male company president requiring female employees to retrieve coins from the front pockets of his pants, we read that some of the women who were exposed to it testified that they did not take it seriously and regarded it as a part of a joking atmosphere at work. As there is no sufficient ground for dismissing these witnesses as unreasonable, their testimony entails that even such conduct would not count as sexual harassment under (2). If (2) were the criterion of sexual harassment, then the notion of sexual harassment would have practically no application.

Some people my be tempted to try to avoid this implication of (2) by arguing, in spite of abundant empirical evidence to the contrary, that most of the conduct that is currently regarded as hostile-environment harassment is in fact unwelcome and offensive to all reasonable people. According to this line of argument, anyone who professes not to be offended by it must be either insincere or unreasonable. The truth of such claims can, of course, be ensured by using a suitably doctored notion of reasonableness, and this is precisely what this strategy does. I would, however, reject it for the same reason for which I have rejected an analogous strategy that was aimed in the opposite direction: it, again, tries to pack more normative content into the notion of reasonableness than the notion is capable of carrying. Doing so is a misuse of the notion of reasonableness, because legal decision-making is obscured when controversial norms are smuggled into it under the innocuous-sounding label of reasonableness.

Quite apart from the fact that each of the above two ways of bringing the notion of a reasonable person into the sexual harassment law has difficulties of its own, a great deal of confusion in thinking about it stems from the simple fact that the difference between the two has not been sufficiently appreciated by either the courts or the commentators. This may strike one as curious, given that the difference appears so perfectly obvious. The source of the problem is that the notion of a reasonable person has been imported into the sexual harassment law from areas of the law that deal with entirely different matters. Typical issues in the law of torts, where the home of that notion is, involve matters in which there is *uniformity* among all reasonable people. They involve issues in which the conduct of every reasonable person is, in the relevant respects, entirely determined by reasonableness, and in which all reasonable persons are therefore interchangeable. That's why in the law of torts it makes sense to speak about the abstract instance of a reasonable person, about *the* reasonable person. In such a context, an ambiguity analogous to that between (1) and (2) would be of no consequence.

The questions as to whether the reasonable person would have repaired the roof of his house under such-and-such circumstances or driven a car in such-and-such way are questions that may well have definite answers, but the question as to whether the reasonable person would have been offended by such-and-such sexual joke has no answer, just as the question as to whether the reasonable person would have liked anchovies on his pizza has no answer. The only answer one can give to such questions is: "Some reasonable persons would, some would not." The notion of reasonableness therefore cannot play in the sexual harassment law the same useful role that it plays in other areas of the law. In sexual matters, the lack of uniformity among reasonable people opens up the gap between (1) and (2), neither of which provides a genuine solution to the demarcation problem.

The deficiencies of (1) and (2) may lead one to interpret the standard of reasonableness as requiring that the conduct complained of, in order to count as sexual harassment, be

> (3) conduct that the *average* reasonable person in the position of the alleged victim would have found unwelcome and offensive.

It seems that this interpretation is bound to generate the results that will be somehow between the two extremes we have considered. Given that what was wrong with the extremes was precisely that they were extremes (i.e., that they covered either too much or too little), it seems to follow that (3) is guaranteed to present an improvement over them.

Unfortunately, (3) is useless for other reasons. In order to see why, we need to first remind ourselves that the meaning of the word "average" is such that the average is the result of applying certain kinds of operations on numerically expressed results of measurements. So, to be able to make sense of the use of that word in a given context we need to know what the *dimension* is, along which the measurements have been made. It is, of course, perfectly permissible to use the word "average" on the basis of rough estimates rather than precise measurements and calculations, but even in such cases we need to know what the relevant dimension is.

Now, if we took the dimension that is alluded to in (3) to be something like income, level of education, the length of work experience and so on, we would quickly see that we have again failed to find a genuine criterion of demarcation, because people of average income, level of education, length of work experience, still differ in what they find unwelcome and offensive in sexual matters. The only dimension that can even appear to hold some promise of making (3) into something that could give us the criterion we are looking for is the dimension that is directly relevant to what is at issue, namely the degree of sensitivity in sexual matters. On that reading, "the average reasonable person" in (3) would be the person whose sensitivity in sexual matters is average for reasonable people.

While one could in principle undertake research that would ascertain what that degree is (or rather what those degrees are, given that the mean, the median, and the mode are not likely to coincide), the criterion such as the one we are considering should not be something that can be applied only by carrying out elaborate empirical research. The criterion can be successful in actually guiding people's conduct only if it can be applied more or less at a glance. The degrees of sensitivity in sexual matters are, however, distributed over people in such a way that no kind of average stands out as such in a way that would be obvious without carrying out actual research.

We could of course solve this problem by saying that "the average reasonable person" in (3) need not be taken to refer to a person whose degree of sensitivity in sexual matter equals *the precise* average; rather it can be interpreted as referring to a person whose degree of sensitivity in sexual matters is in the same *range* as the precise average. This would be in accordance with the way the word *average* is sometimes used in other contexts. For example, when one says that someone's income is average, one is unlikely to mean that it equals the precise average to the cent; it is much more likely that one means that the person's income belongs to the same (more or less wide) range of incomes as the precise average. The phrase "average intelligence" may be used to mean the intelligence that corresponds to the IQ of 100, but it may also be used to mean intelligence corresponding to an IQ in the 90–110 range.

It can be said that although it may be difficult to determine the precise averagc of the degrees of sensitivity in sexual matters for reasonable people, it is not at all difficult to determine, even without elaborate research, what is the range of the degrees of sensitivity within which the precise average is, and thus what the average is in the second, looser, sense of the word. Whether this is true depends on how wide do we allow the range to be. We can't avoid the problem that we had with precise averages unless we allow the range to be fairly wide. If we take it to be narrow, the problem remains: without carrying out actual empirical research it will be difficult to say what that narrow range is.

On the other hand, it is undoubtedly true that we can, without elaborate research, determine the range in which the precise average is, as long as we allow it to be fairly wide. However, as soon as we allow the range to be wide, the variations within the range will reopen the problem that we have had before. If the range is allowed to be wide, there will be quite a few types of conduct that are unwelcome and offensive to some of the people whose sensitivities are within the range, but not to others whose sensitivities are also within the range. In fact as soon as we allow the range to be wide, it becomes misleading to speak about "*the* average reasonable person." The ambiguity analogous to the one between (1) and (2) will recreate itself within the domain of average reasonable people. Admittedly bringing in (3), so interpreted, would be an improvement over what we have had before, but not a great improvement, because much of the conduct that potential harassers may be tempted to engage in would be precisely the conduct that is offensive and unwelcome to some average reasonable people, but not to other average reasonable people.

These problems are enough to render (3) incapable of accomplishing its purpose. But if that problem could be somehow overcome, the criterion would have to face another one. The differences in sensitivity in sexual matters are not only quantitative but also qualitative. Two persons may exhibit the same *degree* of sensitivity, and yet differ widely in *what* they find unwelcome and offensive. One of the two may, for example, be deeply offended by homosexual advances while being relatively tolerant toward conduct of heterosexual nature; the other may not discriminate between homosexual and heterosexual conduct. Or, one of the two may find disturbing any allusions to sadomasochistic sex, but be indifferent to promiscuity, while the other person may dislike any manifestations of promiscuity while being tolerant of references to sadomasochistic sex. Therefore, even people who have the average degree of sensitivity in sexual matters are likely to differ significantly in what they find unwelcome and offensive. Because of such differences, the application of (3) cannot produce any definite results. It does not amount to a genuine criterion at all.

To this it may be responded that the notion of an average could be extended to deal with qualitative differences as well. Thus, it can be said, although the differences among different tastes of food are qualitative rather than quantitative, it doesn't stretch the meaning of the word *average* too much to speak of the average of different tastes of food: that would be the taste of whatever we would obtain by putting all of the relevant food in a blender and letting it run for some time. Or it could be said that although the differences among colors are qualitative, it may make sense to speak of the average color of differently colored things: that would be the color of what we would obtain by mixing all the pigments in the things in question. It is, however, rather unclear how the notion of average that we have in these examples could be extended still further to apply to people's sensitivities in sexual matters. It is not at all clear what would be the analogy of putting it all in a blender when we are dealing with people's attitudes toward sexual matters (or for that matter toward anything else).

It should perhaps be mentioned that my arguments against relying on the average person in this matter have assumed that the person represents the average for the given society taken as a whole. One could conceivably avoid some of my arguments if one allowed for relativizing the criterion to various groups within the society, so that each incident is judged with reference to the average person of the group to which the actual victim belongs. For at least some smaller groups within the society, the question as to what the average member of the group finds offensive in sexual matters may well have a definite answer.

The problem with relativizing the criterion in that way is that each person belongs to many overlapping groups. Every time we attempted to apply such a criterion, we would therefore have to face the question as to which of the many groups to which the person belongs is the relevant one. Should a case of alleged harassment of a Hispanic-American lawyer living in New York City be judged with reference to the average Hispanic-American or the average lawyer or the average resident of New York City? Such questions have no answers; the only way to "resolve" them is by making an arbitrary choice. But the arbitrariness of that choice would mean that any decision based on (3) would be arbitrary as well. Again, we can conclude that (3) would not amount to a genuine criterion at all.

Moreover, even if there were a nonarbitrary way of relativizing the criterion to various groups within the society, that couldn't solve a further problem. One's reaction to conduct of a sexual nature is determined not only by the kind of conduct it is, but also by who it comes from. Coming from one person, certain sexual conduct may be unwelcome and offensive, while similar conduct coming from another person may well be welcome. The behavior that, in someone whom we find generally irritating, strikes us as a manifestation of offensive crudeness, may in a person that we find otherwise appealing strike us as a manifestation of charming clumsiness. According to one empirical study of sexual harassment, one of "the three most commonly endorsed reasons for women being bothered by sexual behavior at work [was] . . . 'I was not attracted to the person,' "[6] which makes it clear that they would not have been bothered by it if they had been attracted by the person. While it is easy to understand how Anita Hill could have found Clarence Thomas's conduct unwelcome and offensive (assuming that the conduct actually took place) it is also true that, as one shrewd British commentator has observed,

> If he had appealed to Professor Hill's idea of an interesting man, his requests for a date would have been pleasurable, not abominable. His conversations might have been teasing, not revolting.[7]

(Just in case anyone thinks that this is relevant, let me say that the journalist who wrote these words was female.)

Even people whose sensitivities in sexual matters are identical in every other respect are likely to differ in *whose* conduct of a sexual nature they find unwelcome and offensive. No version of the appeal to the average reasonable person can abstract from differences of that kind.

It may, at the end of this section, be useful to compare (3) with the way the notion of the average person operates in another, somewhat similar area of the law. It is a well-established feature of the constitutional law about obscenity that something is obscene if "to the average person, applying contemporary community standards, the dominant theme of the material taken as a whole appeals to prurient interest." This formulation comes from the 1957 *Roth* case,[8] and although the test of obscenity has changed in a number of important ways since then (notably by the 1973 *Miller* case[9]), this appeal to the average person remains a feature of the test. Someone might be tempted to argue that if the obscenity law has been functioning since 1957 with tests that incorporate reference to the average person, then it must be possible for sexual harassment law, which after all deals with similar matters, to function with something like (3), in spite of the arguments I have made in this section.

There are three responses that I have to make to this line of argument.

The first is that there is far less variation in people's responses to the question as to whether something "appeals to prurient interests" than to the question whether it is "unwelcome and offensive." There is thus far more chance of something emerging as the response of the average person when we are dealing with the first question than when we are dealing with the second question. It is quite possible for people to agree that something appeals to prurient interests while differing in many other respects in their attitudes to the thing in question. One person may, for example, be deeply disturbed by the very thought of people satisfying their prurient interests, another person may regard the satisfaction of prurient interests as harmless, while a third person may be completely uninterested in whether people satisfy their prurient interests or not. Yet all three may agree on whether the interests that a particular material satisfies are to be classified as prurient. In fact, even people who regularly indulge their prurient interests might not have much difficulty in acknowledging that the interests in question are prurient. The possibility of such agreement on whether something appeals to prurient interests, even among people who otherwise differ in their attitudes toward it, means that the applications of a test that asks whether the average person would regard something as appealing to prurient interests have much better chances of producing definite results than applications of a test embodying something like (3).

The second important difference between sexual harassment and obscenity is that the impact of a piece of work that is likely to be judged for its possible obscenity typically does not depend on who its author is. Once a book, pamphlet, magazine or a movie starts circulating publicly, people's reactions to it are unlikely to be colored by the general attitude that they have toward its author. In fact, in many cases people who are exposed to an item of pornography have no general attitude toward its author simply because they know only vaguely, or not at all, who the author is. One's reaction to, say, a pornographic novel, is thus unlikely to be influenced by whether one finds its author likable or obnoxious. The conduct that may constitute sexual harassment is, on the other hand, much more closely associated with the person engaging in it. As has been observed above, the impact of, say, a sexual advance on the person receiving it sometimes crucially depends on who is making the advance. A consequence of that is that there is far more variation in people's reactions to conduct that is the subject matter of the sexual harassment law than in their reactions to objects that are the subject matter of the obscenity law. This in turn means that we have better chances of finding such a thing as *the* reactions of *the* average person to the latter than to the former.

Finally, we should note that the problems of which I argued that they arise when the sexual harassment law is interpreted as incorporating something like (3) in fact do arise in the law of obscenity as well. Although the average person test of obscenity is, for the reasons outlined above, less liable to such problems than a similar test of sexual harassment would be, it is not entirely immune to them. This is nicely illustrated by the 1975 obscenity case *United States v. Treatman.*[10] In that Eighth Circuit decision we find quoted a note that the jury that had the task of determining the outcome of the case at the district court level sent to the judge during its deliberations. The note asked:

> to be purient [sic], does sexual material have to appeal to the "majority" of the average adults in the so called community or to just "some" of the average?[11]

The Court of Appeals treated the note as showing that

> it is obvious . . . that they [the jury] did not understand that the prurient interest of the average adult must be measured by the synthesis of the entire community. There is obviously no such thing as a minority or majority of "the average adult in the community" or just "some" of the average.[12]

In concluding that the jury had misunderstood the test, the court of appeals refused to realize that these ordinary people had in fact tried to point out something important in their note, something that, when its implications are fully appreciated, threatens to make the whole average person test unworkable.

If one takes the word *average* to mean the precise average, and if there is a way of "averaging" qualitatively different items that is appropriate to this context, then the court is right that there is no "minority or majority of 'the average adult in the community.'" But, as has been argued above, when one takes the notion of an average in that way, then it is very difficult to say what the average in this context is. The court's remark ignores the loose sense of the word, which makes it manageable to say what the average is.

The people on that jury probably interpreted the phrase "average person" the way they did, not because they were unaware of its meaning, but because they assumed that the phrase should be understood so that they, people without specialized expertise, can determine what is involved in being an average person. They therefore took the word in the loose sense. They also had among them enough life experience to see that there is much variety in people's attitudes toward sexual matters, even among those who can legitimately be called average people in that sense, so that no answer to the question at hand clearly emerges as *the* answer of *the* average person. The reaction of this jury thus accords perfectly with the arguments made above.

REASONABLE WOMAN: HISTORY OF THE STANDARD

There has been, within the sexual harassment law, a trend toward replacing the reasonable person standard with that of a reasonable woman. The idea that such a change should be made first appeared on the pages of law reports in 1986 in the dissenting opinion in *Rabidue v. Osceola Refining Co.*[13] In the late eighties, a few district courts appealed to the notion of a reasonable woman[14] (or "a reasonable female employee")[15] in deciding sexual harassment cases, but did not make it very clear whether they thereby intended to introduce a standard significantly different from that of a reasonable person.[16]

It was not until 1990 that a case had actually been decided at the appellate level by using such a standard: that was the Third Circuit case *Andrews v. City of Philadelphia.*[17] It was, however, the somewhat later case *Ellison v. Brady*,[18] decided by the Ninth Circuit in January 1991, that has received more attention and provoked more comments and discussion. The phrase "reasonable woman" admittedly does not appear in the *Andrews* decision, but rather "reasonable person of the same sex in that [plaintiff's] position," while it does appear prominently in the *Ellison* decision, but that difference in wording presumably does not amount to a substantive difference: the plaintiffs in *Andrews* were female, and a footnote in the *Ellison* decision acknowledges that "where male employees allege that co-workers engage in conduct which creates a hostile environment, the appropriate victim's perspective would be that of a reasonable man."[19] (Within this section and the following one I shall set aside the cases in which the alleged victim is male.)

Some commentators[20] treat the 1987 *Yates v. Avco Corp.*[21] case as the first appellate level sexual harassment case to adopt the reasonable woman standard, and the Ninth Circuit in deciding *Ellison* acknowledged[22] its debt to that decision of the Sixth Circuit. The notion of a reasonable woman does indeed play a role in that decision, but invoking the reasonable woman standard announced in that case in the same breath with the reasonable woman standards of *Andrews* and *Ellison* is misleading because they are standards of different things. In *Yates* the notion of the reasonable woman appears in the context of determining whether the resignation of one of the plaintiffs constitutes constructive discharge and *not* in the context of determining whether the conduct complained of amounts to sexual harassment. Thus although it is in a sense true that that case brought the notion of the reasonable woman into the sexual harassment law, it did not bring it into the *criterion* of sexual harassment. The Ninth Circuit thus erred when it said in *Ellison* that *Yates* amounts to an adoption of the standard advocated in the dissenting opinion in *Rabidue*, because the latter was definitely a standard of what constitutes actionable harassment and not of what constitutes constructive discharge.

At about the same time as the *Ellison* decision was made at the appellate level, a federal district court in Florida used the reasonable woman standard to decide *Robinson v. Jacksonville Shipyards*,[23] which has also generated publicity. After the *Ellison* and *Robinson* decisions, the idea caught on, and by now quite a few cases have been decided in which the reasonable woman standard has played a role.[24] These developments have already had some influence even outside the sexual harassment law: in *Harris v. International Paper Co.*[25] a federal district court has introduced the standard of a "reasonable black person"[26] for deciding issues of racial harassment of black people.

Although the enthusiasm for the reasonable woman standard has become widespread among both courts and commentators, the Supreme Court has not endorsed the standard, in spite of the fact that it has had an opportunity to do so. Its decision in *Harris v. Forklift Systems, Inc.*,[27] made after the advent of the "reasonable woman," was based on the reasonable *person* standard,[28] even though the notion of a reasonable woman had been invoked in the original district court decision. To be sure, the Supreme Court has not explicitly rejected the reasonable woman standard, nor indeed made any comment about it, but its use of the reasonable person rather than the reasonable woman standard in *Harris* is conspicuous. Indeed, the Fifth Circuit has gone as far as interpreting the Supreme Court's silence about the "reasonable woman" in *Harris* as equivalent to the rejection of the standard.[29] (The Eighth Circuit, on the other hand, has interpreted the Supreme Court's silence as implying only that the use of the reasonable woman standard is not required, without pronouncing on whether its use is permissible.)[30] It may also be worth noting that the Supreme Court of Michigan has explicitly repudiated the reasonable woman standard.[31]

In a later sexual harassment opinion, issued after the Supreme Court's decision in *Harris*, a judge of the Ninth Circuit said "we use a hypothetical woman in applying our reasonable *person* standard,"[32] and followed that immediately by a reference to *Ellison*, thus implying that this is simply a rewording of the reasonable woman standard. In a still later opinion, the Circuit used the phrase "reasonable person with the same fundamental characteristics [as the plaintiff],"[33] followed immediately by "*Cf. Ellison*." This wording has been characterized by the Circuit, in another decision, as "incorporat[ing] both the Supreme Court's formulation of the standard and that of *Elli-*

son."[34] One gets a sense that the Circuit wishes to keep the reasonable woman standard alive, and, at the same time, to present it in a manner that is not too likely to provoke the Supreme Court's explicit scrutiny.

Reasonable Woman: Discussion

Many commentators have already discussed the issue as to whether the reasonable woman standard is better than the reasonable person one, and most of them have argued that it is. Not much attention has, however, been devoted to the question that needs to be answered before we can even begin considering the question of which of the two standards is better. This is the question of whether there is any difference between them in the first place. The answer to that question is by no means obvious.

The cases that put forward the reasonable woman standard do not make it clear whether its use involves (a) application of some (supposed) standard of *female reasonableness* which is somehow a different *kind of reasonableness* from male reasonableness, or (b) application of *the* standard of (sexless) reasonableness to certain facts about the position of women.[35] The *Andrews* court gives no reasons for introducing the new standard, while the closest that the *Ellison* court comes to providing such a reason is in saying that

> because women are disproportionately victims of rape and sexual assault, women have a stronger incentive to be concerned with sexual behavior. Women who are victims of mild forms of sexual harassment may understandably worry whether a harasser's conduct is merely a prelude to violent sexual assault.[36]

That reason, however, amounts merely to pointing out certain facts about the position of women and does nothing whatsoever to prove that female reasonableness is itself different from male reasonableness. It thus amounts, at most, to a reason for (b).

Commending the standard on the ground that it better reflects women's *experiences*[37] also implies the correctness of the interpretation (b). What experiences people have is a different matter from *how* they reason about the experiences they have: saying that women's experiences are different from men's does not imply that *the ways in which they reason* about the experiences they have are different from men's.

Accepting (b) as the interpretation of the reasonable woman standard is, however, incompatible with regarding it as a new and revolutionary criterion that it is advertised to be, because those who apply the reasonable person standard to the issue have already acknowledged that the application of the standard involves considering "the background and experience of the plaintiff."[38] If (b) is what is meant, then formulations such as "[a]ny reasonable *person* would have to regard these cartoons as highly offensive *to a woman*"[39] express the idea much more accurately than speaking of the new standard of the "reasonable woman."

In general, the good old reasonable person (even when he was called "reasonable man") has always been expected to apply the (class-neutral, age-neutral, sex-neutral and so on) standard of reasonableness to the facts that are being scrutinized, where those facts include the class, age, sex, and so on of the person in question.[40] That this is so with respect to sex was made explicit more than a century ago in *Mich. Cent. R. Co. v. Hasseneyer.*[41] The justices of the Supreme Court of Michigan who decided that case may have made factual assumptions about women that many people today would disagree with, but they had a very clear insight into the conceptual point that taking into account various facts about women in deciding cases does not imply holding women to a different standard than men. This is precisely the conceptual point that the *Ellison* court seems to have been confused about in promulgating the reasonable woman standard.

It may of course be argued that the application of the reasonable person standard to cases involving women has not always taken into account *all* the relevant facts about women; but if this is so we should blame the sloppy application of the criterion, rather than the criterion itself. The fact that a certain legal standard has been applied sloppily in the past is not a reason for changing it, but for applying it more carefully.[42]

Incidentally, everything that has been said above about the reasonable woman standard under interpretation (b) applies even more obviously to the "contextualized reasonable victim standard" for sexual harassment that has been proposed by some theorists.[43] While that standard is also advertised as a new standard that would go still further in improving the sexual harassment law than the reasonable woman standard, it is difficult to see how its application would amount to anything different from the careful application of the reasonable person standard to the circumstances ("context") of the victim.

It should be noted that the confusion between the (alleged) defects that are inherent in the standard itself and the defects in the application of the standard is not something that one finds only in the area of sexual harassment law: much of the recent thinking about the reasonable person standard in general is permeated by that confusion. It has thus become commonplace to claim that the reasonable person standard is inherently biased in favor of white middle-class males, on the basis of arguments that prove, at most, that the actual application of the standard has been so biased. If the Ninth Circuit judges who decided *Ellison* were victims of that confusion, they were certainly not alone in that.

Thus, if (b) is what is meant, which seems to be interpretation that accords with the reasons that are adduced for the standard, then we do not really have a new standard at all, and all the attention that the standard has received is really undeserved. On the other hand, if (a) is what is meant, then we do indeed have a radically new and revolutionary standard. The problem with (a), however, is that it is not at all clear what female reasonableness is supposed to involve, and how it is supposed to be different from male reasonableness. There is nothing in the text of the relevant court opinions that would enable us to answer these questions.

Moreover, whatever precisely female reasonableness is, it is not clear how the standard of female reasonableness could be applied by male judges or jurors (if it were indeed something different from male reasonableness). It could of course be argued that the cases of sexual harassment involving female plaintiffs should be heard only in front of all-female judicial panels and all-female juries, but nowhere in the *Ellison* decision is there any suggestion of anything that radical.

It could also be argued that male judges and/or jurors could be appraised of what female reasonableness involves in a particular case by means of expert testimony.[44] That argument would, however, only shift the problem to another level: the question would then arise as to how could someone's credentials as an expert on female reasonableness be established in front of male triers of facts. How could they be trusted to decide, by using their male reasoning techniques, whether someone is a genuine expert on female reasonableness or merely a spurious one? How could they be trusted to decide, in a case in which different purported experts give different opinions, which one of them is to be believed? If we take seriously the idea that male and female reasonableness differ, shouldn't we expect such applications of male patterns of reasoning to lead to erroneous decisions on who the genuine experts on female reasonableness are?

The problem of male judges and jurors has been pointed out by several commentators,[45] but the problem that hasn't received much attention in the literature and that seems much more fundamental is that of a male potential harasser. If female reasonableness were something different from male reasonableness, and if determining whether something constitutes sexual harassment required application of the standard of female reasonableness, then it is not clear how a male person could ever determine what kind of conduct he is supposed to abstain from.

The reason why various legal rules that are formulated in terms of the "reasonable person" seem, by and large, fair is that being a reasonable person is, in general, within our reach. If I do not foresee something that a reasonable person would have foreseen, then I have failed to accomplish something that I could have accomplished, and it is in virtue of the fact that I could have accomplished it that it is fair to hold me responsible for the consequences. It would be, for example, manifestly unfair to hold us, imperfect mortals, responsible for not foreseeing something that only an angel could have foreseen, because the capacities of angels are beyond our reach. If females were capable of using patterns of reasoning that are beyond the reach of males, then it would be, in exactly the same way, manifestly unfair to hold males responsible for the consequences of not having access to such forms of reasoning.[46]

The *Ellison* court says at one point that "employers may have to educate and sensitize their workforce"[47] and that may appear to be a solution for this problem. But if the putative female reasonableness is something that anyone can acquire by education and something that it is desirable for everyone to acquire, then it is not clear in what sense it is *female* reasonableness. We seem to be pushed again toward the interpretation (b).

Regardless of how we resolve the ambiguity between (a) and (b), in interpreting the reasonable woman standard we shall also have to face the choice analogous to the one we have already encountered in discussing the reasonable person standard. The reasonable woman standard may be taken to require that the conduct complained of, in order to count as sexual harassment, be

> (1') conduct that a reasonable woman in the position of the alleged victim *could* have found unwelcome and offensive.

Alternatively, it may be taken to require that it be

> (2') conduct that *any* reasonable woman in the position of the alleged victim would have found unwelcome and offensive.

Finally, it is also possible to interpret it to require the relevant conduct to be

(3') conduct that the *average* reasonable woman in the position of the alleged victim would have found unwelcome and offensive.

The consequences of our having to make this choice are also analogous to the ones we have already seen in connection with the reasonable person standard. Just like the condition (1), the condition (1') is satisfied by almost all conduct of a sexual nature. For almost any conduct of a sexual nature one can find some reasonable women who would be offended by it, and whose existence proves that a reasonable woman could be offended by it. This is true regardless of what *precisely* is meant by "reasonable" in the "reasonable woman," as long as we assume that the meaning of that word in this context is not very far from its ordinary meaning. The condition (1') thus excludes very little and a prohibition of sexual harassment that would incorporate it would thus still amount to a prohibition of almost all conduct of a sexual nature.

In fact, (1') is included in (1) under either (a) or (b), so if (1') is what is meant, then the whole move to the reasonable woman standard is unnecessary.[48] Yet, some of the things that the *Ellison* court said leave the impression that (1') is precisely what it had in mind as the reasonable woman standard. The court thus said that "a reasonable woman *could* have had a similar reaction" to that of the plaintiff, which suggests that some reasonable women could have had different reactions, and presupposes that (1') is the operative standard.[49] But if that is what is meant, then the court could have also said that "a reasonable person could have had a similar reaction." Whatever satisfies the reasonable woman standard interpreted as (1') is, as a matter of logic, bound to satisfy the reasonable person standard, under the analogous interpretation (1) (assuming that reasonable women are a subset of reasonable persons).

Only a page before the words quoted above, the *Ellison* court, however, formulates the standard as requiring that the conduct be such that "a reasonable woman *would* consider [it] sufficiently severe or pervasive to alter the conditions of employment and create an abusive working environment."[50] That formulation appears to express (2') rather than (1').[51] The court thus appears to have been unclear about the rather crucial distinction between (1') and (2').

Condition (2'), just like condition (2), creates the opposite problem from that created by (1') and (1). Most of the conduct that the current law treats as hostile environment harassment does not, in fact, satisfy (2'). Consequently, (2') cannot be regarded as an articulation of the law as it actually is. If the law about sexual harassment did incorprorate (2'), it would have practically no application. Again, this is so regardless of what precisely "reasonable" means here, as long as the meaning is fairly close to the ordinary meaning of that word, rather than completely arbitrary. Even for the dirtiest of the dirty jokes, even for the crudest of the crude sexual advances, one can find some women who are not offended by them, and who are clearly reasonable in the ordinary sense of the word.

One federal court for example remarked, in dealing with a case in which certain sexual cartoons were introduced into evidence, that

> There were certainly rude, lewd, and ugly pictures . . . and a reasonable person would certainly be entitled to be offended by them. . . . But one of the women who testified at the trial simply laughed at even the crudest of these pictures and said that they did not bother her at all.[52]

There is no suggestion anywhere in the opinion that this witness was unreasonable. Similarly, in *Morgan v. Hertz Corp.*[53] the court noted that some of the women at Hertz who were exposed to the same conduct as the plaintiffs "did not mind, or even participated in the comments and remarks."

In *Johnson v. County of Los Angeles Fire Department* two female firefighters testified that *Playboy* does not make them feel intimidated or uncomfortable.[54] The evidence presented to the federal district court in that case also included market studies that show that "almost two million women read *Playboy* every month."[55]

Or, to take a more drastic example, if the notion of sexual harassment applies to anything, it certainly applies to the practice of men chasing a woman around the workplace, and when they catch her, pulling down her panties. Yet, even that practice does not satisfy (2'): at least one woman is on public record as not objecting to the practice, and moreover as regretting that she wasn't subjected to it when working at a place where it was common.[56] This former secretary is no one else but Helen Gurley Brown, well known as the founder of the *Cosmopolitan* magazine.

In a self-help book written by women for women, we can read that "'Hey, baby!' you get from a cute hardhat" is "not always sexual harassment—said sweetly, it can be fun, and great for your morale."[57] Even Barbara Gutek, a psychologist who devoted her career to presenting sexual harassment as a serious problem, had to acknowledge that "[k]idding around at work is acceptable behavior to many working people, even if it means being touched 'everywhere.' "[58]

Nancy Dodd McCann and Thomas A. McGinn presented 100 working women with 50 "scenarios" involving conduct that may be thought to constitute harassment and asked them whether they would be offended by such conduct.[59] They claim that their respondents were all "reasonable women."[60] The percentage of women who said that the conduct in question would offend them, of course, varied from one scenario to another. What is relevant for my purposes here, however, is that only five of the 50 scenarios were offensive to 100% of the women, and that these five involved quid pro quo harassment[61] and/or physical contact with the parts of the body that are usually regarded as intimate.[62] The precise implications of this research and the significance of specific percentages are debatable,[63] but the fact that *none* of the scenarios that involved verbal hostile environment harassment was offensive to all of the respondents does support the point that I am making here: it is difficult to come up with an example of such conduct that satisfies (2'). (Incidentally, it is also worth noting that, although some of the scenarios in this study depicted behavior of which very few of the women polled said that they would be offended by it, for *every* scenario there were some women who said that they would offended by the behavior in question, which fits what I said above about (1').)

Taking (2') as the meaning of the reasonable woman standard would thus be a radical revision of the law; (2') cannot provide the interpretation of the law as it actually is. It is thus of no help to potential harassers who want to conform their conduct to the prohibition of sexual harassment.

In order to prevent possible misunderstanding of the argument I have just made, it is important to realize that the only thing that is relevant in this discussion of (2') is the empirical fact that *there are* reasonable women who are not offended by dirty jokes, crude sexual advances, and other forms of conduct that are generally treated as paradigms of sexual harassment. I am not saying here anything as to whether it is good or bad that there are such women. One may argue that it is regrettable that there are such women, one may argue that there aren't many of them, but it is difficult to deny the stubborn empirical fact that *there are some*. One may believe that such women deserve some kind of criticism, but there is no reason to believe that all women who accept crude forms of sexual conduct could be dismissed as unreasonable in anything like the ordinary sense of the word "unreasonable."

The considerations invoked by the *Ellison* court in the part of the opinion that has been quoted earlier in this section, namely that women are disproportionately victims of sexually colored violence and that conduct of a sexual nature may be a prelude to violence, are certainly not sufficient to prove that reasonableness compels a negative reaction to all conduct that is currently classified as sexual harassment and that the women who do not have such a reaction are unreasonable. It is probably true that reasonableness compels women to *take into account* the fact that sexual advances and other conduct of a sexual nature are *sometimes* a prelude to violence, but it seems equally true that reasonableness also requires them to take into account the fact that sexual advances, even crude ones, and other openly sexual conduct are in the overwhelming majority of instances *not* a prelude to violence, and are often well-intended. A reasonable woman would presumably be one whose reactions to conduct of a sexual nature would be shaped by balanced consideration of all the relevant facts: she would not allow her reactions to be determined solely by the fact that conduct of a sexual nature is sometimes a prelude to violence. At least that is what seems analogous to how reasonableness operates in other kinds of cases: for example, we expect that a reasonable woman (just like a reasonable man) would not allow her reactions to the idea of flying on a plane to be determined solely by the fact that planes sometimes do crash; rather we would expect her reactions to such an idea to be shaped by balanced consideration of that fact together with the fact that in the overwhelming majority of cases planes bring passengers to their destinations without crashing.

Many people, however, seem to have a strong urge to believe that it is, in spite of all this, somehow still true that all reasonable women are offended by crude sexual behavior, and that something like (2') could thus still provide a workable criterion of demarcation. When confronted with what appear to be obvious counterexamples, they are likely to insulate their belief from empirical refutation by changing the meaning of the word *reasonable.* If one makes it a criterion of a woman's reasonableness that she is offended by behavior that involves sexually explicit jokes and games, displays of pornographic materials, certain forms of sexual advances, and so on, then it of course becomes logically true that all reasonable women are offended by it, because every woman who is not offended by it is *ipso facto* unreasonable, in that new sense of the word.

This maneuver builds a certain very specific substantive outlook on sexual morality into the notion of a reasonable woman. Precisely such a loaded notion of reasonableness is visibly at work in the dissenting opinion in *Rabidue v. Osceola Refining Co.*: "I hardly believe reasonable women condone the pervasive degradation and exploitation of female sexuality perpetuated in American culture."[64] How normatively loaded the word "reasonable" is in this opinion is rendered particularly clear by its being treated as the opposite of "unenlightened."[65]

The effect of using the word *reasonable* in the reasonable woman standard in this way would be to turn the sexual harassment law into a vehicle of legal moralism, which is not what it is supposed to be. Interpreted in this way, the law becomes subject to the arguments of the kind that has been presented in chapter 1. Quite apart from whatever general problems there are with moralistic laws, there is a special problem with a moralistic law that does not make its moralistic character obvious, and the sexual harassment law would be precisely such a law if this interpretation of the reasonable woman standard were accepted. Making the moralistic character of a law unobvious sabotages clear public debate about the law. Those who believe that a moralistic law in this area would be desirable should openly say so and then face the arguments that the opponents of moralistic laws will undoubtedly want to make, rather than hide the moralism behind the word *reasonable*, which is normally used for rather different purposes.[66]

Moreover, although interpreting the reasonable woman standard in this moralistic way would provide a kind of a criterion of demarcation, it would not provide the kind of criterion that is needed here. Knowing that (2') incorporates substantive moral outlook cannot help potential harassers to avoid committing acts that fall under that criterion, unless and until the specific content of that outlook is spelled out. If the content of the outlook were clearly specified (as it certainly has not been in any of the relevant court decisions), then it would be that specification, rather than (2') itself, that would be providing the criterion of demarcation. We are thus driven to the conclusion that under no interpretation can (2') solve the demarcation problem.

The failures of (1') and (2') to solve the problem of demarcation make it tempting to embrace (3'), but that again won't do, for the reasons that were already invoked in the discussion of (3) earlier in this chapter. Even if we agree, for the sake of argument, that the sensitivity of females in sexual matters is higher than that of males, there is still so much variation in the degrees of such sensitivity among women themselves that no particular degree of sensitivity clearly stands out as the average for all reasonable women. Indeed, even an author whose general line of argument is very different from mine readily acknowledges that "we are remarkably uninformed concerning the victim's typical reactions to such abuse or the range of harm it causes."[67]

Moreover, even if the average were easy to ascertain, we would still have the problem caused by the fact that the differences in the sensitivity are not only quantitative but also qualitative: even women who have the degree of sensitivity in sexual matters that is the average for all reasonable women can differ in *what* they find offensive. That would preclude (3') from providing a workable criterion of demarcation.

The root of the failure of the reasonable woman standard, in any of its possible forms, to solve the problem of demarcation, is the simple fact that reasonable women differ in their outlooks on sexuality. In sexual matters there is no such thing as *the* outlook of *the* reasonable woman, and it makes no sense to ask whether the reasonable woman would be offended by this or that conduct. In most cases the only answer that can be given to such a question is: some reasonable women would, some wouldn't. It is remarkable that so many of those writing about sexual harassment appear to be oblivious to the obvious fact that women's outlooks on sexual matters differ. The occasional acknowledgments of the differences among women that one does find in the literature tend to consist of the remarks such as

> the "reasonable woman" standard may exclude the varied perspectives of women of different races, classes, sexual orientations, and abilities[68]

which only confuse the issue and betray that their authors are either unaware of or unwilling to acknowledge the fact that women of the *same* race, class, and so forth, often have radically different outlooks on sexual matters.

OBJECTIONS AND RESPONSES

There are four responses to the argument of chapters 2 and 3 that I have encountered that need to be discussed briefly at this stage.

One response to the argument is that, even if it is sound, it does not point to any "real," practical problem. It could be said that people are unlikely to use the law and the grievance procedures based on the law, unless the particular acts of sexual harassment cause them great distress.[69] This is because the use of legal and quasi-legal mechanisms is burdensome, and also likely to be somewhat distressing itself when the matter concerns one's sexuality. Thus, it could be said that, although the behavior that is very mildly offensive may, strictly speaking, be within the scope of the rules we have discussed, it is unlikely that these rules will ever be applied to such behavior: the victims won't bother to initiate their application. A kind of demarcation that I am looking for could be found in the enforcement mechanisms rather than the relevant rules themselves.

Even assuming that what the response claims is factually true, which is debatable,[70] its moral assumptions are extremely worrisome. What they amount to is that it is okay for a law to be excessively restrictive, as long as potential complainants and plaintiffs can be counted on to use their discretion in a way that will produce acceptable results. The reasoning behind this response thus endorses legal rules that effectively put people at the mercy of potential complainants and plaintiffs and this doesn't seem to be what is normally meant by the "rule of law."

The second kind of response, which some people who haven't carefully followed the argument of chapters 2 and 3 may be tempted to make, is that even if the argument is sound, it only shows that a *part* of what has been intended as the criterion of what constitutes sexual harassment is problematic. The argument at best shows that some forms of hostile environment harassment cannot be demarcated from other forms of sexual interaction, but surely, these people would say, there are other forms of sexual harassment, notably quid pro quo harassment, that are very easy to demarcate from other forms of sexual interaction. This would lead them to conclude that the argument does not affect the sexual harassment law as a whole.

This response, however, manifests a misunderstanding of the logical structure of the argument. It is indeed true that quid pro quo harassment can be easily distinguished from other forms of sexual interaction. However, the only thing that this observation proves is that, *if* the sexual harassment law contained *only* the prohibition of quid pro quo harassment, there would be no demarcation problem. This, however, is not what the law in fact is; the actual law prohibits both quid pro quo harassment *and* different forms of hostile environment harassment. If one of those prohibitions turns out to amount to a prohibition of all interaction of a sexual nature (which is what the argument of chapters 2 and 3 shows) then the law as a whole turns out to be a prohibition of all interaction of a sexual nature. The fact that other prohibitions within the law have more limited scope is irrelevant.

In discussions that I had with people about this argument it often turned out that what interfered with their appreciation of this simple point is the fact that the purported criterion of demarcation in the EEOC Guidelines has the form of a disjunction, together with the fact that they, half-remembering their first-year logic, tended to think that a disjunction must be okay if one of its disjuncts is okay. In order not to be a victim of this confusion one has to realize that what we are dealing with here is a *prohibition* of sexual harassment. That is, we are dealing with a law that requires that we behave in a manner that does *not* constitute sexual harassment. Someone who wants to avoid committing acts of sexual harassment thus has to behave in a manner that satisfies the *negation* of the disjunction found in the EEOC Guidelines, and the negation of a disjunction (as can be found in any first-year logic textbook) is a *conjunction*. It should be obvious to everyone that if one conjunct is practically impossible to satisfy, except by abstaining from all sexual interaction, then the conjunction as a whole is practically impossible to satisfy, except by abstaining from all sexual interaction.

The third line of response that I have encountered in discussions of this argument, and that needs to be dealt with here, is that even if the argument works against one possible interpretation of the law, there surely must be some other interpretation of it that does solve the demarcation problem and avoids the argument. From the viewpoint of the people who want to adjust their conduct to the requirements of this law, it is, however, irrelevant whether you or I might be able to come up with such an interpretation. What they want to do is adjust their behavior to the requirements of the law, as it will be interpreted by the courts. The only thing they can turn to, in order to determine how the courts will interpret the law, are the judicial decisions showing how the law has been interpreted so far. All that, however, has already been taken into account in the argument of chapters 2 and 3. The argument is precisely about the law as it has been interpreted in the relevant judicial decisions. There is no further interpretation that can be relevant to what is at issue here.[71]

The fourth kind of response to my argument so far, that an inattentive reader may be tempted to make, is to dismiss the argument as nothing but a defense of the sexist "male prerogative" to make sexual advances to women. To dismiss the argument in that way would, however, show a misunderstanding of it. Nothing that I have said implies an endorsement of the idea that sexual advances ought to be made by men and addressed to women. The argument I have developed in chapters 2 and 3 hinges on the purely conceptual point that, if sexual interaction of *any* kind is to take place, then *somebody* has to initiate it (i.e., make the relevant sexual advances). Nothing in the argument implies that this somebody has to be male.

Variations on the Theme of Reasonableness

When the U.S. courts invoke the notion of reasonableness in their sexual harassment decisions and consider the allegedly harassing conduct from the perspective of a reasonable person or a reasonable woman, they always consider it from the perspective of a reasonable person/woman *in the position of the alleged victim.* This should strike as somewhat odd, because the notion of reasonableness operates very differently in its original home, the law of torts.[72] The primary issue involving reasonableness in a tort case is typically whether the alleged *tortfeasor* has behaved as a reasonable person would have behaved and not whether the plaintiff has so behaved (nor whether the plaintiff's reactions to the alleged tortfeasor's behavior were reasonable). The reasonableness of the plaintiff becomes relevant only if the issues of contributory or comparative negligence have been raised.

Given that the preceding sections have shown that the way in which the U.S. courts have brought the notion of reasonableness into the sexual harassment law is, in fact, incapable of solving the demarcation problem, it may be worthwhile to consider whether the problem could perhaps be solved by formulating a criterion of sexual harassment that would invoke the notion of reasonableness in a way that is more analogous to the way the notion operates in the law of torts. One possible version of such a criterion would require that, in order to constitute sexual harassment, the conduct complained of be

> (4) conduct of which a reasonable person would have known that it would be unwelcome and offensive.[73]

Now (4), at first sight, seems to be a definite improvement over the criteria we have considered so far. It definitely does prevent the notion of sexual harassment from extending over the whole domain of sexual interaction between people who work together. On the other hand, (4) does not appear, at first sight, to narrow down the scope of the sexual harassment rules as drastically as interpretation (2) of the reasonable person standard or interpretation (2') of the reasonable woman standard. Surely, one could say, there are quite a few cases of what is currently regarded as hostile environment harassment, in addition to deliberate insults, which are such that any reasonable person would know that the conduct is unwelcome and offensive, and these cases would continue to count as cases of sexual harassment under this criterion.

But is that really so? Consider what appears to be the best candidate for such harassment. Suppose that X has already made a number of sexual advances towards Y. Each of the advances was unambiguously turned down by Y. If this is so, isn't it then the case that any reasonable person in X's position would know that the next sexual advance toward Y is bound to be unwelcome and offensive?

Before we rush to say "yes" to this question, we should ask ourselves why, in the situation we are imagining, would X nevertheless go ahead and make the next advance. In any given case, it may be that X is simply unreasonable, but it is difficult to believe that this applies to all cases of this kind that actually occur. The cases in which another sexual advance is made after a number of rejections occur rather frequently, and it is difficult to believe that there are that many unreasonable people around. Another possibility is that X is reasonable, but that the seeming advance is not really a bona fide advance (i.e., that it is not made in the hope of eliciting a positive response), but rather a deliberate attempt to annoy and offend Y. Again, however, it is difficult to believe that this applies to more than a minority of the actual cases of the kind we are considering.

What other explanation could there be of the fact that people so often go ahead and make another sexual advance after several rejections? The main reason for such repetition of sexual advances is that the fact that X has made *n* advances toward Y and that Y has rejected all *n* of them[74] does not entail that *n*+1st advance will be rejected as well. People, including Y, can change their minds about almost anything, including the desirability of a sexual relationship with X. It is always possible that the change of mind[75] will occur precisely between the *n*th and the *n*+1st advance. There is thus always a possibility that the *n*+1st advance will be successful, after all, and it is precisely this possibility that, in a typical case of this kind, makes it worthwhile for X to make the advance.

People thus repeat sexual advances after they have already been rejected for the same reason for which they repeat invitations and offers of other kinds after they have been rejected. X's repetition of sexual advances to Y is analogous to, for example, the conduct of researchers in one empirical study of sexual harassment, who "[i]f the designated respondent refused or broke off the interview, [made] up to four additional attempts . . . to convert that refusal or termination into a completed interview."[76] The researchers presumably did that because they knew that some people change their minds about participation in such research.

We may note that, if *n* is high, then the probability of the *n*+1st attempt being successful is bound to be rather low, and X may well agree with us about that. However, if X regards sexual and romantic fulfillment as very highly desirable, as most people do, and if X finds Y desirable as a potential partner, then X will regard the attempt as worthwhile even if the probability of success is low.

The possibility of such a change of mind is not a purely theoretical possibility. When a magazine intended primarily for women asked its readers to describe their affairs with office colleagues, one of the responses was:

> After my children were grown, I went to work. Little did I know that I would be pursued by the boss, who is ten years my junior. When this man made *extreme* advances, I decided to try it out. What a trip![77]

Another participant in the survey described how, "[a]fter initially resisting [she] finally responded to the advances of her boss. Now, she says, she is filling her heart with 'memories that no one can take away.' "[78] In the case of yet another woman who responded to the survey, the initial resistance went on for a very long time:

> After struggling to stay away from him for more than a year, one afternoon after a "friendly" game of golf, I gave in—like a dog in heat—to my pent-up tumultuous desire and attraction while we were in the high grass.[79]

While the period of resistance in this case lasted more than a year, the affair that eventuated lasted at least ten years (at the time of the survey it was still going on).

Such examples show that people actually do change their minds about the desirability of sexual interaction with another person, and that "extreme" advances, advances that are made in spite of initial resistance (even when that resistance goes on for more than a year) can eventually lead to a great deal of happiness for both of the people concerned. As before, I am not claiming anything as to how often such changes of mind happen, nor am I claiming anything as to whether it is desirable that they happen. The pertinent fact is that they *do* happen, and that a reasonable person knows that they happen.

While many ordinary people regard this possibility of a change of mind from initial rejection to eventual acceptance of someone's sexual advances as a matter of common knowledge, it is never mentioned by the experts writing on sexual harassment. That is curious, given that they often do point out the possibility of a change of mind in the opposite direction, from an initial acceptance to someone's sexual advances to rejecting any continuation of the sexual relationship with that person.[80] Surely, these two ways of changing one's mind are on a par and should be treated as such.

It is because of this possibility of the change of mind on the part of Y, that no person in X's position, no matter how reasonable, can ever know that the advance will, in fact, be unwelcome and offensive (as long as the advance is indeed a bona fide advance). Therefore, even cases of this kind would not count as instances of sexual harassment, if (4) is taken at its face value. So, it seems that we can conclude that (4), taken at face value, just like (2) and (2'), would narrow down the scope of sexual harassment rules far too drastically.[81] Under (4), as under (2) and (2'), law about sexual harassment would be largely inoperative.

The failure of (4) may lead us to consider a criterion of sexual harassment that would only require that the conduct complained of, in order to count as sexual harassment, be

> (5) conduct of which a reasonable person would have known that it *could* be unwelcome and offensive

The problem with (5) is the opposite of the one we have seen with (4). Like (1), (5) does not exclude almost any conduct of a sexual nature. Human sexuality, as we have observed many times within this book, is such that almost any conduct of a sexual nature has some potential for being offensive, and a reasonable person knows that. Almost all conduct of a sexual nature therefore fulfills (5). Thus, when we consider allegedly harassing conduct from the perspective of a reasonable person in the position of the alleged harasser, the dilemma between (1) and (2) re-emerges as the dilemma between (5) and (4). Neither (5) nor (4) can solve the demarcation problem, just as neither (1) nor (2) could.[82]

CONCLUSION

If the argument of chapters 2 and 3 is sound, then the present sexual harassment law is incapable of providing a workable criterion of demarcation between sexual harassment and other forms of sexual interaction, without leaving the latter class empty or almost empty. The prohibition of sexual harassment thus amounts to a prohibition of all sexual interaction between people who work together.

This argument has a certain affinity with the reasoning that led the Supreme Court to declare unconstitutional an ordinance that prohibited people from conducting themselves on sidewalks "in a manner annoying to persons passing by": "Conduct that annoys some people does not annoy others. Thus, the ordinance is vague, not in the sense that it requires a person to conform his conduct to an imprecise but comprehensible normative standard, but rather in the sense that no standard of conduct is specified at all."[83]

The argument of chapters 2 and 3 entails that the present law about sexual harassment is morally unjustified. Crucial to that argument was the examination of the role that the notions of unwelcomeness and offensiveness play in the law: its conclusions thus apply not only to the law as it actually is in the United States, but also to any other sexual harassment law in which the notions of unwelcomeness and offensiveness have a similar role. This includes some of the sexual harassment laws in other developed English-speaking countries, which were often modeled after the EEOC Guidelines. It also includes various forms of possible sexual harassment laws that have been proposed or might be proposed in the future, as long as they retain a role for the words such as "unwelcome" and "offensive" similar to the one they play in the present law.

It should be noted that the argument of chapters 2 and 3 is not based on any positive view of mine as to what the demarcation should look like, but only on the rather minimal assumption (shared, I believe, by most of the people who defend the existence of the sexual harassment law) that there should be some kind of demarcation. My objection to the law is not that it provides a wrong kind of demarcation, but that it provides no demarcation whatsoever.

The argument of chapters 2 and 3 establishes that the current sexual harassment law is unjustified, independently of any possible scrutiny of the reasons that are believed by its defenders to make it morally justified. That the focus of the argument made such scrutiny unnecessary is both its strength and its weakness. It is its strength, because such scrutiny is likely to involve matters far more controversial than anything that appears in the argument. On the other hand, it is its weakness, because the defenders of the law may accept the argument and yet feel that it somehow misses everything that is really important about sexual harassment: they may feel that the argument, so to speak, involves a mere "technicality."

It is indeed true that the arguments that have been made in this book up to this point do not say anything as to whether it would be morally justified to create some law about sexual conduct that would be sufficiently different from the present sexual harassment law to be able to solve the demarcation problem and that would still deserve to be called "sexual harassment law," in that it would attempt to accommodate the concerns that motivate the support for the current law. This is the question to which we now turn.

4
How Much Is Too Much?

Harassment and Interests

Many of those who support the sexual harassment law in its present form or advocate its strengthening seem oblivious to the simple fact that the most typical reason for making a sexual advance is the hope that it will be accepted and that its acceptance will result in some kind of fulfillment and happiness for both of the parties involved. It could even be argued that this is just a conceptual truth about what sexual advances are. This simple fact has been alluded to in much of the discussion of the preceding chapter, but it is worthwhile to explicitly emphasize its significance at this point, because any progress in dealing with the demarcation problem depends on our being vividly aware of that fact.

It is the neglect of that fact that has resulted in lumping together, under the notion of hostile environment harassment, of bona fide sexual advances that turn out to be offensive and acts such as deliberate insults of a sexual nature.

The aim of a deliberate insult of a sexual nature is to give some kind of satisfaction to the person who is making it *at the expense* of the person insulted. In other words, its aim is to increase the well-being of the person making it by decreasing the well-being of the person subjected to it. And not only are deliberate insults intended to produce the decrease in the well-being of the persons to whom they are directed, but they almost always do in fact produce it: in thinking about deliberate insults we may safely ignore the possibility of their having results other than intended ones.

A bona fide sexual advance is, on the other hand, aimed at increasing the well-being of the person making it without decreasing the well-being of the person to whom it is directed. In making a sexual advance, one normally hopes that it will lead to interaction that will be satisfying not only to oneself but also to the other person. In the technical terminology of political theory, this important difference between sexual advances and deliberate insults can be expressed by saying that a bona fide sexual advance is aimed at producing a Pareto-improvement (at least so far as the people directly involved are concerned) while a deliberate insult most definitely is not.

Needless to say, sexual advances do not always produce the hoped-for Pareto-improvements. All too often a sexual advance ends up being directed to a person who is in fact disinclined, sometimes quite strongly disinclined, to pursue sexual interaction of the kind that is being proposed, with the person who is proposing it. Instead of leading to a mutually fulfilling experience, a sexual advance may thus result in making the person to whom it is directed feeling offended, humiliated, annoyed, uncomfortable, or otherwise displeased. This *is* a serious problem for everyone concerned, but it is a problem that is rather different from the problem posed by deliberate insults of a sexual nature.

Moreover, although sexual advances do not always produce the results that those who make them hope for, it is important not to forget that they sometimes do. Sometimes, sexual advances do lead to mutually fulfilling sexual interaction that brings a great deal of happiness to those involved. The kind of fulfillment and happiness that mutually satisfying sexual relationships bring cannot be achieved except by someone making some steps toward its being achieved—steps that can always be characterized as sexual advances. In other words, sexual advances sometimes do lead to Pareto-improvements, and the Pareto-improvements to which they lead cannot be realized without sexual advances being made. This makes sexual advances very different from deliberate insults of a sexual nature, which practically never lead to any Pareto-improvements. Indeed, deliberate insults of a sexual nature typically lead to a net decrease in total well-being, because the decrease in the well-being of the person insulted is typically greater than the increase in the well-being of the person making the insult. This difference is supremely relevant to determining how the problems caused by these kinds of conduct should be dealt with, and yet it often ends up being swept under the carpet in discussions of hostile environment harassment.

Soon after the EEOC issued its Guidelines on Sexual Harassment, the then-acting chairman of the Commission declared that "the Commission sees no justification for treating harassment based on sex any differently than harassment based on race, religion, color, or national origin."[1] The fact that the prohibition of sexual harassment covers the bona fide advances that turn out to be offensive, however, makes it crucially different from the prohibition of these other kinds of harassment. The deliberate insults based on race, ethnicity, and so on are indeed, in many ways, analogous to deliberate insults of a sexual nature, but there are very few examples of conduct involving "race, religion, color, or national origin" that would be analogous to the bona fide sexual advances that turn out to be offensive. The harassment involving race, ethnicity, and so on is almost always intended as harassment; it is very rare for it to turn on unintended consequences of acts that were intended to be mutually beneficial. Insisting that sexual harassment is analogous to racial, ethnic, or religious harassment thus goes hand in hand with ignoring the distinction between deliberate insults of a sexual nature and the bona fide sexual advances that turn out to be offensive.

We should not allow the difference between deliberate insults of a sexual nature and bona fide sexual advances to be obscured by the existence of conduct that we may call mock-advances, namely the conduct that shares some superficial features of genuine sexual advances, but that is not really aimed at mutually satisfying sexual interaction. (In one of the reported cases, for example, the plaintiff was repeatedly asked by her coworkers whether she "wanted to fuck" in the context that strongly suggested that the words were not really intended as invitations to sexual intercourse.)[2] Mock-advances can and should be assimilated to deliberate insults of a sexual nature: they *are* a species of deliberate insults. This being true of mock-advances, however, does not entail anything about bona fide advances, because the two are very different. The theoreticians writing about sexual harassment are often rather careless about the distinction between mock-advances and bona fide advances and sometimes even seem to treat mock-advances as if they constituted the paradigm of sexual advances. This is rather strange given that ordinary people usually have little difficulty in distinguishing between the two.

In the literature on sexual harassment one frequently finds the idea that "sexual harassment has always been primarily about power, only rarely about sex, and never about romance."[3] As one writer has elaborated it:

> Sexual harassment has nothing whatsoever to do with libido and lust. It has everything to do with exploiting, objectifying, and dominating women. It is a manifestation of the extreme loathing so many men bear toward women.[4]

Another author similarly pronounces that

> The underlying attitudes of the men [who engage in sexual harassment] are contempt or at least condescension toward all or most women, not merely toward the one who is currently being harassed.[5]

These claims are fairly plausible as an analysis of what goes on in deliberate insults of a sexual nature, including mock-advances. It is, however, difficult to see how the claim that sexual harassment is about power and not sex is supposed to apply to bona fide sexual advances that turned out to have bad effects on the person receiving them. Consider, for example, the case of Sterling Gray writing to a coworker Kerry Ellison a note in which he said

> I cried over you last night and I'm totally drained today. . . . Thank you for talking with me. I could not stand to feel your hatred for another day.[6]

This note did make Ms. Ellison "shocked and frightened"[7] and a federal court of appeals held (in the *Ellison* case that has been referred to in the preceding chapter) that writing such notes may constitute sexual harassment. But to say that in writing these words Mr. Gray was somehow asserting his *power* over Ms. Ellison stretches the meaning of the word *power* beyond recognition. It is also difficult to see how this note could be interpreted as an expression of Mr. Gray's "extreme loathing" either toward women in general or toward Ms. Ellison in particular, or how it could be taken to indicate his contempt or condescension toward most women.

Many of those who write about sexual harassment proceed as if the whole problem posed by the conduct that is currently so classified amounted to a straightforward clash of interests. They seem to assume that on one side is the interest that harassers have in pursuing harassment, and that on the other side is the interest that the potential victims have in not being subjected to harassment. On that assumption, if harassment takes place, it is the interests of the harassers that are satisfied; if it doesn't take place, it is the interests of those who otherwise would have been its victims that are satisfied. To those who view sexual harassment in that way it appears that the main issue we are facing in deciding what kinds of laws we should have about it is whether we should have the laws that support the interests of harassers in harassing, or the laws that support the interests of potential victims in not being harassed. Once that is taken to be the main issue, the answer seems obvious: of course we should support the interests of potential victims and not of the harassers. This way of framing the issue thus leads those who accept it to advocate the laws that will restrict behavior classified as sexual harassment as much as possible.

This model fits well the harassment that consists in deliberate insults of a sexual nature. The problem posed by such insults can be treated as amounting to the clash between the interest that those who are inclined to make such insults have in the satisfaction that they get out of making them and the interest that the potential victims have in not being insulted.

The reliance on this model, however, seriously distorts the problem posed by bona fide sexual advances that, contrary to what those who are making them are hoping for, turn out to be offensive to those to whom they are directed. That problem does not amount to such a straightforward clash of interests. To be sure, those who may be subjected to such advances do have an interest in not being subjected to them. But those who make the advances that turn out to be offensive do not have any interest in making *them*. What they want is to make advances that will be accepted, not advances that will be offensive. The outcome of a bona fide advance that turned out to be offensive is not only against the interests of the recipient of the advance, but also against the interests of the maker of the advance. The advances that turn out to be offensive are usually a source of at least some embarrassment to those who make them. Moreover, such advances are undesirable even from the viewpoint of the advance-makers who are sufficiently thick-skinned not to suffer such embarrassment, because they constitute a waste of their time and energy. Given that what happens in such advances is against the interests of both parties, the problem posed by it cannot be regarded as a matter of straightforward clash between the interests of the two parties involved.

If the outcomes of such advances are against the interests of those who make them, why do they make them? The answer is, of course, that in making them, they are driven by the interests that they have in making successful advances, namely advances that will be accepted and lead to some kind of fulfillment and happiness. It is in the nature of the kind of cases we are looking at that the makers of offensive advances, at the moment when they are making them, don't know that they are making *unsuccessful* advances; they are hoping that their advances will turn out to be successful. And we should note that when a sexual advance is successful, i.e. when it leads to a fulfilling sexual relationship, its outcome is not only in the interests of the maker of the advance, but also in the interests of its recipient.

We thus have, on one side, offensive sexual advances, which are against the interests of both parties and, on the other side, successful sexual advances, leading to mutually satisfying sexual relationships, which are in the interests of both parties. When these two kinds of cases are considered separately, in neither of them do we have any clash of interests. The problem that we have here does not arise out of anything that could be seen by considering the two kinds of cases separately, but out of the fact that the two kinds of cases are inextricably bound together. What binds them together is the ignorance of the makers of advances as to whether their advances are going to turn out to be successful or unwelcome, offensive, and so on. Successful advances and offensive advances do not result from decisions of different kinds, they both result from decisions of one and the same kind, namely the decisions to make sexual advances, of which one hopes that they will turn out to be successful, but which may turn out to be offensive. Because both kinds of advances result from decisions of the same kind, it is impossible to have laws, or rules of any other sort, that would regulate successful and offensive advances separately. Any rule that by its wording purports to be about advances of only one of the two kinds will still, inevitably, end up regulating the other kind as well.

Unsuccessful, unwelcome, offensive sexual advances are bound with the successful ones in the same way in which losing in gambling is bound with winning. Although losing and winning are different things, they do not result from decisions of different kinds. One does not normally make a decision to lose in gambling. Losing in gambling results from decisions of the same kind that winning results from, namely the decisions to participate in gambling (which are made in the knowledge that both winning and losing are possible, but with the hope of winning). Because of that, there cannot be any rules that regulate losing in gambling without regulating winning as well. A rule that purports to regulate losing only, and does not say anything explicit about winning, would inevitably have an impact on winning as well. For example, a rule that said that losing in gambling is prohibited would clearly amount to a prohibition of gambling itself, and thus of both losing and winning, in spite of, on the face of it, not saying anything about winning.

Even if we focus only on the potential makers and recipients of sexual advances and set aside any interests of the third parties, we need to take into account at least four sets of interests in order to understand the workings of any rule that tries to regulate such advances (including both the present sexual harassment law and any modification of it that might be proposed). These four sets of interests are:

(1) the interests of potential makers of sexual advances in making advances that will lead to mutually satisfying sexual relationships,
(2) the interests of potential makers of sexual advances in not making advances that will turn out to be unwelcome, offensive, and so on to their recipients,
(3) the interests of potential recipients of sexual advances in receiving advances that will lead to mutually satisfying sexual relationships,

(4) the interests of potential recipients of sexual advances in not receiving advances that will be unwelcome, offensive, and so on to them.

Makers of bona fide sexual advances have interests of both the first and the second kind. Those who have interests of the third kind normally also have interests of the fourth kind. Given that one and the same person is often both a potential maker and potential recipient of sexual advances, it is often the case that one and the same person has the interests of all four kinds.

There are also quite a few people who are not, at the given moment, interested in establishing any new sexual relationships, and who thus have interests of the fourth kind without having interests of any of the other three kinds. But although an individual may have interests of the fourth kind only, at a typical contemporary workplace the interests of all four kinds are likely to be represented in some way.

The remarks that I have just made have probably struck some people as spelling out the obvious. These remarks, however, needed to be made because some of the theoreticians writing about sexual harassment appear to be unaware of the existence or significance of the interests of the first three kinds. Mary Radford has, for example, in arguing that conduct of a sexual nature within a workplace should be presumed to be unwelcome, characterized exposure to sexual conduct as "humiliating, severely distracting, and potentially harmful to [people's] ability to perform successfully at their jobs."[8] Characterizing expressions of sexual interest as inherently humiliating is either a sign of remarkable obliviousness of the interests of the third kind, or of the view that they are somehow unworthy of being taken into consideration.

In fact, much of the literature about sexual harassment is written as if the interests of the fourth kind were somehow decisive, as if they were obviously more worthy of legal protection than the interests of the other kinds. This bias is probably a result of the distorting influence of trying to deal with bona fide sexual advances that went wrong by using the same model that is used for dealing with deliberate insults of a sexual nature. It may also be due to the fact that much of the literature about sexual harassment is written by counselors, therapists, and similar professionals, who in the course of their work often have an opportunity to observe the consequences of sexual advances that went wrong, but who, in virtue of the nature of their jobs, do not have comparable opportunities to observe the happiness of the people who find themselves in fulfilling sexual and romantic relationships.

It needs to be emphasized that this bias in favor of the interests of the fourth kind is unfair not only to the makers of sexual advances, but also to all the potential recipients of sexual advances who have interests of the third kind.[9] Unless one believes that human sexuality is somehow intrinsically suspect, it is not at all clear why the interests of the fourth kind should be more important than the interests of the third kind.

The absurdity of treating the interests of the fourth kind as decisive becomes even more obvious if we compare sexual advances to other activities that involve a similar pattern of interests. For example, although we do think that the interests of potential victims of traffic accidents deserve legal protection, we do not think that they are the only interests relevant to our deciding what kind of legal rules to have about motor traffic. If we thought that these interests were decisive, we would have to completely prohibit motor traffic, because that is the only way to ensure that no one will ever suffer a traffic accident. The reason why no one would support such a prohibition is of course that motor traffic is something that brings considerable benefits to both motorists and nonmotorists. In determining what kind of legal regime to have about motor traffic we take into account both the interests that people have in not being victims of accidents and the interests that they (both motorists and nonmotorists) have in the benefits that the existence of motor traffic brings (together with the further interests that they may have in its being cheap, quick, readily available, and so on).

Or, to take an example we have used before, the visits of door-to-door salesmen are bound to cause at least some annoyance or displeasure to some people. People have an interest in not having to deal with door-to-door salesmen who are selling products they are not interested in buying. But again, we do not think that this interest is the only one that is relevant to the question of what kind of legal rules, if any, should there be about door-to-door sales: if we thought that this interest is the only one that is relevant we would have to prohibit door-to-door sales altogether. The reason why most jurisdictions do not have such a prohibition is that we regard other interests as relevant as well: the interests of sellers in selling their goods through door-to-door sales and the interests of potential purchasers in purchasing the goods in this way. In thinking about the annoyance and displeasure that visits of door-to-door salesmen cause, we normally keep it in our minds that this annoyance and displeasure is a by-product of something that is aimed at, and often leads to, mutually beneficial transactions between buyers and sellers.

In fact, most of the day-to-day lives of most of us involve activities to which this pattern of reasoning applies. Setting aside violence and fraud, human interaction in an organized society is normally aimed at Pareto-improvements, and almost no activity that is aimed at Pareto-improvements is guaranteed to produce them: things can always go wrong.

In determining what kind of legal rules should govern a particular kind of activity we normally take into account both the interests that people have in the benefits that the activity brings when it goes well and the interests they have in avoiding the consequences that appear when it does not. In taking different interests into account we pay attention both to the magnitude of benefits and harms that are at stake and to the probability of their occurrence. If we looked only at the magnitude of benefits and harms we would still be led to prohibit all motor traffic, because the harm caused by a traffic accident is usually enormous compared to relatively minor benefits of a successfully completed car trip. The reason why we are, in spite of that, not at all tempted to prohibit all motor traffic is that we take into consideration the fact that it is far more probable that an individual car trip will be successful than that it will result in an accident. Thinking about the probabilities also plays a crucial role in our decision to prohibit particular kinds of driving that significantly increase the probability of accidents, such as driving at very high speeds or under the influence of alcohol. In technical terminology this is usually expressed by saying that we base our decisions on comparing the expected social utility of a practice (the magnitude of the benefits multiplied by the probability of their occurrence) with the expected social disutility or the expected social cost (the magnitude of the harms multiplied by the probability of their occurrence).

Now, what rules about sexual harassment would emerge if we took into account all the relevant interests, in the same way in which we do in all other areas of life? One thing that we immediately notice is that, in most everyday circumstances, the probability that a given sexual advance, that someone is considering making, will be unsuccessful is quite high, far higher than, say, the probability that a given car trip will end in an accident. However, we need to also take into account the fact that, although the probability of a given advance being successful might not be all that high, the magnitude of the benefit that is achieved when it is successful is high indeed. For most people, successful personal relationships that have a sexual component are a source of more intense happiness and sense of fulfillment than anything else. Many people would readily say that romantic and sexual relationships are precisely what makes their lives worth living. Again, it is important not to forget that it is in the nature of such relationships that the benefits in question accrue to both of the parties involved, and not only to the maker of the advance that led to the relationship (i.e., we should bear in mind that the interests of the third kind are at stake, as well as of the first).

In comparison with the benefits that result from successful sexual advances, the harms that result from unsuccessful, unwelcome, sexual advances are usually minor.[10] Having to turn down a sexual advance is annoying, but in most cases it is not anything more than mildly annoying. The harm that results from an unsuccessful sexual advance usually remains small, even if we include in it the embarrassment and other consequences that the advance causes to the person making it (i.e., even if we take into account the interests of the second as well as the fourth kind). In assessing the magnitude of these harms, we need to also take into account that they typically last for only a short period of time. Thus even when the consequences of an unwelcome sexual advance include something more serious than mild annoyance (say anger, or a sense of frustration) the overall magnitude of the harm still remains small relative to the benefits of a successful advance, because the harmful consequences of an unsuccessful advance are likely to dissipate quickly, while the beneficial consequences of a successful advance may last for years.

Much of the literature on sexual harassment emphasizes that unwelcome sexual advances sometimes cause very serious harm to their recipients. That this is so is undoubtedly true, and that is a fact that needs to be taken into account in any deliberations as to what kind of rules should there be about sexual harassment. The literature, however, tends to obscure the fact that it is only *sometimes* that unwelcome sexual advances cause such serious harm and that receiving an unwanted sexual advance and turning it down is usually not a deeply traumatic experience.

When we apply to these facts the patterns of reasoning that we use in other areas of life, we are forced to conclude that sexual advances are often worthwhile and ought to be legally permitted. The fact that the magnitude of the benefits (to both parties taken together) of a successful sexual advance is typically *much* greater than the magnitude of the harms (to both parties taken together)[11] of an unsuccessful sexual advance, entails that sexual advances are typically worthwhile, even when they are not particularly likely to be successful. For example, in most situations it is quite plausible to say that, taking into account the interests of both parties, a sexual advance that has only 10% probability of being successful is still worthwhile, because the benefits that will obtain if it is successful are more than ten times greater than the harms that will result if it is unsuccessful.

These patterns of reasoning also enable us, at least in principle, to isolate the kinds of sexual advances that are not worthwhile. A particularly crude sexual advance, as I have pointed out before, still has some probability of being successful and bringing happiness to the people concerned, but, in assessing whether it is worthwhile, we need to also take into account that it has considerable probability of causing serious harm (and not just mere annoyance). For at least some crude or aggressive advances we will have to conclude that the magnitude of the harm, multiplied by its probability, is so great that the advances in question are not worthwhile, and that it may be desirable to have rules that prohibit them.

Moreover, in determining whether sexual advances of a particular kind would be worthwhile we need to not only compare the making of such advances with not making any advances, but also with making other kinds of advances that can be made under the circumstances. Suppose, for example, that, under certain circumstances, one kind of a sexual advance has 10% probability of being successful, 88% probability of being unsuccessful and causing mild annoyance, and 2% probability of causing serious offense. Considered on its own, such an advance may well seem worthwhile. Suppose, however, that there is a different kind of advance that one can make under these circumstances, that also has 10% chance of being successful, but only 1% probability of causing serious offense (and 89% probability of causing mild annoyance), and that is not any more burdensome to make than the first kind. Surely if we knew all that, we would want to encourage people to make advances of the latter kind: that decreases the risk of harm without affecting anything else. Or, suppose that there is a third kind of advance that can be made under the same circumstances, that would increase the probability of success from 10% to 11%, but that would at the same time increase the probability of offense to, say, 20%. In that case the relevant question to ask would not be whether the 11% probability of success outweighs the 20% probability of offense (together with 69% probability of mild annoyance), but rather whether the *additional* 1% probability of success justifies the additional 19% probability of offense. If the answer to that question is "no," as it may well be (that depends on the precise intensity of the offense), then we may want to discourage people from making advances of this third type, and encourage them to make the advances that are less risky instead. This is exactly analogous to the reasoning that leads us to impose speed limits on motor traffic. We ask ourselves whether any extra benefits that would be gained by people driving at a high rather than moderate speed are worth the extra risk of accidents, and if it turns out they aren't, we impose the speed limit that prohibits driving at high speed.

The patterns of reasoning about sexual advances that have just been sketched are also analogous to the reasoning that is, within the context of torts, expressed in the celebrated Learned Hand's formula. According to that formula, the duty that the law of torts imposes on a potential tortfeasor is the duty to undertake every precaution against causing injuries that is such that the burden of undertaking it is less than the gravity of the injury that is at stake, multiplied by the probability of its occurrence[12] (or, more precisely, by the reduction in the probability that would be achieved by the precautions). There is, according to the formula, no duty to undertake any precautions that would be more burdensome than that. Those who omit to undertake the precautions required by the formula are liable for any damages that do occur, but those who have undertaken such precautions have secured themselves against liability.

Making a crude, aggressive, sexual advance, which is fairly likely to offend, when a more polite, less likely to offend, advance could have been made, is analogous to omitting to take precautions that could have been made. Just as the Learned Hand's formula imposes on potential tortfeasors the duty to take precautions that are not excessively burdensome, so the way of thinking about sexual advances that has been sketched above would lead to the duty to opt for polite rather than crude sexual advances whenever doing so is not excessively burdensome. The burden may, in the case of sexual advances, include the reduction of the probability of success, and whether it is excessive would depend, as in the Learned Hand's formula, on whether it exceeds the magnitude of the harm multiplied by the reduction in the probability of its occurrence that would result from opting for the polite advance. Just like the Learned Hand's formula, this way of thinking would, however, not lead to any duty regarding sexual advances that would be too burdensome. It would not, for example, lead to the duty to abstain from sexual advances altogether simply because people might be offended by them, which is, as I have argued, what the present law about sexual harassment amounts to.

A rule that would say that sexual advances are prohibited if they are not worthwhile in the sense that has been explained above (i.e., for which the difference between their benefits multiplied by the probability of their occurrence and the harms multiplied by the probability of their occurrence is either negative or lower than for other kinds of advances that could be made under the circumstances), and that they are permitted if they are, would thus be a considerable improvement over the rules embodied in the present law about sexual harassment. Saying that bona fide sexual advances that are not worthwhile in the sense explained constitute sexual harassment (together with quid pro quo harassment, deliberate insults of a sexual nature and similar acts), but that worthwhile sexual advances do not, fits fairly well the ordinary meaning of the word "harassment": a body of law that would be centered around such a rule could thus be quite naturally called the law about sexual harassment, in spite of being rather different from the present sexual harassment law.

Such a rule would, unlike the present sexual harassment law, remain neutral among the four kinds of interests that are at stake in sexual advances: it would take them all into account, without treating some of them as more worthy of protection than others. Such neutrality among specific interests that are at stake is precisely what we generally expect from the legal system. (I am, of course, aware that some people believe that some sexual matters are an exception to this general expectation of neutrality. They believe that some interests of a sexual nature, such as the interest in pursuing adulterous affairs, merit legal suppression in virtue of their intrinsic depravity. Such beliefs are, however, versions of legal moralism, which has been set aside in chapter 1.)

There would of course be considerable practical problems in the application of this rule to specific cases, both by the adjudicators and by potential harassers who wanted to avoid committing the acts prohibited by the rule. It is fairly clear that the rule would permit most of the ordinary sexual advances and that it would, under most circumstances, prohibit extraordinarily crude, gross, sexual advances, but there would be numerous puzzling cases that are somewhere in between, and about which there might be uncertainty as to whether they are prohibited or not. This would, however, be merely the familiar problem of fuzzy edges of legal rules that exists in practically every area of the law. The problem of the fuzzy edges is something very different from the radical demarcation problem that we discussed in the preceding two chapters. The problem with the present sexual harassment law, the preceding chapters argued, is not that it provides a criterion of demarcation that is fuzzy, but that it provides no criterion at all. This radical demarcation problem would be solved by the kind of rule that has been presented in this section. The application of such a rule would sometimes be difficult, but it need not be any more difficult than the application of many other legal rules. Potential harassers need not be any more at a loss as to how to go about obeying the rule than potential tortfeasors are as to how to satisfy the duty of care that the law of torts imposes on them.

In fact, it can be said that most people have been following something like this rule in their day-to-day sexual conduct all along and that the rule would simply make explicit what has been implicit in the thinking of many ordinary people. If you questioned people who make polite, considerate, sexual advances, rather than crude, gross, sexual advances, why they do so, you would probably eventually get the response that crude advances carry a considerable probability of offending their recipients without providing any increase in the chances of success, or without providing the increase in the chances of success that would be sufficient to justify the extra risk of offense. If you asked the same people why they make any sexual advances at all (rather than completely abstain from making them), given that even the polite advances carry some risk of being offensive and considerable risk of being annoying, the response would probably be that when all these harms, together with the probability of their occurrence, are taken into account, they are still outweighed by the benefits of a mutually satisfying romantic and sexual relationship, together with the probability of its occurrence.

It could even be said that such choices of what sexual advances to make are precisely the choices that the reasonable person would make. Using the notion of the reasonable person in the context of sexual harassment in this way would accord perfectly with the way the notion has been operating within the law of torts. If we accepted this use of the notion of a reasonable person, then we could say that the rule about sexual advances that has been outlined in this section amounts to the requirement that we do not make any advances that the reasonable person wouldn't make, just as much of the law of torts can be summarized as the requirement that we take the precautions against causing harm that the reasonable person would take. What has been outlined in this section can thus be regarded as yet another possible way of bringing the notion of reasonableness into the sexual harassment law, a way that is radically different from anything we have seen in the preceding chapter. This way of bringing the notion of reasonableness into the law focuses on the alleged harasser rather than the plaintiff, and is in that respect different from the way the notion operates in the present U.S. law on the matter. It is also different from the possible criteria of sexual harassment that we considered at the end of chapter 3 (the criteria nubered (4) and (5)), in that it invites us to ask the question "What would the reasonable person *do,* under the circumstances of a given case?" rather than just "What would the reasonable person *know*?" In short, it invites us to compare the conduct of the alleged harasser with the conduct of the reasonable person, just as we do in the law of torts.[13]

A NOTE ABOUT SEXUAL CONDUCT OTHER THAN SEXUAL ADVANCES

What has been said in the preceding section about sexual advances can be extended to other forms of conduct that are currently covered by the sexual harassment law. For example, when looking at sexual jokes, we need to distinguish the cases in which the purpose of joke-telling is to make the hearers (or some of the hearers) uncomfortable, embarrassed, offended, or otherwise displeased, from bona fide joke-telling; that is, from the cases in which jokes are told in the hope that they will be amusing to those who hear them. The former kind of joke-telling can be assimilated to deliberate insults of a sexual nature, but the latter cannot, even when (contrary to what those who engage in it are hoping for) it ends up causing offense. If we want to understand the working of any rule that attempts to regulate bona fide telling of sexual jokes, we need to take into account:

(1) the interests of potential joke-tellers in telling jokes that will be amusing to their hearers,
(2) the interests of potential joke-tellers in not telling jokes that will turn out to be unwelcome, offensive, etc. to their hearers,
(3) the interests of potential joke-hearers in hearing jokes that will be amusing to them,
(4) the interests of potential joke-hearers in not hearing jokes that will be unwelcome, offensive, etc. to them.

If one takes all of these interests into account and thinks about them in the same way as was applied to sexual advances in the preceding section, one will end up with a rule that would prohibit people from telling sexual jokes if the probability of their being unwelcome, offensive, and so on to their hearers multiplied by the magnitude of the harm that would be involved, is greater than the probability of their being amusing multiplied by the magnitude of the benefit that such amusement would constitute for those concerned.

Sexual jokes, however, differ from sexual advances in one important way: while the benefits of a successful sexual advance can be great (as it can lead to a mutually fulfilling romantic relationship that lasts many years), the benefits of telling an amusing sexual joke are typically minor. If everybody concerned gets a good laugh out of it, that *is* a benefit, but a fleeting, easily forgotten one. That means that, in the case of sexual jokes, it will be much easier for the expected harms to outweigh the expected benefits than it was for sexual advances.

Telling a joke that has, say, 50% probability of being mildly amusing and 50% probability of being mildly annoying to the hearer may thus be prohibited by the rule we are considering here, because the harm of the annoyance, although small, may well be greater than the benefit of the amusement.

Negligence vs. Strict Liability

The rule about sexual advances that has been presented in the first section of this chapter would make sexual harassment a matter of *negligence.* It can be said that those who violate the rule are thereby being negligent as to whether they will cause offense or other harm. Those who follow the rule can be described as exercising due care not to cause offense or other harm, and thus as nonnegligent. The prohibition of sexual harassment in the law as it actually is, on the other hand, covers not only those who negligently cause harm by their sexual advances but also those who cause it without negligence: it thus makes sexual harassment a matter of *strict liability.*

Once the difference between the possible sexual harassment law that has been outlined above and the actual law is put in those terms, there is an argument that will readily occur to those who are familiar with contemporary legal theory that needs to be dealt with. There is a well-known general theoretical argument that proves that the rules of strict liability can be as effective in giving people the incentives to behave in a manner that produces the best balance of expected benefits over expected harms for everyone concerned, as the rules of negligence that explicitly require such conduct.

The argument goes like this. Suppose that a business owner, X, conducts a certain business operation for the client, Y, an operation that is supposed to be mutually beneficial. Suppose, however, that it is also the case that this business operation will cause some damage to Z_1, Z_2, . . . , Z_n. Following the reasoning of the preceding sections, we will want to have the laws that discourage X from pursuing the operation if the expected harms to Z_1, Z_2, . . . , Z_n (i.e., the harms multiplied by the probability of their occurrence) are greater than the expected benefits to X and Y (i.e., the benefits multiplied by the probability of their occurrence), but that do not discourage the operation when the expected benefits are greater than the expected harms. One way to do that is to promulgate the rule of negligence, along the lines of the Learned Hand's formula, that explicitly requires X to behave in precisely that manner. However, having a rule that makes X strictly liable for the damages to $Z_1, Z_2, \ldots, Z_n$ will achieve precisely the same result. If the expected damages are greater than the expected benefits to X and Y then the strict liability rule will deter X from going ahead with the operation, just like a rule of negligence would. On the other hand, if the expected benefits to X and Y are greater than the expected damages, then X would not be deterred from going ahead with the operation by the strict liability rule even though the rule would (unlike the negligence rule) still hold X liable for the damages under the circumstances. This is because X can pay out the full compensation for the damages, as the strict liability rule requires, and, if the benefits are indeed greater than the damages, still be left with some net benefit that makes the operation, from X's viewpoint, worthwhile. What makes X and Y's joint expected benefits relevant to this reasoning, rather than X's alone, is the fact that X can always pass on a part of the cost of strict liability to Y: as long as their joint benefits are greater than the damages, they will be able to make some agreement between themselves that will make it worthwhile for X to go ahead with the operation in spite of having to compensate Z_1, $Z_2, \ldots, Z_n$ for the damages.

Because of this general argument which shows that the rules of strict liability tend to produce the same results, in terms of what is encouraged and discouraged by them, as the rules of negligence, one may wonder why the negligence-based rule about sexual harassment that has been sketched in the preceding sections should be expected to produce results that are any different than the results produced by the present law, which makes sexual harassment a matter of strict liability.

The answer is that the general argument about the interchangeability of negligence rules and strict liability rules applies only when the rules in question are genuine *liability rules*, in the now familiar sense that has been introduced by Calabresi and Melamed,[14] in other words, when they are genuine civil law rules, which do not impose on those who are subject to them any burden other than the burden of compensating people to whom they cause damages, for those damages. From the viewpoint of an individual potential harasser, the present sexual harassment law is, however, not a matter of liability rules, in this sense, at all. This point is very important to understand, because although the sexual harassment law is, in its actual operation, not a matter of liability rules, it masquerades as such: the vocabulary in which it is couched is the one that is characteristic of liability rules and its position in the legal system puts it in the company of liability rules. This discrepancy between what the present law about sexual harassment purports to be and what it cashes into has to do with the fact that it is, on its face, addressed to employers, while its ultimate aim is to regulate the behavior of individual potential harassers. If one concentrates only on what we have in chapter 2 called the upper level of the operation of the sexual harassment law, then it may seem plausible to regard the law as a matter of liability rules, and as not significantly different from other parts of the employment law. However, if one takes into account both the upper and the lower level and views the sexual harassment law from the viewpoint of individual potential harassers, then it turns out to be much more similar to criminal prohibitions than to liability rules. To be sure, people are not sent to prison, nor do they get criminal records, when their conduct gets to be officially classified as sexual harassment, but in almost every other respect, one's being found guilty of sexual harassment has the impact on one's life that is similar to the impact of a criminal conviction. This is so even if the matter is dealt with only at the lower level and never reaches a court of law. Having it in one's employment record that one has been found guilty of sexual harassment can destroy one's life opportunities as effectively as having a criminal record. Someone found guilty of sexual harassment can lose one's job with practically no chance of finding another one. There is a stigma attached to being found guilty of sexual harassment that is comparable to the stigma of being a criminal.[15] When one has been found guilty of sexual harassment, one is an outcast,[16] just as criminals are. In short, the consequences of being found guilty of sexual harassment are such that most ordinary people regard them as something that would ruin their lives just as a criminal conviction would.

All this makes the impact of the sexual harassment law on individual potential harassers very different from the impact that the rules of civil law have on those to whom they apply. Defendants who have lost civil suits can simply pay the damages and get on with their lives. There is no stigma attached to their status and they do not become outcasts. This means that the present sexual harassment law should not be regarded as a matter of liability rules, and that the argument that claims that the rules of negligence and the rules of strict liability tend to lead to the same result is inapplicable.

That the current legal prohibition of sexual harassment is not a genuine liability rule, but rather something akin to a criminal prohibition, is further confirmed by the fact that individuals cannot get insurance against being found guilty of sexual harassment. When the law imposes strict liability by way of genuine liability rules, there normally emerges a market for insurance against such liability, but no insurer would even consider offering such insurance to individual potential harassers. (It is true that *employers* may be able to get insurance against their legal liability for sexual harassment, but that fact is irrelevant to the present argument, which views the law from the perspective of individual potential harassers.)

Although the present sexual harassment law does not explicitly threaten individual potential harassers with criminal sanctions, it creates circumstances in which individual potential harassers are under threat of sanctions that far exceed straightforward compensation for the damages they cause. This fact, coupled with the fact that the law imposes what amounts to strict liability, entails that it deters worthwhile sexual advances that would not be deterred by the negligence-style rule outlined in the first section of this chapter (even if one assumed that the sanctions remained of the quasi-criminal kind).

One may ask, in passing, whether instead of adopting the negligence-style rule of the first section, we couldn't solve the problem posed by the fact that the present sexual harassment law deters worthwhile advances, by making the law into a matter of genuine liability rules, while keeping the liability strict. This would involve eliminating all quasi-criminal sanctions for sexual harassment and simply requiring those who cause annoyance and offense to others by their sexual advances to pay compensation for these consequences. Shouldn't our general theoretical arguments about strict liability lead us to believe that in that case no worthwhile advances would be deterred (just as the business owner X in the above example would not be deterred from worthwhile business activity by being forced to compensate Z_1, $Z_2, \ldots, Z_n$ for the damages caused by it)? The answer is that this solution would indeed work, as long as the world in which it were to be implemented satisfied certain ideal conditions. The fact that I would have to pay a small amount of money to everyone to whom I caused minor annoyance by my advances would not deter me from making the advances. Under such a regime, one would not be deterred from making any advances that would be worthwhile in the sense explained in the first section of this chapter, *provided that* (a) there were no other costs involved, (b) the compensation one would have to pay accurately reflected the cost of the damages, and (c) one were able to claim contributions toward payment of the damages from others who stand to benefit from one's advances, namely the recipients of one's successful advances. In the world as it is, these conditions cannot be satisfied. First, the transaction costs of paying out compensation to everyone who suffers minor annoyance as a result of sexual advances would be enormous (relative to the amount of compensation itself). Second, it would be very difficult to find procedures that would ensure that the compensation accurately reflects the harm, and if they could be found, they could probably be implemented only at considerable extra cost. Finally, it is difficult to see how one could claim contribution from those who will in the future benefit from one's sexual advances, when one hasn't identified them yet (and it is in the nature of the problem that they are bound to be unidentified at the time when the unsuccessful advances are made—if one knew who would welcome one's sexual advances, one wouldn't bother making unsuccessful ones). The possibility of combining strict liability in sexual harassment law with transforming it into a matter of genuine liability rules is thus a purely theoretical possibility.

Inalienability

What we have in the present sexual harassment law are, in the terminology of Calabresi and Melamed, neither liability rules nor *property rules* (rules that protect entitlements by imposing something like criminal sanctions on anyone who removes the entitlements from their holders, but that leave open the possibility of transactions through which the entitlements may be modified, surrendered, transferred, and so on), but effectively *inalienability rules.* They give potential victims of harassment the entitlement not to be harassed, including the entitlement not to be exposed to any unwelcome and offensive sexual advances, which, as we have seen in chapters 2 and 3, is, in its consequences, equivalent to an entitlement not to be exposed to any sexual advances at all; they protect the entitlement by imposing something similar to criminal sanctions on those who interfere with it, and, unlike property rules, they do *not* leave it open to people to negotiate about the entitlement. This is because, as has been pointed out in chapter 2, the notion of a sexual advance extends to any attempt to negotiate about sexual interaction: all such attempts are within the scope of the law, because they can always be characterized as sexual advances (or other conduct of a sexual nature). One's entitlement to be free from anything that can be classified as sexual harassment, in the current legal sense of the term, thus incorporates the equivalent of an "entitlement" to be free from attempts at negotiation about how the entitlement might be modified or under what conditions it might be surrendered. A rule that thus precludes any negotiation about the entitlement that it protects effectively amounts to an inalienability rule, even if it is not couched in the language of inalienability.

Realizing that the present sexual harassment law, contrary to appearances, amounts to neither liability nor property rules, but to rules of inalienability, gives us another way of explicating what is wrong with it (which is, to a certain extent, a reformulation of some of the points made in chapters 2 and 3) and why a modification of it along the lines suggested in the first section of this chapter would be desirable. Legislators can, in general, be justified in protecting an allocation of entitlements by inalienability rules only if they are fairy certain that the allocation is for the best. When they are not certain, then other kinds of rules are called for, rules that enable people to correct any infelicities that the original allocation, given by the legislators, might have. Property rules enable people to change the initial allocation of entitlements through negotiation, liability rules enable them to do it by effectively allowing them to violate the entitlements at the sole cost of compensating the holders of the entitlements.

Inalienability rules, on the other hand, do not provide for any such correcting mechanisms: that is why they are suitable only when the legislators are in the position to know that the allocation they are fixing by the rules is better than the alternatives. Needless to say, it is extremely rare for legislators to be in such a position: by and large, the people directly involved are in a much better position than the legislators to know what allocation of entitlements is for the best. A rare example where legislators may be almost certain that a particular allocation of entitlements is for the best is, arguably, that of the allocation in which everyone has the entitlement to not being a slave: it is thus not implausible to claim that legislators are justified in making the entitlement to not being a slave inalienable. Nothing like that is, however, true in the issue at hand. It is, for reasons spelled out in chapter 2, implausible to claim that the allocation in which everyone has the "entitlement" not to be in *any* form of sexual interaction with the people who work at the same place is for the best, but, even if it were for the best, it would be wildly implausible to suggest that the legislators could know that this is so with anything approaching certainty. A law that fixes that "entitlement" by an inalienability rule, as the present sexual harassment law does, is therefore unjustified.

RIGHTS

In the first section of this chapter it was assumed that what makes a particular legal arrangement desirable is the fact that it leads to the maximization of expected net benefits for everyone concerned, taken together. The argument presented there is thus likely to have an immediate appeal for those who are committed to some form of utilitarianism or law-and-economics in their thinking about what makes a law morally acceptable. There are, however, people who believe that there is more to moral assessment of a law than such cost-benefit analysis. These people have probably been becoming impatient throughout the discussion that I have been pursuing in this chapter so far. Isn't it true, they are probably tempted to say, that people have *rights* and that it is one of the tasks of a legal system to protect those rights? Moreover, they could also say, shouldn't a legal system try to ensure that the benefits that accrue to people under it are *fairly* distributed, rather than being solely preoccupied with how to increase the total amount of benefits? When the issues of rights and fairness are brought under consideration, do the arrangements sketched in the first section of this chapter continue to seem as morally desirable as they may have seemed at first?

Let us begin by considering rights. The relevant right here is presumably the right not to be exposed to sexual advances that are offensive to oneself. It is not immediately obvious that there is such a right, but let us assume that it is plausible to say that there is. However, it is equally (if not more) plausible to say that people also have the right to pursue happiness and fulfillment through romantic and sexual interaction. Given that it is practically inevitable that sexual advances made in good faith will sometimes turn out to be offensive to their recipients, the only way to give complete legal protection to the first right is to completely prohibit sexual advances and that amounts to a violation of the second right. If we want to decide, by thinking in terms of rights, what legal rules about sexual advances would be morally desirable, we therefore need some way of *balancing* these two rights. Right-based theorists are notoriously evasive when it comes to questions of how conflicting rights are to be balanced, but even without having the balancing procedure spelled out in detail, it is almost certain that it would lead to a departure from the present law, because, speaking in terms of rights, the present law doesn't seem to be a result of such balancing at all: it simply protects people's right not to be exposed to offensive sexual advances, while completely ignoring the right to pursue happiness and fulfillment through romantic and sexual interaction.

In fact, it is difficult to see how the application of the balancing procedure to the problem of sexual advances would amount to anything radically different from the reasoning we pursued in the first section of this chapter, only couched in the vocabulary of rights. The appeals to rights therefore don't seem to have the potential to significantly affect the outcome of the arguments made so far.

In order to avoid any possible misunderstandings, let me emphasize that in saying what I have just said, as in most of this chapter, I have been focusing only on bona fide sexual advances. The matter is different when it comes to deliberate insults of a sexual nature: there it is quite plausible to say that the potential victims of such insults have the right not to be insulted while the potential makers of the insults don't have any right to make them. It could thus be said that when it comes to deliberate insults we do not need any balancing procedure: if we enact a legal prohibition of such insults, we are simply protecting the only right that is at issue. However, that result of right-based thinking again fits well with what we have said in the first section of this chapter, when we separated deliberate insults of a sexual nature from bona fide sexual advances that turn out to be offensive.

FAIRNESS

The appeal to fairness poses a more important challenge to the kind of rule about sexual advances that was sketched in the first section of this chapter than the appeal to rights. It is quite plausible to say that the rules of negligence, after which that rule was modeled, sometimes do produce results that are unfair.

In order to see why this is so, let us return to the example of X who causes harm to $Z_1, Z_2, \ldots, Z_n$, while operating a business that benefits X and Y. If X is conducting the business in a nonnegligent way and if the rule that governs the case is one of negligence, then X won't be liable for any harm that the operation of the business might cause to $Z_1, Z_2, \ldots, Z_n$. However, it is quite possible that some harm to $Z_1, Z_2, \ldots, Z_n$ will be caused: in most real-life situations the precautions required by the Learned Hand's formula, which are sufficient to make X nonnegligent, will not reduce the risk of harm all the way down to zero. When we are confronted with this type of case, the question arises: is it fair that $Z_1, Z_2, \ldots, Z_n$ suffer such harms and not be compensated for them? In the situation we are imagining, conducting the business operation produces some net benefits for all concerned taken together, but when we look at how the benefits are distributed, we see that only X and Y reap them, while $Z_1, Z_2, \ldots, Z_n$ suffer losses. Given that X's and Y's benefits and Z_1's, Z_2's, . . . , Z_n's losses have a common cause, it looks as if X and Y gain their benefits at the expense of $Z_1, Z_2, \ldots, Z_n$. Isn't that unfair? Isn't it unfair for a law to force $Z_1, Z_2, \ldots, Z_n$ to suffer uncompensated losses for the sake of X's and Y's benefits, as the Learned Hand's formula does? Wouldn't it be morally better to have legal rules that would force X and Y to use some of their benefits to compensate $Z_1, Z_2, \ldots, Z_n$ for their losses, even when no negligence is involved? This is precisely what rules of strict liability do. As we have observed before, such rules will not deter X and Y from pursuing the business in the kind of case we are considering, because they will still have some net benefits left for themselves after they compensate $Z_1, Z_2, \ldots, Z_n$.

Arguments such as these may be used to defend strict liability rules as, in at least some areas of activity, morally preferable to the rules of negligence. Considerations such as these have partially motivated the moves from negligence to strict liability in many areas of the law of torts over the last few decades.

This problem about fairness can be transposed to the issue of sexual harassment, and this may lead us to wonder whether a negligence-style rule about sexual harassment, of the kind that has been outlined in the first section of this chapter, is really fair. Suppose that X makes a sexual advance toward Y, which turns out to be successful and leads to a relationship that makes both of them happy. Suppose also that, before making that successful advance to Y, X made a number of unsuccessful advances to $Z_1, Z_2, \ldots, Z_n$ and that as a result of that $Z_1, Z_2, \ldots, Z_n$ were all annoyed and that some of them were perhaps even offended. Suppose moreover that all these advances were worthwhile in the sense explained in the first section of this chapter, so that X has not in any way violated the rule about sexual advances sketched there. Given that the successful advance that led to X's and Y's happiness is a part of the very same pattern of advances that led to Z_1's, Z_2's, . . . , Z_n's annoyance and offense, it again looks as if X and Y are gaining their happiness at the expense of $Z_1, Z_2, \ldots, Z_n$. Isn't that unfair? Why should $Z_1, Z_2, \ldots, Z_n$ have to put up with uncompensated annoyance and offense for the sake of X's and Y's happiness?

As long as one looks at the one case of X, Y, $Z_1, Z_2, \ldots, Z_n$ in isolation, this question has no good answer. Having $Z_1, Z_2, \ldots, Z_n$ suffer, even if only mildly, for the sake of X's and Y's happiness seems manifestly unfair, and a legal rule that seems to endorse that unfairness (as the rule sketched in the first section of this chapter does) consequently also seems unfair.

The appearance of unfairness, however, dissipates if we stop looking at X's sexual advances in isolation. X wouldn't be the only person making sexual advances under the rule we are considering. Many other people would be making them as well. Moreover $Z_1, Z_2, \ldots, Z_n$ themselves may choose to make their own advances. As a result of that, chances are that $Z_1, Z_2 \ldots, Z_n$ will sooner or later receive or make sexual advances that will make them happy. The advances that will lead to Z_1's, Z_2's, . . . , Z_n's happiness belong to the very same practice of advance-making, made possible by the rule that we are considering, as X's advances that make them annoyed or offended. We can thus think of Z_1's, Z_2's, . . . , Z_n's putting up with that annoyance and offense as their supporting the practice that will make them happy. In other words, we can say that, when $Z_1, Z_2, \ldots, Z_n$ are annoyed and offended by the advances they receive from X, they are not suffering for the sake of X's and Y's happiness. Rather, they are suffering for the sake of their own happiness, which will result from other advances that will be made within the same practice. When we look at the matter that way, we see that Z_1's, Z_2's, . . . , Z_n's sufferings do not really remain uncompensated. They don't get compensated by X and Y, but they do get compensated by the further operations of the same practice of advance-making. The rule that was sketched in the first section of this chapter does not explicitly say anything about compensation for the annoyance and offense that it allows, but it makes possible a practice that spontaneously provides the compensation for the harm that it creates. When the matter is looked at in that light, the rule can be seen to be perfectly fair.

The fact that this rule allows fairness to be achieved in the way that has just been explained, through spontaneous operations of a social practice, makes it preferable to any rule that would attempt to effect compensation on a case-by-case basis through legal and quasi-legal mechanisms. This is because the operation of legal mechanisms is costly and cumbersome: in the case at hand it would be exceedingly costly and cumbersome, because the harms in question are difficult to measure and distributed over a very wide population (practically all adults). If fairness can be achieved without costly and cumbersome legal interventions, then it is best to let it be so achieved, and to keep legal mechanisms for the cases where fairness cannot be achieved otherwise. In the case of sexual advances that means that legal and quasi-legal mechanisms should be used only against those sexual advances (say very crude and aggressive ones) that overstep the boundaries of the inherently fair forms of advance-making. This is precisely what we would have if we were to accept the rule about sexual advances that was sketched in the first section of this chapter.

The argument about fairness that I have just made may, however, be subject to one possible objection. It can be said that the argument seems plausible as long as one assumes that the ratio between benefits and burdens that the practice of advance-making brings to different people is roughly the same for everyone. This, it can be claimed, is far from the truth.

Compare, for example, the cases of A and B. After a few years of dating during A's college years, A got married at the age of 22. Now, more than 20 years later, A is still happily married to the same person. A has never had an extramarital affair and doesn't have the slightest intention to have one in the future, nor does A have the slightest intention of getting divorced. Yet, during all those years, people who were not fully aware of A's circumstances kept making sexual advances toward A, which A found annoying and sometimes offensive.

B's life, on the other hand, went differently. B, who is now the same age as A, has been through a number of romantic relationships. One of those relationships was a formal marriage, but after a number of years B got divorced. When a relationship is dissolved, B spends a period of several months (and sometimes even several years) looking for a new partner. When the new partner is found, B enters into a relationship that may last anywhere from a few months to a few years. When that relationship comes to an end, B enters again into a period of looking for a new partner and so on. At the point of entering into a new relationship, B may hope that it will last long, but knows that it is, in fact, unlikely to last more than a couple of years.

We can all easily find, among our friends and acquaintances, actual people whose lives approximate that of A and people whose lives approximate that of B. A and B are both representatives of large classes of people that exist in the actual world.

Now, it could be claimed that my argument about fairness would be sound, if the world consisted solely of people like B. People who were all like B would all tend to benefit equally from the practice of advance-making, and would also be equally exposed to the annoying and offensive by-products of that practice. None of them could be accused of gaining something out of the practice at the expense of others. However, given that in the actual world there are both people like A and people like B, my argument about fairness, it could be claimed, doesn't really work.

The basis for this objection to my argument is that it appears that, although A did benefit from the practice of advance-making at the early stage of A's life, A does not stand to gain from the practice any more. Now that A is in this happy relationship, A, unlike B, doesn't seem to need the practice of advance-making. Once A enters the happy relationship, there seem to be no further benefits that the practice of advance-making can bring to A, and yet throughout the rest of A's life, A will continue to be exposed to the annoying and offensive aspects of the practice. In that respect A is unlike B to whom the practice continuously brings a stream of both benefits and burdens, in which the benefits outweigh the burdens. Because of that it could be argued that the practice of advance-making is, contrary to the claims I made above, unfair: it brings benefits to people like B at the expense of people like A, to whom it brings nothing but annoyance and offense. We therefore need, the argument could continue, legal arrangements that, unlike the rule sketched in the first section of this chapter, rectify that unfairness.

There are two responses that can be made against this move, and in defense of my claim that the practice of advance-making is fair as long as it fits the rule sketched in the first section of this chapter. The first response is that although A's marriage may in fact continue to be happy and last for the rest of A's life, A has no way of knowing that in advance. A may be too much in love to consider such matters seriously, but if A were to think in a cool manner, A would have to acknowledge that there is a possibility that at some point in the future, things in A's present relationship will start going badly, and that A will eventually come to be in the position in which it will be necessary to look for a new partner. After all, there is ample empirical evidence that marriages and marriage-like relationships that were as happy as A's is now, often fall apart eventually. For all A knows, A may thus still come to need the practice of advance-making in the end. Because of that possibility, A, contrary to what may appear at first sight, has a reason to support the practice of advance-making. We can say that, even though A might not think about that, the existence of the practice of advance-making is a good thing for A, in the same way in which having an insurance policy is a good thing for oneself, even if one never in fact comes to make any claims under the policy. The difference between A and B can then be regarded as analogous to the difference between a person who has an insurance policy, but is so fortunate that he never suffers the harms that the policy applies to, and thus never makes any claims, and another person insured under the same scheme who does suffer the harms and therefore does receive specific payouts from the scheme. We normally don't think that there is anything unfair about the latter difference, therefore we shouldn't think that there is anything unfair about the difference between A and B. We can say that A's exposure to occasional annoyance and offense due to unwelcome sexual advances is not any more unfair than paying an insurance premium is: in exchange for that A gets the benefit of continuous availability of a practice that A might come to need.

Pursuing the analogy of insurance further, someone might ask: shouldn't A at least get some discount on the "premium"? The answer is that, in the world as it is, A is probably already getting the discount: happily married people generally receive fewer sexual advances than others. Moreover, the rule outlined in the first section of this chapter does allow for somewhat different treatment of advances directed at people who are known to be in a position like A's and those directed at people known to be in a position like B's. This is because the rule takes into account the probability that an advance would be successful and the probability that it would be offensive. For advances directed at people known to be in A's position these probabilities are different than they are for advances directed at people known to be in B's position: the rule can thus place the boundary between what is permitted and what is prohibited somewhat differently in these two kinds of cases.

An alternative way of arguing that the comparison between A and B does not point to any unfairness is to say that, even if one sets aside the possibility that A might come to need the practice of advance-making in the future and concentrates only on what has already happened, it simply isn't true that B has benefited more from the practice than A. It can be argued that it is misleading to say it was only in A's youth that A benefited from the practice of advance-making. It is true that A has entered into A's present relationship at that time, but it is also true that A has been in that relationship ever since, and every day of A's being in that relationship can be regarded as increasing the benefit that has its roots in A's having made or received some sexual advance in A's youth. It can thus be said that as long as A stays in that relationship, A continues to benefit from the practice of advance-making. When the benefit that A gets from the practice of advance-making is viewed that way, we see that it is great indeed: it is not any smaller than B's. So we can again conclude that the practice of advance-making is not unfair to people like A.

In order to assure ourselves that the rule outlined in the first section of this chapter is not unfair, we, however, still need to ask ourselves whether it is perhaps unfair to people like C. At the early stage of C's life, C decided that romantic and sexual pursuits should not be allowed to interfere with some other pursuits that C regarded as more important, say, religious ones. C consequently made a vow of celibacy, and has so far been faithful to that vow. If C gets exposed to a sexual advance, chances are that the experience will make C upset. The practice of advance-making thus causes some loss to C and it is difficult to see how it could be providing any benefits to C. Given that C is not and has never been in a romantic relationship, the second argument that we have used in the case of A clearly does not apply. Under no interpretation could the harm that sexual advances cause to C be regarded as a payment for benefits that C has already received from the practice of advance-making: *ex hypothesi* there have been no such benefits. The first argument that we used about A can be applied to the case of C insofar as it could be argued that it is always possible that C's outlook will change and that C will eventually want to give up celibacy. How much force that argument will have in the case of C, however, depends on the details of C's case: if C's vow of celibacy was just a youthful whim, then it will have considerable force, as the probability of the change of mind will be considerable.

On the other hand if the vow springs from a deep religious conviction and is a part of C's joining a religious order, then the argument will have much less force. The fact that C, under such circumstances, does not have as strong reasons to uphold the practice of advance-making as B or A, however, does not count against the rule about sexual advances outlined in the first section of this chapter. That rule may require C to put up with some unwanted sexual advances but it will not require C to put up with the same number and kind of advances as B or A. This is, again, because the rule is sensitive to both the probability and magnitude of the harm caused by unwanted sexual advances. If we imagine that C is known to be a deeply convinced member of a celibate religious order, then the probability that a sexual advance directed at C will cause harm is far greater than in the case of B or A. Other things being equal, the magnitude of the harm is also going to be greater. Moreover, the probability that sexual advance directed toward C will be successful, although higher than zero, is substantially lower than in the case of advances directed toward B or A. As a result of that, many kinds of advances that would be worthwhile if directed to a person known to be in B's or even A's position will not be worthwhile when directed to a person known to be in C's position. The rule outlined in the first section of this chapter will thus prohibit people from directing at those known to be in C's position many kinds of advances that it permits when they are directed at those known to be in B's or A's position. The example of C therefore does not give us any ground to regard the rule as unfair.

5
Sexual Harassment and Freedom of Speech

The Issue

Suppose that the arguments that I have been developing in the preceding chapter get generally accepted and that the purported criterion of demarcation from the EEOC Guidelines gets replaced by a rule of the kind that has been sketched in the first section of that chapter. Would the sexual harassment law then be morally acceptable? Contrary to what one may have been led to expect from the arguments of the preceding chapter, the answer to that question that I want to defend is "No." While such a change would certainly be an improvement over the law as we have it now, it would not on its own solve the problems that beset the present sexual harassment law. The reason why I have been discussing that rule at some length is not that its introduction would in itself solve the problems of the sexual harassment law, but rather that the discussion of that rule helps to put our thinking about sexual harassment on the right track.

There are several problems with the present sexual harassment law that are independent of the fact that it makes no distinction between worthwhile sexual advances and conduct of a sexual nature that is not worthwhile, and these problems would remain even if the sexual harassment law were modified along the lines outlined in the preceding chapter.

Out of these remaining problems the one that this chapter will be devoted to concerns the fact that the sexual harassment law prohibits a great deal of what is in its own terminology called "verbal conduct" and what is otherwise called "speech" in both plain English and in legal terminology.[1] It also covers various forms of nonverbal expressive conduct, which are in many ways akin to speech and which are usually also classified as "speech" in the legal sense of the word. It is thus a serious question whether the sexual harassment law is compatible with the deep commitment that the Western civilization has to freedom of speech, commitment that, in the Unites States, is embodied in the First Amendment.

Indeed, the very fact that the sexual harassment law uses the phrase "verbal conduct" should make us pause. In legal contexts other than that of sexual harassment, the word "conduct" has usually been used to mean nonverbal conduct. In discussions of freedom of speech, conduct has thus been contrasted with speech. The introduction of the phrase "verbal conduct" into the sexual harassment law seems to have been an attempt to blur the distinction that the law has been making between speech and (nonverbal) conduct and to make less obvious the law's vulnerability to criticisms based on the principle of freedom of speech. Judging from the fact that such criticisms of the sexual harassment law have started appearing only recently, this attempt has been fairly successful.

The first full-fledged criticism of the sexual harassment law on the basis of First Amendment considerations is an excellent article by Kingsley Browne, "Title VII as Censorship: Hostile-Environment Harassment and the First Amendment," published in 1991.[2] My discussion of the matter in this chapter is heavily indebted to Browne's article, and those who are interested in the details of the issue are advised to turn to the article itself. A somewhat later article by Jules Gerard, although different in tone, essentially concurs with Browne's.[3]

The conflict between the sexual harassment law and the First Amendment has also been commented on by Nadine Strossen in 1992,[4] but that article, despite being written by the ACLU president, avoids pursuing its arguments to a definite, clear conclusion. Instead of such a conclusion, Strossen, at crucial points, gives her readers unhelpful, evasive remarks, such as "one cannot make blanket assessments about the protected or unprotected nature of any type of speech."[5]

While the conflict between the sexual harassment law and the established First Amendment jurisprudence has not been fully appreciated by many of those who are otherwise concerned about protecting freedom of speech, it has been understood all too clearly by a legal scholar who is well known for her advocacy of large-scale expansions of legal restrictions of freedom of speech. Catharine MacKinnon's book *Only Words*,[6] which is largely devoted to a criticism of the established First Amendment caselaw (formulated with rhetoric flair that is characteristic of that author), presents the sexual harassment law as an area of the law that is exceptional in that, within it, the courts have dealt with speech "[w]ith a fine sense of reality"[7] and "real comprehension that what might be called speech . . . are in fact acts of inequality."[8] She seems to regard the way in which the sexual harassment law deals with "what might be called speech" as a paradigm for a wholesale revision of the way in which the legal system handles the freedom of speech. The fact that she and her followers appear to be poised to use the sexual harassment law as a springboard for advocating a rejection of the way in which the First Amendment has traditionally been understood, provides a reason why everyone (including those who are not particularly concerned about sexual harassment itself) should try to understand the relationship between the sexual harassment law and the First Amendment.

There is one possible source of misunderstanding of the conflict between freedom of speech and the sexual harassment law that needs to be dealt with immediately. It has been suggested[9] that whether such a conflict exists is of no great consequence, because employees generally do not have much freedom of speech at their workplaces anyway: the nature of one's job, as specified by one's employer, often imposes considerable constraints on what one may say at work and how one may say it. This suggestion confuses the issue by encouraging inattentiveness to the incompleteness of the phrase "freedom of speech." The freedom of speech that the Western political tradition cherishes, and that the U.S. Constitution guarantees, was never meant to be freedom from every conceivable impediment to speech; it was meant to be freedom from *government-imposed* restrictions on speech. The ability that private employers have to restrict the speech of their employees in all manner of ways is entirely irrelevant to *that* freedom. The strength of one's constitutional right not to have one's speech controlled *by the government,* in no way diminishes when one enters one's workplace (notwithstanding that one's employer may control one's speech there).[10] If various rules about sexual harassment had been enacted by private employers for some reasons of their own, then they could be amalgamated to other employer-imposed restrictions on speech, and this chapter would not need to be written. But the sexual harassment law is *law,* that is, an instrument of the government's power. The restrictions on speech that it generates are thus government-imposed restrictions, and that's why the question of whether they are compatible with freedom of speech cannot be dismissed easily.

In much of the discussion in the preceding chapters, I have concentrated on the problems posed by legal prohibitions of bona fide sexual advances that are contained in the sexual harassment law, and have proceeded as if legal prohibitions of deliberate insults of a sexual nature and similar acts, which are also contained in the law, were unproblematic. However, even deliberate insults constitute speech, and that makes it problematic to prohibit them by law, in face of our general commitment to the idea that speech should not be prohibited by law. Indeed, some of the insults that are covered by the sexual harassment law, namely those that express or imply a certain general view about the proper position of women in the society, or about their suitability for particular occupations,[11] can be construed as political in character, and thus close to the very core of the concerns that motivate the ideal of free speech. The main rationale for endorsing the principle of the freedom of speech is that it provides for open political debate and it is thus usually held that whatever else the principle might protect, it certainly protects all speech that has political character.[12]

Although that is not essential to my argument, it may be worth noting that the political speech that the law applies to might include some criticisms of the law itself. The possibility of a law stifling criticism of itself seems particularly worrisome.[13] The law can also be used to stifle criticism of specific instances of its use: it can be applied to the conduct that expresses disapproval of complaints of sexual harassment[14] (but not to the conduct that expresses support for them).

Some of the insults that are subject matter of sexual harassment complaints take the form of displays of nonverbal symbols or graphic representations and thus do not constitute speech in the everyday sense of the word, but legal prohibitions of such nonverbal insults are as much at odds with the principle of freedom of speech as the prohibition of verbal insults, because that principle is usually taken to extend to the nonverbal expressions that are akin to speech and not only to speech in the literal sense. Within the context of First Amendment jurisprudence, the term "speech" is used to cover such nonverbal expressions as well.

FIGHTING WORDS

It may seem at first that the prohibition of insults of a sexual nature, embodied in the sexual harassment law, could be reconciled with the principle of freedom of speech, as embodied in the First Amendment, by invoking the doctrine of "fighting words." Since the 1942 *Chaplinsky v. New Hampshire* case, the "fighting words," namely the words "which by their very utterance inflict injury or tend to incite an immediate breach of the peace"[15] have been held to constitute an exception to the First Amendment's general protection of freedom of speech.

Some scholars have expressed the opinion that, although the *Chaplinsky* doctrine of fighting words has never been formally overruled, some later Supreme Court decisions about freedom of speech amount to "a covert overruling of *Chaplinsky*,"[16] but I shall here set such views aside, so as to examine the conflict between the First Amendment and the sexual harassment law in the light that is most favorable to the latter.

While it is indeed true that *some* of the speech that is prohibited by the current sexual harassment law could be regarded as fighting words, that doctrine cannot provide a general reconciliation between the sexual harassment law and the First Amendment, because that law prohibits far more than just the fighting words in the sense of constitutional law.

First, it is an essential feature of fighting words that their utterance has to be addressed to someone specific. The sexual harassment law, on the other hand, extends to many forms of expression, such as displaying pornographic materials or writing graffiti that contain general remarks of a sexual nature, that are not addressed to anyone in particular.

Moreover, although the Supreme Court's definition of fighting words has the form of a disjunction (words which "inflict injury *or* tend to incite an immediate breach of the peace"), and although the definition has been repeated in that form many times by the Court, in actual application of the doctrine, the Court has in fact always ignored the first disjunct. Indeed, given that the original case in which the doctrine was formulated involved a possibility of "immediate breach of the peace," the first disjunct can arguably be regarded as a *dictum.* While it has never explicitly repudiated the first disjunct, the Supreme Court itself has paraphrased the definition of fighting words in a way that completely omits it.[17]

It is thus the concern that people to whom certain words are directed will respond by engaging in literal, physical fights that is central to the fighting words doctrine. That concern, however, does not apply to typical cases of sexual harassment. When the insults that typically feature in sexual harassment complaints are made, it is, in most cases, extremely unlikely that those to whom they are directed would retaliate by entering into a physical fight or anything even remotely similar. Those who uphold the current sexual harassment law in fact often seem to think that one of the crucial reasons for giving the victims of such insults legal protection is precisely that they would otherwise be unlikely to respond to the insults. The main rationale for the "fighting words" exception to the First Amendment, namely that it makes it possible for the state to prevent "breaches of peace," thus fails to apply to typical cases of sexual harassment.[18]

Finally, even if one were to treat the first, generally ignored, disjunct in the *Chaplinsky* definition of "fighting words" (the one about inflicting injury) as valid law, one could still not effect a reconciliation between the sexual harassment law, in anything like its present shape, and the First Amendment. Whatever precisely "injury" might mean in that disjunct, it would have to be construed very narrowly, in order to ensure the consistency of the construal with various later pronouncements of the Supreme Court, such as that "the fact that society may find speech offensive is not a sufficient reason for suppressing it,"[19] or that "[s]peech does not lose its protected character . . . simply because it may embarrass others."[20] While it may be true that the conduct that is currently classified as hostile environment sexual harassment typically causes injury in some possible sense of that word, that injury often amounts to no more than offense or embarrassment, and thus fails to amount to injury in the narrow sense in which the word "injury" in the definition of fighting words must be taken. Because of that, the current sexual harassment law cannot be subsumed under the "fighting words" exception to the First Amendment, even if one were to invoke the first disjunct of the *Chaplinsky* definition.

VIEWPOINT NEUTRALITY

While there are a number of other constitutional doctrines that provide exceptions to the First Amendment's general guarantee of freedom of speech, there is, as Kingsley Browne's article shows, one problem that is fatal to any attempt to subsume the sexual harassment law under these established exceptions. Legal restrictions on the freedom of speech are expected to be, as a minimum, viewpoint neutral. "[T]he First Amendment forbids the government to regulate speech in ways that favor some viewpoints or ideas at the expense of others."[21] This means that, when dealing with speech on any issue on which people may hold different views, the law may not restrict the expression of some views, while allowing unrestricted expression of other views on the same issue: if the law, under certain conditions, restricts the expressions of a certain viewpoint on a given issue, then it must, under the same conditions and in the same way, restrict the expression of all other viewpoints that may be held on that issue. In other words, the state may not use its power to promote a particular viewpoint on a given issue by suppressing expression of disagreements with that viewpoint. This requirement of viewpoint neutrality of any restriction on the freedom of speech is a consequence of the general requirement of neutrality that the liberal political tradition imposes on the state.

It needs to be understood that the requirement of viewpoint neutrality is different from the stronger requirement of content neutrality. Most exceptions to the guarantee of freedom of speech also require the state to maintain content neutrality in restricting the freedom of speech, but the requirement of viewpoint neutrality has wider application: even when the state is allowed to discriminate on the basis of the content of speech (i.e., when it is allowed to restrict speech on certain topics while permitting unrestricted speech on other topics) it must not discriminate on the basis of the viewpoint expressed (i.e., within discourse on a certain topic, it must not promote some viewpoints by suppressing others). For example, a city may, under certain circumstances, prohibit political advertising on vehicles of its public transit system while permitting commercial advertising on those vehicles,[22] but that does not authorize it to prohibit advertising in favor of certain political viewpoints while permitting advertising in favor of competing political viewpoints. Similarly, military authorities may prohibit political campaigning on a military reservation while permitting, say, entertainment and religious services, but again that does not mean that they may prohibit campaigning by some candidates while permitting campaigning by the opposing candidates.[23] A city's zoning ordinance may impose restrictions on the presentation of sexually explicit movies that it does not impose on the presentation of movies on other topics, as long as it does not, among sexually explicit movies, discriminate on the basis of "whatever social, political, or philosophical message a film may be intended to communicate."[24] The Supreme Court has not always distinguished the requirements of content neutrality and viewpoint neutrality with as much clarity as constitutional scholars would have appreciated,[25] but its commitment to viewpoint neutrality is nevertheless clear enough.[26]

Can the law about sexual harassment satisfy the requirement of viewpoint neutrality? The answer is that there is only one way in which it could be made to satisfy it, but that it comes at too high a price. It would involve basing the criterion of demarcation on a purely subjective standard, by making the law proscribe *whatever* is unwelcome or offensive to the person in question. In promulgating and enforcing *such* a law, the state would arguably maintain its neutrality, because it would not specify in advance the viewpoints that the law could be applied to: whether such a law would make actionable the expressions of a particular viewpoint in a given case would depend entirely on the reactions of the alleged victim, and not on the government's agreement or disagreement with the viewpoint.[27] However, taking that approach involves giving up any attempt to overcome the difficulties presented in chapter 2. We have seen there that a subjective standard is incapable of providing a workable criterion of demarcation. As soon as we try to overcome those obstacles and replace the purely subjective standard by a rule that says something definite about what the law prohibits and what it does not prohibit, we are on our way toward abandoning the viewpoint neutrality that the First Amendment requires. As long as the sexual harassment law continues to apply to speech, there is no obvious way out of this dilemma: either we say that it applies to whatever speech is in fact offensive to its recipients, in which case the argument of chapter 2 becomes inescapably fatal, or we specify the character of the speech in some way that is not recipient-relative, in which case the law comes to be in conflict with the First Amendment.

But couldn't there be, one might ask, a way of specifying what speech is prohibited by the sexual harassment law that wouldn't be recipient-relative and that would still maintain viewpoint neutrality? The reason why no interpretation or modification of the sexual harassment law can be expected to satisfy that requirement is that the sexual harassment law is a part of the antidiscrimination law. The restrictions on the freedom of speech that are embodied in it thus have to target the speech that expresses or can be construed as expressing discriminatory viewpoints, without targeting the expressions of the opposite, antidiscrimination viewpoints on the same issues. Because of that, the restrictions on the freedom of speech that are embodied in the sexual harassment law are bound to violate the requirement of viewpoint neutrality. Thus, for example, the expressions of hostility to the presence of women in the workforce will often violate the sexual harassment law, while otherwise similar expressions of a welcoming attitude to the presence of women in the workforce will be allowed. The expressions of the view that women are incapable of pursuing a certain occupation may be illegal under the law, but the expressions of its denial, namely of the view that they are capable of pursuing it, remain legal.

This argument, which is central to Kingsley Browne's article, that the present sexual harassment law in the United States is unconstitutional because it is essentially biased in favor of a particular viewpoint on a controversial issue, while constitutionally permissible restrictions on the freedom of speech must be viewpoint neutral, is a very powerful one.[28] However, an argument of comparable power has yet to be made in actual litigation. In fact, the issue as to whether the restrictions on the freedom of speech made in the name of combating sexual harassment are compatible with the First Amendment has not often been raised in the courts at all.

The *Robinson* Case

The most influential of the small number of cases in which the question of the compatibility of restrictions of freedom of speech made in the name of combating sexual harassment and the First Amendment has received some attention from the courts, is *Robinson v. Jacksonville Shipyards, Inc.*[29] The federal district court that decided the *Robinson* case made seven responses to the defendants' appeal to the First Amendment. The brief discussion of these responses in this section will again largely be based on Browne's article.

The first response of the court was that the defendant Jacksonville Shipyards was, by its own admission, not trying to "express itself through the sexually-oriented pictures or the verbal harassment by its employees [and that thus n]o first amendment concern arises."[30] That argument is, however, a red herring, because the First Amendment rights that were invoked were obviously not those of the shipyards corporation itself but, rather, of the individual workers whose conduct the corporation was, according to the plaintiff's theory, supposed to constrain.[31]

The court's second response (partially inspired by Marcy Strauss' article "Sexist Speech in the Workplace")[32] was that "the pictures and verbal harassment are not protected speech because they act as discriminatory conduct."[33] In support of that claim the court quoted the Supreme Court opinion that "potentially expressive activities that produce special harms distinct from their communicative impact . . . are entitled to no constitutional protection."[34] The district court, however, does not make it at all clear how the opinion expressed in that quotation is supposed to apply to the issue at hand.[35] On the face of it, it seems that the harm that the comments such as "there's nothing worse than having to work around women"[36] cause to women is indistinguishable from their "communicative impact," rather than distinct from it, which is what the quotation requires. (Catharine MacKinnon seems to confirm this when she observes that the typical harms of sexual harassment are "harms of communication as such.")[37] It is true that such remarks can make it more difficult for a woman to do her job and that that effect can be characterized as discrimination, but it seems that the discrimination in question is essentially tied to the emotive impact of such remarks, and, as the Supreme Court has explicitly stated in another case, "'[t]he emotive impact of speech on its audience is not a "secondary effect"' unrelated to the content of the expression itself."[38] (The implications of the last quoted statement to a problem that is in many respects analogous to that of sexual harassment can be seen in *U.S. v. Lee,*[39] where an application of an antidiscrimination statute to clearly racist expressive conduct was held to be a violation of the First Amendment.)

The third argument that the court made was that "the regulation of discriminatory speech in the workplace constitutes nothing more than a time, place, and manner regulation of speech,"[40] which is the kind of speech regulation that is well established as constitutionally permissible. The court then went on to observe that "time, place, and manner" regulation of speech must be content neutral, but that "[t]o the extent that the regulation here does not seem entirely content neutral, the distinction based on the sexually explicit nature of the pictures and other speech does not offend constitutional principles."[41] What this response ignores, however, is that when the restrictions on freedom of speech are allowed not to be content neutral, they must still be viewpoint neutral, and that the regulation in question was most definitely not viewpoint neutral. In this argument the court has thus come close to, but still avoided coming to grips with what is, from the First Amendment standpoint, the central problem in the sexual harassment law.

The same observation applies to the fourth argument of the court, which is that the employees who were exposed to harassing speech constituted a "captive audience" and that regulation of speech when the audience is captive has been held to be constitutionally permissible.[42] While it is indeed true that this exception to the constitutional guarantee of freedom of speech has been recognized, the court ignores the requirement that the regulation of speech made under this exception be viewpoint neutral. It is also debatable whether the employees in question really constituted a captive audience in the relevant sense: at least one scholar has made arguments that imply that they did not.[43]

The fifth argument of the court was that the interests protected by the First Amendment need to be balanced against "the governmental interest in cleansing the workplace of impediments to the equality of women."[44] Assuming that we agree that the interest that has been invoked here is so exceptionally important, or, in legal jargon, "compelling," that such balancing is appropriate,[45] the court's argument is still, at best, incomplete. The court itself acknowledges that the balancing can justify only those restrictions of freedom of speech that are "narrowly tailored" to serve the interest in question, but it does not show that the restrictions at issue were in fact "narrowly tailored."[46] Even if this argument of the court could be supplemented to show that the "interest in cleansing the workplace of impediments to the equality of women" justifies an exception of some sort to the constitutional guarantee of freedom of speech, it is unlikely that the argument could be made so strong as to override the requirement that the exceptions to the First Amendment's guarantee of freedom of speech be at least viewpoint neutral.

The sixth argument of the court was that the government's requiring private employers to restrict the freedom of speech of their employees by sexual harassment rules was analogous to the government's restriction of the speech of its own employees.[47] Given that it is well established that the restrictions of the latter kind can be justified by all kinds of reasons, such as reasons that appeal to the interest in maintaining discipline and order in the workplace, it follows, the court claims, that the requirements of the former kind can be justified by similar reasons, and the interest in preventing the harms caused by sexual harassment surely provides as good a reason as the interest in maintaining discipline and order in the workplace.

This analogy is not convincing. Crucial to the cases about freedom of speech of public employees is the distinction between the government acting in its capacity of the sovereign and the government acting in its capacity of an employer. The Supreme Court provided a very clear explication of the distinction in its opinion in *Waters v. Churchill.*[48] That case is relatively recent, but the Court has made it clear that its account of the distinction is merely an explication of something that has been a part of the law all along. What makes it permissible for the government to restrict the workplace speech of its employees in a way in which it may not restrict the speech of the people at large (nor indeed of the public employees themselves as long as they speak as citizens rather than employees) is the fact that in creating such restrictions the government is acting as an employer rather than the sovereign. This, however, is not what we have when the government requires private employers to restrict the speech of their employees by sexual harassment rules: in that case it is clear that the government is involved as the sovereign.[49]

Incidentally, a similar instance of willingness to use what the government may do as employer as a model for what it may do as sovereign is exhibited in the *amicus curiae* brief of the American Civil Liberties Union and the American Jewish Congress in the *Harris* case.[50] It is curious how an organization such as ACLU could have been oblivious to the fact that the very point of making the distinction is that the government as sovereign may *not* do everything that it may do as employer.

The last, seventh argument regarding the First Amendment in the *Robinson* case points out the important differences between the antipornography ordinance that was at stake in *American Booksellers*

Association v. Hudnut[51] and sexual harassment rules.[52] That argument, however, need not concern us here because it is merely a refutation of one specific argumentative strategy used by the defendant in the case before the court. Even if we agree that that argument of the court is sound, it cannot on its own solve the conflict between the sexual harassment regulation and the First Amendment. The argument could contribute to solving that conflict only in conjunction with some other argument, but we have seen that none of the other arguments invoked by the court is persuasive.

The decision in which the district court has made these arguments has been appealed, but the defendant Jacksonville Shipyards then ceased its operations and the Eleventh Circuit consequently never had the opportunity to scrutinize the arguments of the district court.[53] In spite of their significant shortcomings, these arguments have exercised nationwide influence,[54] and, in 1999, received appellate-level endorsement of the Tenth Circuit in *Baty v. Willamette Industries, Inc.*[55]

OTHER DEVELOPMENTS

Between *Robinson* in 1991 and *Baty* in 1999, the issue of the compatibility of the restrictions of the freedom of speech made in the name of combating sexual harassment with the First Amendment has been litigated in a few other cases, with a wide range of different results.

In *Black v. City of Auburn, Ala.* a federal district court in Alabama dismissed an alleged harasser's appeal to the First Amendment as frivolous.[56] This outcome is largely a result of the fact that the court subsumed the case under the rules about the workplace speech of public employees. Under those rules, the speech is entitled to First Amendment protection only if it relates to a "matter of political, social, or other concern to the community"[57] and the court concluded that this condition was not satisfied by the speech of the alleged harasser in this particular case.

Subsuming the issue in *Black* under those rules was, however, a fundamental mistake. As has been remarked above, there is a distinction between the government acting as sovereign and the government acting as employer. While the government as employer is not entirely immune to First Amendment constraints, it is not subject to them in their full strength with which they apply to the government as sovereign. The role of the rules about freedom of speech of public employees within constitutional law is to spell out the precise ways in which the First Amendment applies and the ways in which it does not apply to the government as employer. These rules, however, do not in any way limit the ways in which the First Amendment applies to the government when it acts as sovereign.

Now it is true that government as employer is involved in the operation of the sexual harassment law: the government as employer enacts and enforces various regulations about sexual harassment at what I have called the lower level, just like private employers do. However, the government as employer does not enact and enforce these regulations for reasons of its own. Just like private employers, it enacts and enforces them because it is obligated to do so by the government as sovereign. It is in its capacity of sovereign that the government enacts the sexual harassment law at what I have called the upper level.

Because of that involvement of the government as sovereign, the First Amendment constraints apply here in their full strength, and not in the limited form articulated in rules about freedom of speech of public employees. These rules are irrelevant to the problems posed by the sexual harassment law, because they are intended for cases where the government is involved only as employer and not as sovereign. In subsuming the issue in *Black* under these rules, the district court has effectively ignored the crucial role of the government as sovereign in enacting and enforcing the sexual harassment law. In a way, it is rather unfortunate that the First Amendment issues have been raised in *Black* by a public employee: if they had been, with otherwise similar facts, raised by an employee of a private employer, it would have been impossible to ignore the fact that the government as sovereign is involved.

While an alleged harasser's appeal to the First Amendment was unsuccessful in *Black*, a couple of months later such an appeal turned out to be successful in *Silva v. University of New Hampshire.*[58] Deciding about the alleged harasser's motion for a preliminary injunction against his employer, the court ruled that he "is likely to succeed on the merits of his First Amendment claims."[59] Those who believe that there is a conflict between the sexual harassment law and the First Amendment should certainly regard this decision as a step in the right direction, but there are several reasons why they should not celebrate it as a major victory.

First, throughout its discussion of the First Amendment issue,[60] the court treats the problem as due to the way in which the employer has *applied* its sexual harassment policy to the particular case. It carefully avoids saying anything that would imply that the policy itself or the law on which the policy is based might be in conflict with the First Amendment. In other words, in acknowledging the existence of a

First Amendment problem in the case before it, the district court in *Silva* treats it as merely an unfortunate aberration that was probably caused by the idiosyncrasies of one particular employer at one particular moment, rather than as a predictable consequence of a systematic defect in the law itself. In the terminology that I have used before, we can say that in discussing the First Amendment issue, the *Silva* court concentrated solely on what happened in the application of the employer's lower level regulations, and did not deal with the far more reaching question as to how regulations at the lower level and their application may have been influenced by the upper level.

Consistently with this treatment of the problem as due to the idiosyncrasies of the particular employer, the court regards it as relevant that the employer in question is public, and this leads it to investigate whether the speech in question satisfies the conditions for the First Amendment protection of the speech within public schools or of the workplace speech of public employees in general. The court's finding was that these conditions were satisfied in the case before it, and the case therefore turned out differently from the *Black* case mentioned above. Despite that difference in outcome, in regarding these conditions as relevant in the first place, the reasoning of this court is significantly similar to the reasoning that we have seen in *Black.* By confining its discussion to the operation of the law at the lower level, the *Silva* court has, just like the *Black* court, avoided facing the fact that the government is involved as sovereign at the upper level of the law and that this involvement of the government as sovereign triggers the First Amendment constraints in their full strength, rather than in their more limited form in which they apply to the government as employer.

Moreover, the crucial instances of alleged harassment in *Silva* occurred within the alleged harasser's teaching, and a significant part of the court's discussion is devoted to arguing that academic freedom is specially deserving of First Amendment protection.[61] While one can easily agree with the court about that, these appeals to academic freedom to a certain extent confuse the issue, because one is left wondering whether they are essential to the court's opinion, or whether they were brought into discussion merely to reinforce a case that would have been strong enough anyway. In other words, the presence of these appeals to academic freedom makes it unclear whether the court would have decided the same way on otherwise similar facts that occurred outside an academic setting.

After the district court in *Silva* granted the alleged harasser's motion for preliminary injunction, the parties decided to settle, rather than pursue further litigation.[62] While that may well have been beneficial for those directly involved, it is unfortunate from the viewpoint of those who are concerned about the state of the law in this area, because it means that the opportunity has been lost for something of more definite precedential value to emerge out of this case.

Whatever limited impact *Silva* might have on the law in this area appears to be countered by *Rubin v. Ikenberry*.[63] Like *Silva*, *Rubin* involved remarks of a sexual nature, most of which were made in the course of teaching at a public university. The *Rubin* court, however, found that the alleged harasser's remarks did not satisfy the conditions for the First Amendment protection of speech within public educational institutions, and thus declined to interfere with the university's decision to treat these comments as sexual harassment. Despite the obvious parallels, *Silva* is not mentioned anywhere within the opinion in *Rubin*. The alleged harasser's insistence that his remarks were "pedagogically correct" and his apparent belief that they enabled "him to keep the interest of his students"[64] in the course of his classes, were dismissed by the *Rubin* court as not even raising a serious issue (the decision in *Rubin* was on a motion for summary judgment and not a result of a trial). It is, incidentally, noteworthy that out of thirty-three students, all of them female, who were enrolled in the course in which the remarks were made, only two chose to complain. None of the remaining students claimed to have been offended by the remarks. In fact, five of them stated in the course of the University's investigation that "the comments were appropriate in the context in which they were made."[65] It also appears that most of the students in the course were angered by the fact that the complaints were made.[66]

A case that should also be briefly mentioned here is *Johnson v. County of Los Angeles Fire Department*.[67] In that case a fire captain succeeded in obtaining a declaratory judgment that the sexual harassment policy of his employer was unconstitutional insofar as it prohibited his private possession, reading, and consensual sharing of *Playboy* at the fire station. He also obtained a permanent injunction against the enforcement of these aspects of the policy.

That case has generated some publicity, but its impact on the problem that we are concerned with in this chapter is, in fact, extremely limited. What was at issue in that case was only one particular aspect of the sexual harassment policy of the particular employer, namely its prohibition of *private* possession, reading, and consensual sharing of *Playboy*. The court made a point of emphasizing that other aspects of the policy are not at issue in the case.[68] While this employer is certainly not the only one to issue such a prohibition (the facts of *Tunis v. Corning Glass Works*,[69] for example, included the employer's prohibition of an employee's possession of a postcard-sized pinup-type picture that was affixed on the *inside* cover of his tool box), the prohibition is at the extreme end of what is done in the name of combating sexual harassment. The decision in this case implies nothing whatsoever about the First Amendment concerns related to the prohibitions of employees' making their own spoken or written comments of a sexual nature. In fact, the issue in this case was so narrowly drawn that it concerned only the use of one particular magazine, *Playboy*, and the court partially based its decision on the features of that magazine. It therefore doesn't follow without further argument that the decision implies anything even about private use of other publications. (The court has, for example, relied on the fact that *Playboy* "contains articles relating to politics, sports, arts and entertainment"[70] and that its cover does not contain nudity;[71] it is thus unclear whether the decision would have been the same if it involved private use of a more straightforwardly pornographic publication.) Finally, the decision was partially based on the peculiar circumstances of a firefighter who sometimes needs to be continuously present at the fire station for several days in a row so that the station effectively becomes his "residence as well as his workplace."[72] Because of that, this case cannot without further argument be invoked by employees with more usual working hours.

In spite of all these limitations in the scope of the actual decision, the court's discussion in the *Johnson* case is noteworthy for the appeal to "fundamental principle of First Amendment law that the government cannot regulate material in order to prevent the readers from developing certain ideas."[73] A reaffirmation of that principle in the context of a sexual harassment case was badly needed, because many supporters of the law and some courts[74] seem oblivious to it.

In 1995, the Fifth Circuit came close to having to deal with the conflict between the sexual harassment law and the First Amendment in *DeAngelis v. El Paso Municipal Police Officers Association*, which reached the court in May 1995.[75] However, although the court acknowledged the seriousness of the problem in no uncertain terms,[76] it avoided making an actual decision about the conflict. The court found that the aspects of that case that did not involve the First Amendment provided conclusive grounds to decide the case for the defendant-appellant and that that made it unnecessary to decide the First Amendment issue.

A month later, the decision of the Supreme Judicial Court of Massachusetts in *Bowman v. Heller*[77] was described in the media as a "sex-harassment ruling" in a case "pitting free-speech rights against protection from sexual harassment."[78] However, although some of the plaintiff's claims in this case did involve the sexual harassment law, the court dealt with those claims only in a footnote (without invoking the First Amendment)[79] and then proceeded to examine whether the First Amendment provides a defense against the claims that the plaintiff made within the law of torts. These claims legally had nothing to do with the sexual harassment law (although they concerned the same conduct), and the court's decision in this case therefore implies nothing whatsoever about the relationship between the sexual harassment law and the First Amendment. Petition for a review of this case was made to the federal Supreme Court, but the Court declined to take it up.[80]

In 1996, *Cohen v. San Bernardino Valley College*, a case involving the conflict between the First Amendment and the prohibition of sexual harassment, reached a federal court of appeals.[81] The alleged harasser won the case, but (similarly to the alleged harasser in *Silva*) he did so only on the basis of the court's finding that the *application* of the employer's sexual harassment policy to his case violated his First Amendment rights, not on the basis of any scrutiny of the policy *itself* or of the law behind the policy. Moreover, the focus of the court's opinion in *Cohen* is on the *vagueness* of the policy (as applied in the specific case), and the court explicitly limited the impact of its decision by saying "[w]e do not decide whether the College could punish speech of this nature if the Policy were more precisely construed by authoritative interpretative guidelines or if the College were to adopt a clearer and more precise policy."[82] Because of these limitations, and because the text of the opinion is relatively brief, the Ninth Circuit's decision in *Cohen* does not do much to illuminate the conflict between the First Amendment and the sexual harassment law.

In 1998, in a federal district court, a professor at a public university won a summary judgment finding the sexual harassment policy of his employer unconstitutional.[83] While the implications of that decision concern only public employment, they are much less limited by the details of the specific case than the implications of *Silva, Johnson,* and *Cohen.* Unlike the decisions in *Silva* and *Cohen,* which concerned only the ways in which the employers' sexual harassment policies were applied to specific incidents, and not the policies themselves, the decision in this case, *Booher v. Board of Regents, Northern Kentucky University,* found that the employer's sexual harassment policy was itself unconstitutional. Unlike the decision in *Johnson,* which dealt only with one very specific aspect of the employer's sexual harassment policy, the decision in *Booher* dealt with the employer's sexual harassment policy as a whole. As the policy in question does not seem to be particularly unusual, *Booher* seems to imply that sexual harassment policies of quite a few public employers are unconstitutional. The *Booher* court was, however, keen to ensure that its condemnation of the policy not be construed as implying that the law itself is unconstitutional. As the wording of the employer's policy was, in fact, quite closely guided by the law, the court was able to distinguish the two only at the cost of making some rather problematic argumentative moves. The court, for example, interpreted the university's prohibition of "verbal conduct" as a prohibition of speech and argued that its prohibiting speech made it different from the law itself, which prohibits verbal conduct and not "pure" speech.[84] Exactly what the difference between verbal conduct and speech was supposed to be is something that the opinion left less than clear.

Unlike the decisions in *Silva* and *Johnson*, the decision in *Booher* went unnoticed by the media. The potential impact of *Booher* on the development of the law is limited by the fact that the decision has not been published in a reporter of decisions (its text is available only electronically).

THE *R. A. V.* CASE: A PREVIEW OF THE SUPREME COURT'S VIEW ON THE ISSUE?

As has been observed above, the issue of the compatibility of the restrictions of freedom of speech made under the Title VII and the First Amendment has not been raised often before the courts, and it has thus never reached the Supreme Court. However, in 1992 the Court decided the case of *R. A. V. v. City of St. Paul, Minnesota,*[85] which is highly relevant to this issue, although it is not itself a sexual harassment case. In that case, the majority of the Court has very strongly reaffirmed the principle that the constitutionally permissible restrictions on the freedom of speech must be viewpoint neutral. Thus the court has observed that

> The government may not regulate use [of fighting words] based on hostility—or favoritism—towards the underlying message expressed.[86]

The opinion treats content-based restrictions of the freedom of speech as generally suspect but as sometimes constitutionally permissible,

> so long as the nature of the content discrimination is such that there is no realistic possibility that official suppression of ideas is afoot[87]

that is, as long as the restrictions remain viewpoint neutral. According to the Court, the problem with the St. Paul ordinance that was at issue in that case was that it was impermissibly content-based, but also that

> In its practical operation, moreover, the ordinance goes even beyond mere content discrimination, to actual viewpoint discrimination. Displays containing some words—odious racial epithets, for example—would be prohibited to proponents of all views. But "fighting words" that do not themselves invoke race, color, creed, religion, or gender—aspersions upon a person's mother, for example—would seemingly be usable *ad libitum* in the placards of those arguing *in favor* of racial, color, etc., tolerance and equality but could not be used by that speaker's opponents. . . . St. Paul has no such authority to license one side of a debate to fight freestyle, while requiring the other to follow Marquis of Queensberry rules.[88]

A clearer reaffirmation of the requirement of viewpoint neutrality would be difficult to formulate.

What is of particular relevance to our problem, however, is the fact that the court has in its *obiter dicta* explicitly addressed the issue of whether the restrictions of freedom of speech made under the sexual harassment law are compatible with its reasoning in this case, and claimed that they are:

> Moreover, since words can in some circumstances violate laws directed not against speech but against conduct (a law against treason, for example, is violated by telling the enemy the Nation's defense secrets), a particular content-based subcategory of a proscribable class of speech can be swept up incidentally within the reach of a statute directed at conduct rather than speech. Thus, for example, sexually derogatory "fighting words," among other words, may produce a violation of Title VII's general prohibition against sexual discrimination in employment practices. Where the government does not target conduct on the basis of its expressive content, acts are not shielded from regulation merely because they express a discriminatory idea or philosophy.[89]

It is, however, highly problematic how much of the regulation of freedom of speech that is currently made under the umbrella of Title VII is in fact covered by this remark of the Court. As has been observed above, when the sexual harassment law proscribes utterances such as "there's nothing worse than having to work around women," it seems to be proscribing precisely on the basis of the "expressive content," and it is thus difficult to see how such restrictions can be regarded as "swept up incidentally within the reach of a statute directed at conduct rather than speech."[90]

That this reasoning of the majority does not really apply to typical cases of verbal hostile environment harassment has, in fact, been observed by the four justices who concurred with the final decision reached by the majority but who disagreed vehemently with its reasoning.[91] These justices argued that, if the majority had pursued its reasoning consistently, it would have concluded that the prohibitions of verbal hostile environment harassment are unconstitutional. It needs to be noted, however, that these justices did not intend their argument as a proof that the prohibitions were in fact unconstitutional but rather as a *reductio ad absurdum* of the reasoning of the majority.

In trying to gauge the implications of the quoted remark of the majority, we should also take into account the fact that the majority uses the phrase "sexually derogatory 'fighting words' " to characterize the type of expressions that it may be constitutionally permissible to proscribe under Title VII. The notion of "fighting words," as has been observed above, in fact covers only a small part of "verbal conduct" that is within the scope of the sexual harassment law. The quoted remark of the majority thus really says less than it may seem to say at first about the issue that interests us. The remark does not give us a good ground to predict how the justices would deal with the issue of the compatibility of the sexual harassment law with the First Amendment if it came to be actually litigated in front of them. It is to be hoped that the remark will not deter potential litigants who may be in the position to raise that issue from pursuing it all the way to the Supreme Court.

We should mention in passing that arguments pointing out the existence of First Amendment problems in the sexual harassment law have been presented to the Supreme Court in two *amicus curiae* briefs in *Harris v. Forklift Systems*[92]: that of the ACLU and the American Jewish Congress, and that of the Feminists for Free Expression. The latter brief, which was the more forceful of the two, was partially based on Browne's article. The Court, however, has ignored these arguments, and rightly so, because, although intrinsically important, they were only remotely related to the specific issue in the case.

It may, be worth noting that the dissenting opinion in the recent Supreme Court case *Davis v. Monroe County Board of Education* refers several times to possible conflicts, at least within educational settings, between combating sexual harassment and respecting First Amendment rights.[93] These remarks, made by four of the justices, including the Chief Justice, suggest that the Court may be poised to take on, in the near future, a case that involves such a conflict, and should thus encourage more vigorous litigation in this area.[94]

Freedom of Speech of Employers

The preceding sections of this chapter were devoted to the question whether the sexual harassment law is compatible with the general principle of freedom of speech insofar as that principle applies to individual employees. That question has not yet received sufficient attention from the courts or the commentators, but it has nevertheless, as the preceding pages show, received some attention. The question that has gone almost completely unnoticed, however, is whether the sexual harassment law might not also be in conflict with the principle of freedom of speech as it applies to employers.

The principle of freedom of speech, as it is usually understood, concerns not only one's right to speak as one sees fit, but also one's right not to speak on any given topic, if one so chooses, and in particular, one's right not to speak in favor of some particular government-endorsed viewpoint on a given issue. In other words, the principle of freedom of speech not only makes it problematic for a government to prevent people from speaking, but also to force people to speak in a particular way. "[T]he choice of a speaker not to propound a particular point of view . . . is presumed to lie beyond the government's power to control."[95] It is certainly an established element of the First Amendment jurisprudence that its guarantees cover such a right not to speak as well as the right to speak.[96]

When the principle of freedom of speech is understood to include both of those components, it entails that, while a government may require those within its jurisdiction to do all manner of things, it cannot require them to do these things with enthusiasm. In a liberal society, it is always permissible to comply with laws grudgingly. The government can require me to pay certain taxes, for example, but we would regard it as monstrous if it also required me to sing praises to the system of taxation that is currently in force while paying my taxes. We think that taxation laws must be formulated in such a way that compliance with their provisions is perfectly compatible with active criticism of those very same provisions. The government may require me to install five fire extinguishers in my building, but it may not require me to publicly declare that I believe that five is the ideal number of fire extinguishers for such a building. It may not require me to pretend that five is the number of fire extinguishers I would have chosen myself. My compliance with fire safety regulations must be compatible with my silence on the issue of whether they are good regulations and even with my active lobbying for their change.

The sexual harassment law does not satisfy this implication of the principle of freedom of speech. At what I have called the upper level of its operation, that law requires employers to enact and enforce regulations against sexual harassment within their businesses. However, numerous cases make it clear that an employer's having sexual harassment regulations "on the books" and enforcing them when complainants choose to invoke them, is not enough to shield it from the upper-level legal liability. What else is required? In the words of the EEOC:

> Prevention is the best tool for the elimination of sexual harassment. An employer should take all steps necessary to prevent sexual harassment from occurring, such as affirmatively raising the subject, expressing strong disapproval, developing appropriate sanctions, informing employees of their right to raise and how to raise the issue of harassment under Title VII, and developing methods to sensitize all concerned.[97]

The requirement that employers affirmatively raise the subject means that they are not really allowed to remain silent on the topic. This would in itself be sufficient to raise some freedom-of-speech concerns, but the requirement that employers express "strong disapproval" is even more at odds with the principle of freedom of speech. This means that in speaking on a matter which is, in fact, controversial the employers have to express one specific viewpoint: the viewpoint that the government regards as the correct one. Notice that the requirement that strong disapproval be expressed applies to all employers regardless of whether they in fact disapprove of all the conduct that the law regards as sexual harassment: those who do not disprove of it are still expected to comply, presumably by feigning disapproval, or maybe by somehow inducing the disapproval in themselves. This feature of the sexual harassment law effectively makes it impossible for employers to obey the law grudgingly: employers who fail to display real or feigned enthusiasm for the aims of the law are under the threat of a significantly higher risk of legal liability than employers who do display it. This makes the sexual harassment law rather unlike the laws that one normally finds in societies that are committed to freedom of speech.

By requiring employers to express, on the matter of sexual harassment, the position that is endorsed by the government, the law of course makes it practically impossible for them to express positions that the government regards as incorrect. Imagine an employer whose considered opinion is that much of the conduct that the law currently treats as sexual harassment is in fact a wholesome expression of human sexuality and general *joie de vivre*, that it should be encouraged rather than discouraged, that only people whose sexuality has been damaged by puritan upbringing would object to it, that such people should be helped to overcome their repression rather than indulged in their neuroses, and that the current sexual harassment law is therefore utterly misguided. It is difficult to see how such an employer could at the same time publicly express this opinion and satisfy the expectation that it express strong disapproval of the conduct that the law currently classifies as sexual harassment. If the employer tried to do both, say by producing and distributing one set of pamphlets that stated its actual opinion and another set of pamphlets in which it pretended to hold the government-endorsed view, then it would be on record as having made mutually contradictory statements on the topic. This would mean that neither of its aims would be accomplished. The existence of the materials in which it pretended to hold the government-endorsed view would interfere with its effective communication of the view that it actually holds. On the other hand, the existence of the materials that express its true view would give rise to doubts as to whether the expressions of strong disapproval were made in good faith (which, of course, they were not) and that would put it in a precarious position in possible sexual harassment litigation. If it wishes to avoid that result the employer must remain silent about its real opinion on sexual harassment. This is something that seems to be in direct opposition to the First Amendment.

6
A Tale of Two Levels

The Two-Level Operation and Restrictiveness

Another set of problems that precludes us from making the sexual harassment law morally acceptable just by replacing the purported criterion of demarcation from the EEOC Guidelines with something like a rule that has been discussed in chapter 4 has to do with the fact, which has already been pointed out in chapter 2, that the sexual harassment law operates on two levels: the upper level at which the government requires employers to see to it that there is no harassment in their businesses and the lower level at which employers require their employees to abstain from harassment. At the end of chapter 2 we have seen how this two-level operation of the law prevents the effects of the severe-or-pervasive test, which is used at the upper level, from percolating to the individual potential harassers. The arguments made there do not apply only to the severe-or-pervasive test: they can be generalized to other possible tests of what is actionable at the upper level, including a test that would be based on chapter 4.

Whatever test gets accepted at the upper level, the employers will need a margin of safety against their upper-level liability, and this will lead them to proscribe, at the lower level, more than is actionable at the upper level.[1] This general need for a margin of safety is due to the same factors that have been listed in chapter 2 in the context of discussing the severe-or-pervasive test: the imprecision of the upper-level rules and their openness to interpretation (which can be reduced by careful formulation of the rules, but which can never be eliminated), the fact that lower-level rules need some time to operate, and the fact that employers will normally want to ensure not only that they will win any cases that may be brought against them, but also that they will not be sued in the first place. Moreover, the benefits of a wide margin of safety that an employer gets by having highly restrictive lower-level rules are not countered by any costs that the employer would have to bear.[2] The main costs of highly restrictive rules, namely the lost opportunities for romantic and sexual fulfillment, are borne by individual employees: employers have no incentive to be concerned about those costs. Employers do have some reason to be concerned about the cost of operating the lower-level enforcement mechanisms, but these costs do not necessarily increase with the severity of the rules: in fact, it is quite likely that highly restrictive rules will be cheaper to enforce than the rules that would require the employers to engage in some delicate balancing of different interests.

An employer that rationally deliberates how restrictive to make its lower-level rules is thus bound to reach the conclusion that they should be quite restrictive: the more restrictive they are, the more it stands to benefit from a wider margin of safety, and there is, in general, nothing that it stands to lose by making them highly restrictive. This remains so regardless of the specific content of the upper-level rules. No amount of effort spent on trying to formulate the ideal criterion of demarcation between sexual harassment and other conduct of a sexual nature is therefore on its own going to solve the problems of the present sexual harassment law. Even if we succeeded in formulating a criterion that would be ideal in that it would put the demarcation exactly where it should be (wherever that is), and that ideal criterion got accepted at the upper level, the consequences at the lower level would still be less than ideal. It can thus be said that the fact that the sexual harassment law unduly restricts people's freedom to pursue happiness and fulfillment through sexual interaction is to a considerable extent due to its two-level mode of operation and not to the specific provisions of its upper level. No amount of adjustment and fine-tuning that the legislators and/or judges might engage in will ever create acceptable results at the lower level, because the very fact that the operation of the law involves intermediaries, namely employers, creates a crude push toward restricting individual freedoms.[3]

Understanding how the separation between the upper and the lower level of the law's operation increases its restrictiveness is essential to reaching an informed moral judgment about the law. Unfortunately, very few commentators (let alone members of the general public) understand this feature of the law. The fact that the law imposes liability on employers and, in general, not directly on individual harassers, is sometimes even presented as if it somehow made the law deplorably lenient,[4] which, as we have seen, is exactly the opposite of the truth.

It has sometimes been claimed that the present two-level arrangement is more efficient (i.e., produces a better balance of benefits over costs) than the available alternatives, because employers are in the position to most efficiently minimize the incidence, and thus the harm, of sexual harassment.[5] That reasoning is, however, misguided. The problem with it is that it omits from the calculation the considerable costs of missed opportunities for romantic and sexual fulfillment that the enforcement of the sexual harassment law generates.

To reformulate the argument I have made above in the jargon of economics, the problem with the present sexual harassment law is that it makes these costs an externality. The two-level system makes the operation of the law at the upper level principally a matter between employers and alleged victims, while these costs are largely borne by third parties. There is nothing in the present law to make employers internalize the costs of lost romantic and sexual opportunities of their employees. As a result, these costs end up being generated quite liberally. The law thus ends up being inefficient overall (even if it is, for the sake of argument, granted that it may be efficient as between employers and alleged victims).

In thinking about the way in which the two-level structure of the law increases its restrictiveness, one should not allow oneself to be befuddled by the fact that an employer may designate some of the mechanisms that it provides for dealing with the allegations of sexual harassment as informal, and others as formal. Employers create both kinds of mechanisms for the same reason: to reduce the risk of being found liable for sexual harassment at the upper level. The so-called informal proceedings should therefore be regarded as a part of the lower level of the operation of the law, just like the (more) formal ones. These "informal" proceedings are conducted under the auspices of the employer's *formal* regulations (where they are *formally* designated as informal), and are presided over by people in whom the employer has vested *formal* authority to do so. While the "informal" proceedings may not result in anything that would be formally designated as punishment, their purpose is still to control individual conduct.[6] As that control wouldn't be taking place were it not for the state action that puts employers under the threat of upper-level liability, we should think of what happens in the "informal" proceedings as a part of a system by means of which the state controls the conduct of its citizens, even though the state is not directly involved in these proceedings.

It may also be worthwhile to observe (although it is not essential to my argument) that most workers are informed about the lower-level rules that apply to them in the context of various "training" programs that are designed either by the "human resources" departments of their employers or by the consultants who specialize in such services. These "training" programs often do not clearly separate the content of the rules themselves from various pieces of advice that may go beyond what the rules require.[7] The confusion between the rules and the advice may sometimes be inadvertent, but one suspects that it is often deliberate: the people who design the "training" programs typically see it as their mission to scare their audiences into not coming anywhere close to violating the rules against sexual harassment. They do not see it as their role to assist people in coming as close to violating the rules as possible without actually violating them. If one is not very attentive and intellectually sophisticated, one can thus easily be left with the impression that various pieces of advice that are offered within such "training" are themselves parts of the rules, when they are, in fact, not. This confusion amplifies the restrictiveness of the lower-level rules. It should be noted that this confusion is made possible by the separation between the upper and the lower level: it would be unthinkable of the state itself to perpetrate a confusion between what is legally required and what might be otherwise regarded as desirable.

The Two-Level Operation and Due Process

The fact that it leads to this restriction of *substantive* individual freedoms is, however, not the only problematic consequence of the two-level operation of the sexual harassment law. The two-level operation also significantly affects the availability of *procedural* safeguards to the accused.

There is a well-established tradition, within legal systems of the Western world, of holding the state to a very high standard of "due process" whenever it seeks to impose penalties on individuals for their engaging in prohibited conduct. On the other hand, while there is also an expectation that private institutions, including private employers, will provide some form of due process to those over whom they exercise power, the standards of due process that apply there are far less stringent. Now, the proceedings in which the guilt of individual alleged harassers is ascertained and penalties imposed on them take place at the lower level: they are administered by employers rather than the state. In spite of the fact that the employers conduct these proceedings because of the threat of upper-level liability, the proceedings do not constitute "state action" in the technical legal sense of that phrase, and thus do not trigger the stringent standards of due process that apply to the state's dealings with its citizens.[8] Given that private employers are not subject to the same due process standards as the state,[9] alleged harassers have far less procedural protection under the present two-level law than they would have if the law operated on a single level. One article written for employers, on the topic of how to handle lower-level sexual harassment investigations, for example, explicitly advises them *not* to allow those accused of harassment to be represented by a lawyer, because "[a] lawyer will only make the interview more adversarial and will restrict the amount of information that the investigators glean from the perpetrator."[10] Putting people in jeopardy of a serious deprivation while precluding them from being represented by a lawyer would of course be unthinkable if the state were involved directly. By "franchising out" the application of its prohibition of sexual harassment to employers (which is what the two-level operation of the law effectively amounts to) the state thus bypasses the due-process constraints that would have to be respected if the application were carried out by the state itself. We thus have a situation in which the state imposes significant restrictions of individual freedoms on its citizens (we should not forget that employers do not enact and enforce the lower-level rules on their own accord, but *because* the state requires that through its upper-level rules) without providing them with the kind of due process that is normally expected of it (because it leaves the dirty work to be done by employers). Indeed, the mere fact that one attempts to defend oneself can be held against one in the lower-level proceedings. A man who was fired for having said to a coworker two or three times "I'm gonna flirt with ya," was, for example, told in the memorandum informing him of the firing, "that he had been argumentative about the significance of his words."[11] An opinion of at least one court appears to imply that employers are free to retaliate with impunity against their employees who attempt to defend themselves against sexual harassment charges.[12]

The two-level operation of the sexual harassment law makes it possible for the state to overcome the constraints that the traditions of Western societies have imposed on it, without explicitly repudiating those traditions. In the two-level operation of the sexual harassment law we have a dangerous new device for expansion of the power that the state has over the individual. It is important to realize that the conduct that is currently labeled sexual harassment is not the only kind of conduct that is susceptible to control by a two-level law. If this consequence of the manner of operation of the sexual harassment law is not subjected to public criticism (and so far there has been practically none), the state could in principle choose to control an almost unlimited range of different types of conduct in the same manner: whenever it wished to prohibit a certain type of conduct without giving to those subject to the prohibition the full benefits of due process, it could simply enact a law that would require *employers* to see to it that their employees do not engage in that conduct. For conduct that cannot be effectively controlled by employers, other analogously situated intermediaries could be used: educational institutions could be required to control the conduct of their students, and hotel operators could be required to control the conduct of their guests.[13] That's why the problems associated with this mode of operation of the sexual harassment law deserve attention even from those who are not particularly concerned about other aspects of that law.

The point of this section is nicely illustrated by the case of Austen Donnellan, a British student who was accused by a fellow student of raping her. The alleged victim chose not to report the incident to the police, but did lodge a complaint against Mr. Donnellan with the internal authorities of the college. He regarded himself as innocent, but was afraid that the internal authorities of the college would nevertheless probably find him guilty and expel him from the college, which would have practically ruined his chances of pursuing any kind of a respectable career. In other words, he was concerned that his chances of defending himself successfully in front of a body whose mode of operation was very different from the mode of operation of a court of law, were limited. How different the two modes of operation are can be seen from the fact that the college authorities, as the college "solicitor" (attorney) has later confirmed, would have relied on hearsay evidence.[14]

In order to save his reputation and his career, Mr. Donnellan decided to go to the police himself and insist on being charged with rape. The police did that and he thus secured for himself the right to a trial in a court of law with all the procedural safeguards that characterize criminal trials in civilized countries. The college authorities were sensible enough not to pursue their internal procedure any further once the criminal investigation started, although they were technically under no obligation to do so. The final outcome was that Mr. Donnellan was acquitted and unambiguously cleared his name. (In case anyone thinks that that is relevant, there were nine women on the jury that acquitted him.)[15]

What made it possible for Mr. Donnellan to obtain a proper trial and thus clear his name was the fact that what he was accused of under the internal rules of the college was also a criminal offense. The option of going to the police is, however, not available to those who are accused of sexual harassment that does not amount to a criminal offense. Such people are completely at the mercy of various "kangaroo courts" that are set up by their employers or educational institutions.[16]

A related problem concerns the standards of proof that are used in the proceedings against the alleged harassers. Normally when the state seeks to impose on an individual a criminal sanction, we expect the individual's guilt to be proven beyond reasonable doubt.

Now, as I have already observed in chapter 4, being found guilty of sexual harassment, although not technically a criminal matter, often has similar effects on the individual's life as a criminal sanction would: it is severely stigmatizing, it makes one an outcast, it significantly narrows down the range of one's opportunities; in short, it is capable of, colloquially speaking, ruining one's life. Being found guilty of sexual harassment is in that respect definitely closer to being found guilty of a criminal offense than to losing a civil suit: a defendant who loses a civil suit may have to pay the damages, but his life is otherwise unaffected. However, in spite of the fact that the effects of being found guilty of sexual harassment are akin to criminal sanctions, the evidence sufficient for one's being found guilty of it need not come anywhere close to proving the guilt beyond reasonable doubt.

This is again a consequence of the fact that the law operates at two levels. Given that what happens at the upper level is a civil and not a criminal matter, the evidence is weighed there by the standard of preponderance of evidence, as in any other civil matter. This is not problematic in itself, given that the sanctions that the employers are subjected to if they lose are indeed typical civil sanctions. However, the fact that they will lose upper-level suits if the existence of harassment can be proven by preponderance of evidence means that employers cannot afford to use the beyond-reasonable-doubt standard, or any other standard that would be more stringent than the preponderance-of-evidence standard in deciding about the guilt of individual alleged harassers at the lower level, in spite of the fact that the sanctions at the lower level are more similar to criminal than to civil sanctions.[17] Moreover, while the upper level thus constrains employers not to use any standard that would be more stringent than the preponderance-of-evidence one, it, in the majority of cases, leaves them free to use a standard that is less favorable to the alleged harasser. This is because an alleged victim who is dissatisfied with the employer's findings of facts is always entitled to move the matter to the upper level and have the facts ascertained there, while such an option is not generally available to the alleged harasser (even when he has a contractual right not to be fired except for a good cause and the penalty for harassment is firing).[18] Due to the employers' understandable desire for a margin of safety, the asymmetry effectively encourages employers to give less weight to exculpatory than inculpatory evidence.[19]

The two-level operation thus enables the state to affect people's lives in the manner that is usually reserved for the criminal law, without having to prove their guilt beyond reasonable doubt. Again, we should not forget that although the state is not directly involved at the lower level, it is involved indirectly: what happens at the lower level happens *because* of the state action at the upper level.

This concern about the state's bypassing the standards of proof that would otherwise apply is also independent of what one thinks about the justifiability of the substantive content of the sexual harassment law, because similar bypassing maneuvers could easily be applied elsewhere. The danger that this might happen is more than just a theoretical possibility, because some feminists seem to regard the standard of proof beyond reasonable doubt as more of a nuisance and an obstacle to doing justice than as an important limit on the power of the state over individuals, and were able to gather considerable support from congressmen who, as Andrea Dworkin observed at the time, "don't understand the meaning of the legislation they pass,"[20] for a law that effectively made it possible to bypass the criminal procedures in cases of all "crimes of violence motivated by gender."[21]

The two-level operation of the law also enables the state to bypass the tradition that requires that the proceedings through which the state asserts its power over individuals generally be open to the public. The lower-level sexual harassment proceedings are almost always confidential. Their confidentiality means, first, that the full impact of the sexual harassment law is not open to public scrutiny. Second, the secrecy exacerbates the demarcation problem, discussed earlier: as the ordinary employees of a particular business have no way of knowing how the sexual harassment regulations of their employer have been applied so far, they cannot use the past application of the regulations as an indicator of what it is that the regulations require of them. Third, the secrecy means that, when someone is found guilty of sexual harassment in the lower-level proceedings, those around him will usually come to know only *that* he has been found guilty of sexual harassment, and not specifically what it is that he has done, and what his defenses were. Given that the notion of sexual harassment encompasses conduct that ranges from well-intended courtship to rape, this lack of information has the consequence that people who have committed acts of very different degrees of moral gravity all, unfairly, carry the same stigma. Unlike those who are accused of crimes in a court of law, the people accused of sexual harassment at the lower level are not given the opportunity to present their version of the facts to the world at large.

ASYMMETRY BETWEEN THE POSITIONS OF COMPLAINANTS AND ALLEGED HARASSERS AT THE LOWER LEVEL

The preceding section has shown how the two-level structure of the law enables the state to get around the standards of due process that otherwise govern its dealings with individuals. The problem with the state's evasion of the established standards of due process is not merely that the state is unfaithful to some venerable tradition, but that the unfaithfulness creates definite procedural injustices. We can appreciate the significance of the evasion better if we reflect on some further details of what typically goes on at the lower level.

In order to shield themselves from the upper-level liability, it is generally not enough for employers to enact the lower-level regulations and provide a mechanism for enforcing them when they are invoked: employers also need to actively assist the complainants in articulating their complaints. An employer that has sexual harassment regulations "on the books," but fails to make it easy for potential complainants to use them, runs a considerable risk of finding itself at the losing end of a sexual harassment suit. Moreover, as soon as a complaint, or anything that could be construed as a complaint, is made, the employer is under an obligation to deal with it, even if the complainant appears unmotivated to pursue the matter further. (If the complainant expresses a wish that the matter not be pursued, but later chooses to sue anyway, the complainant's earlier expression of that wish will not be sufficient for the employer to defend itself.)[22] Employers thus need to have in place not only adjudicators, but also something analogous to public prosecutors of sexual harassment complaints.[23]

On the other hand, employers are not under an obligation to provide those accused of sexual harassment with the assistance comparable to that provided to the complainants, and they typically do not provide it. The only person responsible for the accused's defense is the accused. The employer may permit the accused to bring a sympathetic coworker or a union representative to harassment hearings, but there is no real analogue of public defenders in lower-level harassment hearings. This is in sharp contrast with criminal proceedings in a court of law, where the accused always has not only a very definite right to professional assistance and representation, but also the right to be provided with it at the state's expense if he cannot otherwise afford it.

Furthermore, many employers do not maintain a sharp separation between those who draft their sexual harassment regulations, those who adjudicate disputes under these regulations, and those who assist the complainants. These functions may all be carried out within the same office. There is nothing analogous to the clear separation, that one finds in the law proper, between the legislature, judiciary, and public prosecution. That lack of separation is exacerbated by the fact that the educational background of those who are entrusted with handling sexual harassment complaints is often such that they strongly disdain the very idea of the adversarial process, and that they regard it as their professional role to help the victims of sexual harassment (even when exercising purportedly neutral functions). Employers are also advised to ensure that the investigators of harassment complaints (whose job is presumably to find the truth in an unbiased way) "are people with whom the claimant will feel comfortable."[24]

In the cases in which the person accused of sexual harassment does have an advisor of some kind in the lower-level proceeding, chances are that the advisor will not enjoy the same kind of close relationship with the adjudicators as is enjoyed by those assisting the complainant. Moreover, nobody advises the employers to worry whether the accused is "comfortable" with the investigators, and chances are that the investigators specially selected to make the complainant comfortable will not make the accused equally comfortable. There is thus a significant asymmetry between the positions of the accused and the complainant in the lower-level proceedings. (The reader should remember that these are the proceedings that are supposed to ascertain whether the accused is guilty or not; they therefore ought not to reflect an assumption that he is guilty.)

From the viewpoint of justice, this asymmetry is already worrisome in itself. It, however, becomes even more worrisome when we take into account one important feature of the theory that typically informs the work of those who assist the complainants in lower-level sexual harassment proceedings. Empirical research often reveals that only a minority of those who have been exposed to conduct that the researchers regard as sexual harassment think of themselves as victims of sexual harassment.[25] The researchers never regard this fact as casting any doubt on their identification of what is harassment: they are confident that what they classified as harassment really is harassment "irregardless [sic] of whether the victim labels it as problematic."[26] The conclusion that they typically draw from that fact is that some people need professional help to realize that they have been harassed:

> college administrators will have as their task moving students who are the objects of these behaviors along the cognitive path from tolerance

to identifying the behaviors as unacceptable, labeling them as sexual harassment, and then to reporting them through official channels.[27]

Those whose job it is to handle sexual harassment complaints often wholeheartedly embrace this kind of a view. As a consequence, they routinely encourage people who have not spontaneously thought of their experiences as sexual harassment to think of them that way, and to proceed accordingly. They regard it as their professional duty to convert ambiguous and vague expressions of dissatisfaction, whenever possible, into complaints of sexual harassment.[28]

Now, the ideology that is behind this professional dedication to boosting sexual harassment complaints may well deserve criticism,[29] but it is not my aim at this point to engage in that criticism. My aim is rather to point out that the structure of the lower-level sexual harassment proceedings allows this dedication to play a *role* that is problematic from the viewpoint of procedural justice, independently of the merits or demerits of the underlying ideology. The effects of that dedication to boosting sexual harassment complaints on the lower-level proceedings is very different from the effects that the zeal of a prosecutor has in a well-structured legal system. A zealous prosecutor may perform an invaluable function in a properly functioning justice system, as long as he confronts comparably trained defense in front of impartial adjudicators. Even an overzealous, ideologically minded prosecutor cannot do much damage under such circumstances. These are, however, not the circumstances that prevail at the lower level of the sexual harassment law. At a typical workplace or a typical educational institution, there are no people whose paid job is to assist those who are accused of sexual harassment in preparing their defenses. (We have already noted that employers are discouraged from allowing the accused to bring an attorney, even at his own expense.) The accused can usually get only the help of what are essentially amateurs, who are no match for the dedicated professionals who are involved in articulating and, effectively, prosecuting the complaints. The amateurs cannot be counted on to keep the professional's dedication to boosting sexual harassment complaints in check. As there is no clear separation between the prosecution and adjudication (and as the two are anyway likely to share the same ideological background), the adjudicators cannot be counted on keeping the dedication in check either.

Moreover, it is not only the ideologically driven dedication that boosts sexual harassment complaints. Once handling sexual harassment complaints becomes a paid job, the prestige and job security of those who hold that job are likely to be proportional to the number of cases they handle. They thus have, even if only subconsciously, an incentive to convert as many ambiguous occurrences as possible into unambiguous cases of sexual harassment.

The imbalance between the assistance provided to complainants and the assistance provided to those accused of sexual harassment thus has two effects: it increases the chances that, in any given case, the accused will be found guilty, and the number of complaints themselves (and thus the chances that any given person will be accused of sexual harassment).

Nor is that all. Employers are sometimes held liable, at the upper level, even if no lower-level complaint has been made on the ground that they should have known about the harassment. Employers consequently cannot afford to wait for complaints to be made: the law gives them an incentive to be constantly alert to anything within their businesses that might be regarded as, or turn into something that might be regarded as, sexual harassment. This effectively includes all sexual interaction between their employees. One author thus advises employers that they are

> also required to monitor interoffice dating to ensure that requests for sexual favors or dates are not a condition of employment and are not creating a hostile working environment.[30]

The law thus encourages employers to monitor intimate lives of their employees in ways that would be an unthinkable invasion of privacy if carried out by the state itself.[31]

It is a mistake to think of the problems outlined in this section as primarily due to the ideological proclivities of those who create and implement lower-level sexual harassment rules. It is, of course, true that these proclivities play a role in how sexual harassment cases are handled, but in thinking about that fact, one should always bear in mind that it would have never occurred to most employers to hire people with such proclivities to create and implement sexual harassment rules, were it not for the fact that the state imposes on employers upper-level liability for harassment. The morally worrisome asymmetry between the position of the complainants and the alleged harassers in the lower-level sexual harassment proceedings is primarily due to the incentives that the upper level of the law gives to employers. The responsibility for that asymmetry thus ultimately belongs to the state, and it is that fact that makes it deeply problematic. If a particular private employer spontaneously, for some reasons of its own, created a comparable asymmetry, that would be morally worrisome too, but not nearly as worrisome as it is for the state to create such an asymmetry.

PUNISHMENT OF THE INNOCENT

The asymmetry between the positions of the complainant and the alleged harasser continues to manifest itself even if the lower-level proceedings result in the finding that no harassment actually took place. The complainant enjoys legal protection against any adverse reaction in such a case; the adverse reaction would constitute retaliation, and retaliation for making a complaint of sexual harassment is illegal, regardless of the disposition of the complaint. On the other hand, employers are encouraged by professional advisers to "consider separating the victim and perpetrator due to hard feelings engendered during the investigation" even if "the investigators conclude that victim's sexual harassment allegations cannot be substantiated."[32] If neither the complainant nor the alleged harasser wishes to move, this separation will have to be effected by moving the latter (moving the complainant may result in a suit for retaliation). This effectively means that an employer may need to punish an alleged harasser even if he is found not to be guilty.

Employers are also advised that "it may . . . be appropriate to instruct" those who were accused of sexual harassment to stop the conduct complained of (which amounts to the lower-level analogue of an injunction), even if the lower-level investigation has determined that the conduct did not constitute sexual harassment, in order to "reassure the [complainant] that the complaint was taken seriously [and to] increase the likelihood that other employees will not hesitate to come forward with more serious complaints of unwelcome sexual conduct."[33] Reassuring the complainant and encouraging future complaints is thus supposed to be a higher priority for employers than ensuring that the wrongly accused is not affected by the accusation.

Another source of advice for employers says that they should

> If the facts and circumstances warrant, consider placing a memo in the accused's personnel file that states simply that a sexual harassment allegation was raised on a given date, against this individual, and that after a complete investigation, results were inconclusive. In the event a similar situation develops later, this notice may help the employer implement a

higher level of discipline than might have been possible without the prior documentation.[34]

This means that an allegation of a particular incident of sexual harassment can result in additional punishment for a later incident, even though a "complete" investigation has not revealed a sufficient reason to hold the accused guilty of the first incident. It is, moreover, not uncommon for somebody who has been accused of sexual harassment and found not to be guilty in lower-level proceedings, to nevertheless be subjected to specially close supervision afterwards. These aspects of lower-level proceedings all mean that the fact that these proceedings have failed to prove one's guilt does not put one back in the position in which one would have been if the allegation had not been made.

It is noteworthy that the experts on sexual harassment appear to be reluctant to ever say that the accused has been found not to be guilty: when the investigation does not prove the that the accused is guilty, they characterize the result as "inconclusive" or say that the "allegations cannot be substantiated." Such terminology is indicative of the position in which an allegation of sexual harassment puts the person accused.

Allegations of sexual harassment that have not been adjudicated either way can also have consequences for the alleged harasser: one author appears to encourage employers to mention such allegations in giving references about the alleged harasser to prospective future employers.[35]

There is a worry that the employers' attempts to avoid upper-level liability may eventually move in the direction of obliterating the very distinction between being guilty and not guilty: they may choose to not hire the applicants whom they *believe* to be *likely* to commit acts of sexual harassment, regardless of whether these people have ever committed or even been alleged to have committed any actual harassment.[36] The fact that efforts have been made to develop "personnel selection tests which might be used in screening management applicants who have some proclivity to sexually harass"[37] suggests that this is not a merely speculative worry.

The Two-Level Operation and the Public Debate

The two-level operation of the sexual harassment law thus creates problems of both substantive and procedural nature. But the two-level operation not only creates such problems, it also obscures these and other problems in this area of the law, and thus makes it more difficult to criticize it. The two-level operation of the sexual harassment law has, to a considerable extent, been successful in shielding the law from the scrutiny it otherwise would have received.

Let us imagine that no one has ever thought of creating sexual harassment law in anything like the two-level form it ended up having, but that someone has instead proposed that the state enact a single-level law that would be otherwise similar to the actual sexual harassment law. Imagine, for example, that a criminal statute has been proposed that would make it a misdemeanor for an individual to engage in unwelcome sexual advances or other conduct of a sexual nature (including purely verbal conduct), which has the effect of creating an intimidating, hostile, or offensive working environment for that individual's coworkers.

It is quite possible that some people would have supported even such a proposal. But it is clear that such a proposal would have instantly encountered significant opposition. It would have been obvious to practically everyone that such a proposal runs counter to the widely held view that the mere fact that people are offended by an individual's conduct is not a sufficient justification for the state's interference with that conduct. Those who hold such a view would have immediately seen its relevance to the proposal, and many of them would have thus been led to articulate their opposition to it. Alarm bells would have started ringing at the headquarters of the ACLU and similar organizations as soon as such a proposal had been formulated, and they would have rung far more loudly than they ever have in the actual history of the sexual harassment law. The veterans from the political battles about censorship of pornography and other issues of freedom of expression and/or legal control of sexuality would have immediately seen the analogies between these old issues and the new one, and at least some of them would have adapted to the new issue the arguments that have been sharpened through the decades of debating the similar old ones.

In other words, if a law similar to the actual sexual harassment law had been originally proposed as a single-level law, it would have been immediately perceived by many as a potential threat, and that would have led to its being very carefully scrutinized by all those who cherish the tradition of respect for individual freedoms. The supporters of the proposal could have tried to argue that threat is not as serious as it seems, or that it is outweighed by other considerations, but it is clear that, in the face of such serious opposition, they would have had a very heavy burden of proof.

Some of the reasons why there was no public outcry at the introduction of the actual sexual harassment law in the mid-seventies, and why the opposition to it has only recently begun to be heard, have been discussed in chapter 1. But an important additional reason for the relative absence of timely public reaction to the introduction of the sexual harassment law has to do with its two-level structure. It is the two-level structure that explains why many of those who are otherwise alert to the threats to individual freedoms have, until recently, been silent on the issue of sexual harassment.

This silence has to do with how the idea that the state ought not, without a very strong reason, to interfere with individual freedoms, is currently interpreted. In the political history of the last half-century, the prevailing interpretation of that idea came to be the one that takes it literally, as applying only to *individuals,* and as not extending the same protection against the power of the state to private *corporations.* It is debatable whether such a narrow understanding of the idea is justified or not, but it is obvious that it, rightly or wrongly, became a part of the present-day political culture. Most people nowadays are used to the state restricting and regulating the conduct of private corporations in all manner of ways, and regard that as morally unproblematic and as perfectly consistent with respect for individual freedoms.

As a result of the dominance of such understanding of what protection of individual freedom involves, most of the watchdogs that carefully monitor the political, legislative, and jurisprudential developments that might endanger individual freedoms tend to be disinterested in the laws that regulate the conduct of corporations. Given that the sexual harassment law presents itself as, and at its upper level really is, an instance of the state's regulation of the conduct of employers, which are practically always corporations rather than individuals, it generally remained outside the scope of interest of those who are concerned about individual freedoms. The way in which the sexual harassment law is formulated, and its place in the legal system, make it rather unlike paradigm instances of laws that raise concerns about individual freedoms.

In order to perceive the sexual harassment law as a law that raises such concerns, it is necessary to take off its mask of a law that only regulates the conduct of corporations. In other words, it needs to be vividly appreciated that the upper level of the law is not all there is to it, that it also has the lower level, which does interfere with conduct of individuals in a very direct way, and that what goes on at the lower level is an unavoidable consequence of the upper level.

Public debate about the law is hindered still further by the fact, discussed at the end of the preceding chapter, that the law effectively requires employers not only to prohibit sexual harassment in their businesses, but also to display real or feigned enthusiasm about doing so. (Remember that, according to the EEOC Guidelines, employers should *express* strong disapproval of sexual harassment, not merely inform their employees that the state disapproves of it.) The required displays of employers' enthusiasm for the prohibition of sexual harassment obscure the fact that it is ultimately the decision of the state that the freedom of individual employees is to be restricted by that prohibition.

We would all agree that there are certain things that the state may not do to its citizens. It is debatable whether restricting their sexual expression, in the way in which the sexual harassment law does, is one of those things. The two-level structure of the law, however, makes it difficult even to debate the matter, because it makes it appear that in that area of the law the state does not do anything to individuals: it can claim that it only imposes some restrictions on employers, and that if individual freedoms are restricted, they are restricted by employers, not by the state. The two-level structure of the law thus makes it less than a straightforward matter to subsume the issues raised by the law under the general principles about the relationship between the state and the individual; if the law had been a single-level law, that would have been perfectly straightforward. This, in turn, considerably slows down the public debate about the law.

The importance of understanding this aspect of the law, again, goes far beyond the importance of specific freedoms that the law affects. Even those who do not particularly care about the forms of sexual expression that the law restricts have a reason to be concerned about the mechanism by which the two-level structure of the law obscures the fact that the state restricts individual freedoms through the law. As has been pointed out above, this mechanism can be easily transposed onto entirely different subject matters. If this mechanism is not exposed in the case of sexual harassment, the state may be tempted to pass, in the future, laws that will restrict some entirely different freedoms through intermediaries such as employers. The state may sometimes be justified in restricting individual freedoms, but it should *never* be allowed to avoid the *responsibility* for restricting them by getting such intermediaries to do the dirty work, and then pretending that it is not really restricting individual freedoms, but merely regulating conditions of employment, or something similar. This concern is perfectly general and independent of the significance of specific freedoms that may be at stake in a particular case. In other words, the state should not be allowed to use the creation of two-level laws as a mechanism for bypassing the traditions of respect for individual freedoms.

7
Sexual Harassment and Discrimination

Sexual Harassment and Employment

After everything that I have said about the problematic character of the two-level operation of the sexual harassment law, one may wonder why is it that the two-level operation seems unproblematic to so many people, including both lay people and theoreticians discussing the law. The reason is that those people have accepted the view that sexual harassment is a form of sex discrimination, and that it is therefore quite proper for the laws against it to be a part of the antidiscrimination laws. Given that the whole body of antidiscrimination law, which has been created and developed well before anyone thought of the notion of sexual harassment, is addressed to employers, it seems quite proper for the sexual harassment law to also be addressed, in the first instance, to employers.

The idea that sexual harassment is a form of sex discrimination is at the very core of the sexual harassment law as it actually is. The law came into being through litigation under Title VII of the Civil Rights Act of 1964, which is an antidiscrimination statute.[1] It came into being when a federal court accepted that idea for the first time, in *Williams v. Saxbe.*[2] It is this idea that gives the sexual harassment law its legal "home" within the antidiscrimination law. If this idea cannot survive scrutiny, then the whole structure of the present sexual harassment law collapses. If the idea is refuted, then those who still want there to be some kind of a sexual harassment law have to start from scratch.

Treating sexual harassment as a form of sex discrimination also plays a considerable role in making the sexual harassment law appear morally justified. Most people agree that antidiscrimination laws are, in general, morally justified. So, if it is accepted that the phenomena characterized as sexual harassment are really instances of discrimination, it seems relatively easy to prove that laws against them are morally justified.

But is sexual harassment really a species of sex discrimination? This chapter will be devoted to examining that question.

In discussing the question I shall set aside the demarcation problem and proceed as if it had been resolved in some satisfactory way (such as the way sketched in chapter 4). I shall also assume, for the sake of argument, that the majority of people are right in thinking that antidiscrimination laws, and specifically laws against discrimination in employment on the basis of sex, are, by and large, justified. For the purposes of this book, I shall simply set aside any general criticisms that could be made against antidiscrimination laws, such as the ones that have been made by Richard Epstein.[3] What I want to investigate is whether, assuming that the laws against sex discrimination are, by and large, justified, the idea that they can provide a legal "home" for the sexual harassment law can withstand scrutiny.

Let me say at the outset that I readily acknowledge that there are *some* instances of conduct that is currently classified as sexual harassment that are, at the same time, instances of sex discrimination. For example, if men at some workplace that has until recently been all-male submit female coworkers to a campaign of sexual insults that is intended to make the women's lives so miserable that they will be forced to resign, then it may well be quite plausible to say that the women are victims of sex discrimination. The existence of such examples, however, in no way proves that all of the conduct that is currently classified as sexual harassment constitutes sex discrimination. The literature on sexual harassment often generalizes, without argument, from such examples to all of sexual harassment. The issue that is relevant here, and that I will be discussing in this chapter, is not whether there are *overlaps* between sexual harassment and sex discrimination (there clearly are), but whether sexual harassment can be *subsumed* under the notion of sex discrimination.

An interesting detail from the history of the sexual harassment law, that the surveys of the law routinely mention and that deserves to be mentioned here as well, is that, when the argument was first made that Title VII should be interpreted as including the prohibition of sexual harassment, it was outright rejected by the courts. In *Corne v. Bausch and Lomb Inc.*,[4] the court thus concluded that the conduct complained of cannot constitute discrimination in employment, because it

> appears to be nothing more than a personal proclivity, peculiarity or mannerism. By his alleged sexual advances, [the alleged harasser] was satisfying a personal urge. Certainly no employer policy is here involved. . . .[5]

The court contrasted the alleged harasser's "personal proclivity, peculiarity or mannerism" with the conduct that had been at issue in Title VII suits that had been successful up to that point, which had involved "company policies" and had always been "employer designed and oriented."[6] The court also observed that in these other cases "[t]here was apparently some advantage to, or gain by, the employer," while in the case in front of it,

> rather than the company being benefited in any way by the conduct of [the alleged harasser], it is obvious it can only be damaged by the very nature of the acts complained of.[7]

The district courts in *Miller v. Bank of America*[8] and *Barnes v. Train*[9] expressed opinions similar to that of the *Corne* court. These decisions were later reversed on appeal.[10]

A novice in the area of sexual harassment law is, after reading *Corne v. Bausch and Lomb, Inc.,* likely to think that there must be some crucial argument that has been made in the later cases that somehow refutes the *Corne* argument, and that it is because of that refutation that the sexual harassment law came into being under the umbrella of Title VII. When one turns to *Williams v. Saxbe,*[11] the first case in which a sexual harassment suit under Title VII was successful, and thus the case with which the history of the sexual harassment law, as we know it, started, one finds that the crucial argument is, in fact, elusive. In that case the court decided that what the alleged harasser was claimed to have done can be characterized as his "policy or practice" and then immediately proceeded to impute that "policy or practice" of the alleged harasser to his employer, by simply saying, without argument, that

> if this was a policy or practice of plaintiff's supervisor, then it was the agency's policy or practice, which is prohibited by Title VII.[12]

This sentence is the sole link that can be found in *Williams* between the kind of conduct that *Corne* characterized as "personal proclivity, peculiarity or mannerism" and the employment law.

The link is, in fact, highly problematic. If I always wear a paisley tie with my gray suit, then it is perhaps true, although certainly unnecessarily pompous, to say that it is my "policy or practice" to wear a paisley tie with the gray suit, but it most definitely does not follow that it is the "policy or practice" of my employer that I wear such an outfit, even if I in fact often wear it to work. This remains so if my position is a supervisory one. (I am assuming here that my employer does not have any kind of a dress code that would govern the matter.)

The reason for treating sexually harassing conduct as something that is importantly connected with employment, and thus subject to the employment law, remained elusive through much of the first two decades of the development of the law. When the Supreme Court first addressed the topic, it pronounced that the courts should "look to agency principles for guidance in this area," but declined to spell out what that implies.[13]

Some courts declared that employers should be liable for sexual harassment because sexually harassing conduct was within the scope of the harassers' employment.[14] Such declarations are, however, at odds with the traditional understanding of what "scope of employment" means, which excludes from the scope of employment any act of an employee that "is done with no intention to perform it as a part of or incident to a service on account of which he is employed."[15] Clearly, people who perform acts classifiable as sexual harassment practically never think that these acts contribute to the fulfillment of the duties of their employment.[16]

A few appellate opinions from the eighties, however, succeeded in producing a reasonably plausible argument for imputing sexually harassing conduct to harassers' employers. That argument analogizes the employers' liability for harassment to the liability that they have under the established rule of the law of agency which says that a "master" is subject to liability for a tort committed by a "servant" of his, even if the servant acted outside the scope of the employment in committing the tort, provided that "the master was negligent or reckless, or . . . the servant . . . was aided in accomplishing the tort by the existence of the agency relation."[17] (Because of the historical roots of this area of the law, the terms "master" and "servant" are often used in it to characterize the relationships that would not be so characterized outside legal contexts: in that technical sense, employees are servants of their employers.)

That the harasser was "aided in accomplishing" the harassment by "the existence of the agency relationship," that is, by his position in the institutional structure set up by the employer, is true in quid pro quo harassment and in a narrow range of cases of hostile environment sexual harassment.[18] (For example, if a harasser was able to perform the acts of hostile environment harassment only because he, in virtue of his official position, had a key allowing him to access the locked room in which the victim worked,[19] then it is arguable that he was aided in accomplishing the harassment by his position in the company.) The rule that a "master" is liable for the torts of his "servants" if "the master was negligent or reckless" in hiring or supervision[20] of the "servants" can provide a reasonably convincing analogy with the remaining cases of sexual harassment.[21]

These analogies with the established law of agency can thus provide an argument for imputing sexually harassing conduct to the harasser's employer, but they were developed with clarity only in a small number of cases, until the Supreme Court in 1998 decided *Burlington Industries, Inc. v. Ellerth*[22] and *Faragher v. City of Boca Raton*,[23] which decisions unambiguously endorsed the argument.[24] In making it clear that the grounds for imputing the conduct to the employer are either the fact that the harasser was aided in accomplishing the harassment by the existence of the agency relationship[25] or the employer's negligence or recklessness, the Court explicitly criticized the idea that sexual harassment could generally be regarded as within the scope of the harassers' employment.[26]

SEXUAL HARASSMENT AND THE PROHIBITION OF DISCRIMINATION

That argument for imputing the conduct to the employer, outlined in the preceding section, can, however, justify the current law only if the conduct is discriminatory. Title VII is a law about discrimination in employment; in order to justify treating sexual harassment as a violation of that law, it needs to be shown not only that it is significantly connected with the alleged victim's employment, but also that it constitutes sex *discrimination* in the first place. Obviously if the conduct in question cannot be characterized as discrimination in the relevant sense, it follows straightforwardly that it cannot constitute discrimination in employment for the purposes of Title VII and similar laws, even if it is granted that it can be imputed to the harassers' employers.

The argument that led the court in *Williams* to classify sexual harassment as sex discrimination was almost disarmingly simple. According to the allegations in that case, the harasser directed the conduct at issue only to females and never to males. That in itself means that, in deciding to whom to direct such conduct, he was discriminating between males and females. Once we accept the terminology of "policy or practice," it follows that it can be said that he had a "policy or practice" that was sexually discriminatory.

This argument can be readily applied to most instances of conduct of a sexual nature. The overwhelming majority of people tend to direct their sexual advances and similar acts to persons of one sex rather than another: heterosexuals direct them to members of the opposite sex, homosexuals to members of their own. In other words, it can be said that people typically discriminate between the sexes in deciding to whom to direct conduct of a sexual nature.

Thus, if the reasoning that led the court in *Williams* to connect sexual harassment and sex discrimination is accepted as sound, it becomes easy to claim that such a connection exists in almost every case of sexual harassment, and that it is thus quite proper to think of sexual harassment in general as a form of discrimination. Since *Williams*, this argument has been endorsed by courts at all levels, including the Supreme Court,[27] but the endorsement has largely been implicit: the matter has rarely received much discussion. It was observed, in 1994, that neither of the Supreme Court opinions on sexual harassment delivered up to that point (*Meritor*[28] and *Harris*[29]) had "discussed in any significant detail the doctrinal basis for classifying sexual harassment as sex discrimination."[30] That observation remains largely true: the Supreme Court's 1998 decision in *Oncale v. Sundowner Offshore Services, Inc.*[31] endorses the argument somewhat more explicitly than *Meritor* and *Harris*, but hardly in a way that could be characterized as a detailed discussion. It is also noteworthy that the EEOC, in promulgating its Guidelines on Sexual Harassment (which are officially an interpretation of Title VII) never made it clear how their content was supposed to follow from Title VII; it simply declared that it did.[32]

Given that the above-sketched argument that subsumes sexual harassment under the notion of sex discrimination plays such a crucial role in the legal approach to sexual harassment, we need to examine its soundness. Later in this chapter I shall show that the argument is not sound. But before embarking on that discussion, let us examine one general theoretical assumption behind the decision to subsume sexual harassment under the notion of sex discrimination.

"Sex Plus" Criteria and Discrimination

The conduct complained of in a typical case of sexual harassment is usually not directed to all employees of a particular sex. It may be true, for example, that a particular person accused of sexual harassment has been directing the conduct in question only to females and never to males, but it is almost never the case that he has been directing it to *all* females in the workplace. Rather, it could be argued, such a person is likely to be selecting the females to whom to direct the conduct on the basis of some such criterion as finding them attractive. Because the quality on the basis of which the conduct is directed to someone is thus, say, perceived attractiveness, rather that the simple fact that the person is of a particular sex,[33] it may appear that the discrimination cannot be characterized as sex discrimination. It could be characterized as, say, discrimination on the basis of perceived attractiveness, but that kind of discrimination is not covered by Title VII and similar laws.

The response of those who support treating sexual harassment as a form of sex discrimination is that, although it is true that perceived attractiveness and similar features typically play a role in determining whether particular conduct of a sexual nature will be directed to someone, it still remains true that being of a particular sex plays a role too. The kind of criterion that typically guides the conduct that is at issue in sexual harassment cases has thus been described in the literature as a "sex plus" criterion: it is that the person to whom the conduct will be directed must be of a particular *sex, plus* have some additional features, such as attractiveness.[34] In the philosophical terminology, the point can be made more clearly, by saying that, within such a criterion, being of a particular sex functions as a necessary but not a sufficient condition.

The actual words of Title VII simply prohibit discriminating against an individual "because of such individual's . . . sex."[35] That wording is arguably ambiguous. The first interpretation that comes to mind is that it prohibits only discrimination on the basis of criteria that take being of a particular sex as a sufficient, or perhaps both necessary and sufficient, condition for unfavorable treatment. But perhaps it does not stretch the meaning of these words too far to interpret them as prohibiting discrimination on the basis of criteria that take being of a particular sex as merely a necessary condition for unfavorable treatment.

Whether discrimination on the basis of such a "sex plus" criterion constitutes sex discrimination is an issue that has been discussed at some length by both the courts and the commentators. The *Williams* court itself, in defending its decision to regard sexual harassment as a form of sex discrimination, invoked two earlier cases in which discrimination on the basis of a "sex plus" criterion had been held to be discrimination on the basis of sex. They involved discrimination against women with preschool children[36] and discrimination against married women.[37] In both cases the discrimination was not based solely on whether one was a female, but it nevertheless was discrimination in which being female played a part. It was directed against the females who had the further feature of having preschool children or being married (i.e., it was based on "sex plus" criteria), but that did not prevent the courts that considered these cases to treat it as sex discrimination.

The *Williams* court regarded these two cases as analogous to a case of sexual harassment, but it is questionable whether they really are. The employer in the first case, which discriminated against women with preschool children, also dealt with men with preschool children. The claim of discrimination on the basis of sex in such a case can then be easily sustained by comparing the employer's treatment of women with preschool children with its treatment of similarly situated men, namely men with preschool children. Similarly, when an employer discriminates against married women, the claim of sex discrimination can, in principle,[38] be easily sustained by comparing its treatment of married women with its treatment of similarly situated men, that is, the men who are married. Analogous comparison cannot, however, be made in the case of, for example, a heterosexual male who directs his sexual advances to women he finds attractive. In order to make such a comparison, we would have to compare his treatment of these women with his treatment of men who are relevantly similar. If one follows the pattern from the preceding two cases, then the relevantly similar men would have to be the men he finds attractive in the similar manner and to the similar degree, and it follows from the hypothesis that he is heterosexual, that there are no such men. The comparison therefore cannot be made.

A better analogy to sexual harassment is provided by discrimination on the basis of pregnancy. Such discrimination can also be characterized as "sex plus" discrimination: it is directed against women who have the additional feature of being pregnant. Unlike the cases of women with preschool children and married women, and like the case of sexual harassment, the case of pregnancy does not allow for straightforward comparison with relevantly similar men. The relevantly similar men would seem to be pregnant men, and obviously there aren't any such men.

The issue of whether discrimination on the basis of pregnancy is a case of discrimination on the basis of sex (and thus actionable under Title VII) came before the Supreme Court in *General Electric Co. v. Gilbert*,[39] which was decided a few months after *Williams*. In that case the Court took the position that discrimination against pregnant women does *not* constitute discrimination on the basis of sex, thereby rejecting the feminist reasoning that would treat discrimination on the basis of "sex plus" criteria as sex discrimination. The decision has, however, caused a considerable uproar, and the feminist arguments that have failed to convince the Supreme Court seem to have won the battle for public support in the aftermath of the decision. That eventually led to the Supreme Court's position about discrimination on the basis of pregnancy being legislatively overridden in 1978 by the Pregnancy Discrimination Act[40] which declared the discrimination on the basis of pregnancy to be a form of sex discrimination, and in 1991, to the codification,[41] in general terms, of the idea that "sex plus" discrimination constitutes sex discrimination.

In 1989, in a different context, the Supreme Court appeared to endorse the general principle that "sex plus" discrimination constitutes sex discrimination when it pronounced that the prohibition of discriminating "because of" sex is

> meant to condemn even those decisions based on a mixture of legitimate and illegitimate considerations. When, therefore, an employer considers both gender and legitimate factors at the time of making a decision, that decision was "because of" sex . . .[42]

In 1993, however (partially as a result of changes in the membership of the Court), the majority of the court again displayed hostility to treating "sex plus" discrimination as sex discrimination. In *Bray v. Alexandria Women's Health Clinic* the Court held that interfering with rights of women seeking abortions did not constitute discrimination against women as a class.[43] That decision, however, was not made under Title VII, but under an older antidiscrimination statute,[44] which sexual harassment plaintiffs invoke only occasionally. It is thus debatable to what extent *Bray* is relevant to the majority of sexual harassment cases that reach the federal courts, which are litigated under Title VII.

Notwithstanding this hostility of the Supreme Court and some commentators,[45] the idea that discrimination on the basis of a "sex plus" criterion constitutes sex discrimination has earned considerable respectability and cannot be dismissed lightly. When the idea is applied to sexual harassment, it becomes obvious that the fact that a typical harasser does not harass all people of a particular sex within a workplace does not count against treating sexual harassment as a form of sex discrimination, as long as the harasser harasses only people of one sex and never those of the other (as is almost always the case).

The Pregnancy Discrimination Act, however, still pays respect to the need for comparison with relevantly similar men for a finding of sex discrimination to be justified. It purports to solve the problem created by the emptiness of the class of pregnant men by simply stipulating that the comparisons should be made between women disabled by pregnancy and men similarly disabled by other causes. Looked at on its own, in isolation from the overall purpose of the act, this solution can easily appear ad hoc, because it simply declares, by legislative *fiat*, that the obvious differences between pregnancy and other forms of disability are irrelevant. There is no argument that would be compelling on its own for specifying the class for comparison in the way in which the Pregnancy Discrimination Act does. Therefore, if one regards, as many people do, the provisions of the Act as, on the whole, justified, that must be because of one's general commitment to regarding discrimination based on "sex plus" criteria as sex discrimination.

Given that the idea that "sex plus" discrimination constitutes sex discrimination has achieved such wide acceptance in thinking about issues other than sexual harassment, one cannot succeed in making any specific argument against the sexual harassment law by entering into the debate about the idea.[46] I shall henceforth assume, for the sake of argument, that the idea is unproblematic, and that whatever might be problematic about treating sexual harassment as discrimination, it is not due simply to the fact that it involves a "sex plus" criterion.

A Digression on the *Huebschen* Case

In connection with the discussion of "sex plus" discrimination in the preceding section, it may be worthwhile to note that the courts deciding sexual harassment cases do not always seem to appreciate all the implications of the idea that "sex plus" discrimination constitutes sex discrimination and of its centrality to the sexual harassment law. In *Huebschen v. Department of Health and Social Services,*[47] a case involving harassment of a man by his female supervisor, the Seventh Circuit stated

> Rader [the alleged harasser] did indeed react spitefully towards Huebschen. . . . But Rader's motivation in doing so was not that Huebschen was male, but that he was a former lover who had jilted her. Furthermore, we note that there is no evidence that Rader discriminated against other men in the office or that she attempted to have romances with other men in the office.
>
> Thus the proper classification, if there was one at all, was the group of persons with whom Rader had or sought to have a romantic affair. It was this group, of which Huebschen may have been the only one, that Rader sought to disadvantage.[48]

The court seemed unaware that this reasoning, taken at face value, amounted to a repudiation of the doctrine that discrimination based on a "sex plus" criterion constituted sex discrimination and was thus at odds with the very foundation of the sexual harassment law. Given that Rader was a heterosexual, Huebschen's maleness, although not sufficient, was a necessary condition of his membership in "the group of persons with whom Rader had or sought to have a romantic affair," and the treatment that he was exposed to was thus partially based on his sex. The facts appealed to in the above quotation were perfectly analogous to those of a multitude of successful sexual harassment suits, in which it was also true that the victim belonged to the group of persons with whom the harasser "had or sought to have a romantic affair." If the court's argument that discrimination against those with whom one "had or sought to have a romantic affair" is not sex discrimination were taken literally and applied consistently, the whole structure of the sexual harassment law would begin to unravel.

Predictably, the decision in *Huebschen* has been invoked by defendants in a number of later sexual harassment cases, causing the courts that had to deal with their arguments a great deal of embarrassment. When the Seventh Circuit itself faced such an argument it "distinguished" *Huebschen* by claiming that it applied only to cases in which "a consensual romance disintegrated."[49] That maneuver is, however, manifestly at odds with the above quoted language of *Huebschen* which clearly covers not only the treatment of those with whom that alleged harasser had an affair but also of those with whom the alleged harasser "sought to have a romantic affair."

In a later case in which the defendant invoked *Huebschen* in arguing that the conduct at issue was not sex discrimination, *King v. Board of Regents of the University of Wisconsin System,* the Seventh Circuit dismissed the argument in the following way:

> [The alleged harasser] claims that King [the alleged victim] was not a member of a protected class since she was simply a member of the class of people whom [he] desired to have an affair with. But King was and remains a woman. That is all that is required.[50]

It is difficult to comprehend how that was supposed to distinguish *Huebschen,* given that it can be equally truly said that Huebschen "was and remains" a man. As the dissenting judge in *King* has remarked

> The only way *Huebschen* would not apply is if we were to say that classification of the target of a romantic affair applies only to men and not to women.[51]

A few months later, the judge who wrote that dissenting opinion sat on an otherwise different panel of the Circuit, which determined that *Huebschen* did apply to a case involving a female victim.[52] The panel argued that its decision was not inconsistent with the line of cases in which sexual harassment was held to be discrimination on the basis of sex, but its argument is less than clear. At the crucial point in the argument, the court elucidated the notion of discrimination the basis of sex by quoting "had [the female plaintiff] been male, she would not have suffered as she did"[53] and then, without explanation, proceeded as if that was not true in the case in front of it, while it manifestly was.

One other court attempted to sweep the difficulty created by *Huebschen* under the carpet by claiming that its language was "not a model of clarity."[54] That was not really true: the language, as anyone who looks at the above quotation from the case can see, was quite clear and clearly inconsistent with regarding "sex plus" discrimination as a species of sex discrimination.

The Bisexual Objection

In this section I begin to outline what I regard as conclusive objections against treating sexual harassment as a form of sex discrimination.

What I shall call "the bisexual objection," in its original form, invites us to consider a possible case of a bisexual who directs a certain kind of sexual conduct to both males and females, with the same intensity, frequency, and so on. Let us suppose that the conduct is such that we would all agree that, if directed to individuals of one sex, it would constitute sexual harassment.

The problem posed by this case is that the argument for subsuming sexual harassment under the notion of sex discrimination, outlined above, simply does not apply to it. The bisexual from the example *ex hypothesi* does not discriminate between males and females in any sense of the word "discriminate": he treats them both in the same way. If the bisexual does not discriminate, then it seems that there is no discrimination that we can impute to the bisexual's employer. And if there is no discrimination to be imputed to the employer, then it follows that Title VII and similar antidiscrimination laws simply cannot get a foothold in the case.

That is a problem because it entails that one's entitlement to a legal remedy for the losses caused by the harassment depends on whether some other people have also been harassed. That implication is profoundly counterintuitive. If we really think that the suffering and losses caused by a particular kind of harassment are serious enough to warrant legal remedy when caused by someone who subjects only people of one sex to such conduct, then it seems utterly bizarre that we should think that the very same suffering and losses would not deserve the remedy if they were caused by someone who subjects the people of the other sex to it too. If Petra and Paula have been subjected to similar suffering and losses through similar forms of treatment, then it seems manifestly unfair that Petra should receive a legal remedy while Paula should not, on the sole ground that Paula's harasser has also harassed Paul, while Petra's harasser has not harassed anyone else. When a harasser who has been harassing a female starts harassing a male as well, we intuitively think that the mischief committed has doubled; thinking of sexual harassment as discrimination entails not only that it hasn't increased at all, but, perversely, that the harasser's harassing a male somehow annuls the harm that has been done to the female. It is this absurd consequence of thinking about sexual harassment as discrimination that the bisexual objection seeks to expose.

The bisexual objection has been sketched already in *Corne v. Bausch and Lomb, Inc.*,[55] and it has been made particularly forcefully in the dissent from denial of hearing *en banc* at the Court of Appeals level in *Vinson v. Taylor*:

> Perhaps some of the doctrinal difficulty in this area is due to the awkwardness of classifying sexual advances as "discrimination." Harassment is reprehensible, but Title VII was passed to outlaw discriminatory behavior and not simply behavior of which we strongly disapprove. The artificiality of the approach we have taken appears from the decisions in this circuit. It is "discrimination" if a man makes unwanted sexual overtures to a woman, a woman to a man, a man to another man, a woman to another woman. But this court has twice stated that Title VII does *not* prohibit sexual harassment by a "bisexual supervisor [because] the insistence upon sexual favors would . . . apply to male and female employees alike." *Barnes v. Costle.* 561 F.2d at 990 n. 55; *Bundy v. Jackson*, 641 F.2d at 942 n. 7. Thus, this court holds that only the differentiating libido runs afoul of Title VII, and bisexual harassment, however blatant and however offensive and disturbing, is legally permissible. Had Congress been aiming at sexual harassment, it seems unlikely that a woman would be protected from unwelcome heterosexual or lesbian advances, but left unprotected when a bisexual attacks. That bizarre result suggests that Congress was not thinking of individual harassment at all but of discrimination in conditions of employment because of gender.[56]

These opinions were critical of subsuming sexual harassment under the notion of discrimination and used the bisexual objection to make their point. The strategy of the courts and the commentators which support treating sexual harassment as discrimination, in dealing with the bisexual objection, has mostly been to acknowledge the implications that the objection outlines (i.e., that equal harassment of males and females by a bisexual harasser would not be actionable under laws that prohibit discrimination on the basis of sex) and to then simply pretend that these implications do not cause any theoretical problems.[57] Insofar as there is any attempt to actually respond to the objection, it usually consists simply in pointing out that such cases involving bisexual harassers are unlikely to actually occur.[58] It is then suggested that the issue of what would be the proper way of dealing with such cases, if and when they occur, is of no relevance for dealing with the typical cases of sexual harassment.[59]

Dismissing the bisexual objection by pointing out that the kind of case it invokes rarely occurs shows a misunderstanding of the character of the objection.[60] Unusual cases can often illuminate our thinking about the principles that inform our approach to the more usual ones. Indeed, unusual cases can sometimes provide insights into the underlying principles that typical cases cannot. This is true of the scenario presented by the bisexual objection.[61]

Those who support the law about sexual harassment as it is, advocate a certain pattern of thinking about the phenomena that the law covers. In order to show that a *pattern* of thinking is defective, it is enough to show that it *can* lead to obviously absurd results. Once an example, even if only hypothetical, has been provided in which a pattern of thinking leads to obviously absurd results, the pattern cannot be relied on any more. This is what the bisexual objection shows with respect to the pattern of thinking that treats sexual harassment as discrimination. When a pattern of thinking has been shown to be unreliable, we should stop relying on it even in those cases in which the results are not obviously absurd. An unreliable pattern of thinking cannot provide a sound foundation for anything.

If classifying sexual harassment as discrimination adequately captured our intuitions on what is wrong with it, then we would not perceive as absurd the claim that harassment by the bisexual harasser is not wrong in the same way. We would not have the intuition that the harassment by the bisexual harasser is wrong in exactly the same way and for the same reasons as otherwise similar harassment by the more common heterosexual and homosexual harassers. But we in fact do have that intuition, and it is rather strong. (This point is not affected by the disagreements that people may have about what acts that are currently classified as sexual harassment are really wrong, because practically everyone *agrees* that *whatever* is wrong when done by heterosexual and homosexual harassers is wrong in the same way when done by bisexual harassers.) Intuitions are of course not conclusive in such matters, but a rather powerful argument would be needed to override such an intuition. Such an argument has not been produced by the supporters of the present sexual harassment law. In the absence of such an argument, the bisexual objection entitles one to conclude that classifying sexual harassment as discrimination fails to capture the nature of its wrongness.

The bisexual objection also cannot be refuted by observing, as one court did in an apparent attempt to refute it, that "[i]t would be exceedingly perverse if a male worker could buy his supervisors and his company immunity from Title VII liability by taking care to harass sexually an occasional male worker, though his preferred targets were female."[62] The bisexual objection, stated precisely, invites us to consider a case in which the relevant conduct is directed to men with the *same* frequency, intensity, and so on, as it is to women, and not a bisexual who harasses men only occasionally and whose "preferred targets" are female. Moreover, the point of the bisexual objection is precisely that classifying sexual harassment as sex discrimination has a logical consequence that *is* perverse, and that this shows that the classification is problematic.

The positive lesson that can be learned from the bisexual objection is that sexual harassment is a noncomparative wrong. Discrimination, on the other hand, is an essentially comparative wrong. In order to be able to say that someone has been discriminated against, I need to show that his position is worse than that of someone else. What the bisexual objection brings out is that wrongness of sexual harassment does not involve such comparisons.

In spite of the considerable force that the bisexual objection has in the form that has been outlined above, I am afraid that many people will still misguidedly continue to dismiss it on the irrelevant ground that there aren't many bisexual harassers around. I am therefore going to end this section by offering a new objection to treating sexual harassment as discrimination, which does the same job as the bisexual objection, by means of a realistic scenario that does not involve bisexuals.

Let us recall that the sexual harassment law typically imposes liability for harassment on employers. Now, among the employees of almost any employer there will be some who typically direct sexual advances and similar conduct to males (heterosexual women and homosexual men) and some who typically direct such conduct to females (heterosexual men and homosexual women). In virtue of that, it can be said that every employer is, metaphorically speaking, bisexual.

Now let us imagine (and this scenario is not at all fanciful) that one employee (say a heterosexual male) of a particular employer engages in conduct that would otherwise be harassing toward females, and another employee (say a heterosexual female) engages in similar conduct with similar frequency, intensity, and so on, toward males. Both of them, unlike the bisexual harasser, discriminate on the basis of sex, but the crucial question for the antidiscrimination law is whether the *employer* is discriminating by allowing such conduct to go on, and to that question the answer must be "no." The discrimination carried out by each of the two, so to speak, cancels out the discrimination carried out by the other. Therefore, when the conduct of both is imputed to their employer, there doesn't seem to be any discrimination that the employer can be accused of. The employer can say, with perfect truthfulness, that its male and female employees are treated the same: they get subjected to the sexual conduct in question with the same frequency, intensity, and so on. When males and females are treated the same, it seems clear that there is no ground for any accusations of sex discrimination. If the wrongness of sexual harassment consisted in its being a form of sex discrimination by employers, then we would have to agree that in such a case no wrong has been committed. But we all have the intuition that the mischief done by the harassment of females is added to, rather than canceled out by, the harassment of males.

Thus, this realistic scenario, just like the scenario in the original bisexual objection, shows that treating sexual harassment as discrimination does not capture our intuitions on what is wrong with it.

A Possible Response to the Bisexual Objection

In the 1994 case of *Steiner v. Showboat Operating Co.*[63] the Ninth Circuit made remarks that may be read by some as a persuasive response to the bisexual objection. That case dealt with deliberate insults of a sexual nature, rather than sexual advances, and it thus did not literally involve a bisexual, but it still exhibited the crucial feature of the scenario invoked by the bisexual objection: the behavior in question was directed to both men and women.

The defendant in the case argued that, because the alleged harasser "consistently abused men and women alike" there could have been no discrimination and thus no violation of Title VII.[64] The court's first response to that argument was that, although he may have been abusive to both men and women, some of the facts suggested "that his abuse of women was different."[65] The second response, which is the one that is of theoretical interest here, was that "even if [he] used sexual epithets equal in intensity and in an equally degrading manner against male employees," there would still be a difference in how these epithets affected their male and female recipients: "words from a man to a man are differently received than words from a man to a woman."[66] This second response has been foreshadowed by Catharine MacKinnon's remark that "[a]rguably, a sexual requirement placed on both a man and a woman would not have the same impact upon each."[67]

The move that the court is making here is of the same nature as the moves that have already been made elsewhere in the area of antidiscrimination law. It is effectively a move from what is known as "disparate treatment" theory of discrimination to "disparate impact" theory. The latter theory, unlike the former, claims that there is discrimination whenever certain ways of treating people have different impact on the sexes (or races, ethnic groups, and so on), even if these ways of treating them are in every other respect exactly the same. Within the court's opinion, that move toward the "disparate impact" theory of discrimination is supposed to work together with the court's endorsement of certain psychological theories (which also motivated the same court's enunciation of the reasonable woman standard in *Ellison v. Brady*),[68] according to which sexual conduct may affect women differently than the analogous conduct affects men.

Although the court made these remarks in the context of a specific case, they can be readily generalized and applied to the scenario that is invoked in the original bisexual objection, as well as to the scenario from my modification of the bisexual objection. Thus it can be said that even when males and females in a workplace receive exactly the same sexual advances (either from one and the same bisexual, as in the original objection, or from different people, as in my modification), there is still discrimination going on in that such conduct may be more disturbing to the females than to the males.

Do the court's remarks thus constitute an answer to the bisexual objection? The remarks could certainly be attacked on two general grounds: one can challenge the appropriateness of the "disparate impact" theory of discrimination for this type of a case and/or the soundness of the psychological theory about the differences in male and female responses.[69] I shall, however, not pursue these challenges here, because I believe that even if they are waived, these remarks of the court do not significantly affect the bisexual objection.

If we accept the "disparate impact" approach to discrimination and the psychological theories referred to above, then, in order to cast the same kind of doubt on classifying sexual harassment as discrimination, as is cast by the objections of the preceding section, we only need to change them slightly. In the preceding section, we imagined that sexual advances that were the same in kind, frequency, intensity, and so on were directed at both males and females. Now we need to imagine that males and females receive the advances that are different in these respects, but with the differences so gauged that the impact of these advances is the same for both sexes. Surely if certain advances are more likely to offend women than men, then there must be some other advances (perhaps somewhat gentler, less persistent, and so on) that would have the same expected offensiveness for women as the advances of the first kind have for men. Those who accept the reasoning of the *Steiner* court are committed to the conclusion that in *that* case there would be no discrimination, and the laws that make all other kinds of sexual harassment actionable should not make that particular kind of harassment actionable. That conclusion seems as absurd as what we considered in the preceding section, and its absurdity thus provides as strong an argument against treating sexual harassment as discrimination as the ones we considered in that section.

Sex Discrimination and Sexuality

The bisexual objection shows that, insofar as sexual harassment is wrong, the ground of its wrongness must be something other than sex discrimination. In this section I wish to supplement the bisexual objection by showing that one crucial element of standard cases of discrimination in employment is, in fact, missing in the case of sexual harassment.

Let us consider carefully what is involved in a paradigmatic case of sex discrimination in employment. Suppose that John works for XY Corporation, and that he is often involved in making hiring decisions on behalf of the corporation. Suppose moreover that John systematically turns down female candidates for jobs with the XY Corporation, even when they are, by all usual criteria, clearly the best qualified ones. As a result of John's actions, very few women get hired by the corporation. John obviously discriminates against women. The overwhelming majority of people nowadays would readily agree that such discrimination is seriously wrong (assuming that no special circumstances are present).

Although there is a clear sense in which the discriminatory actions in this example are performed by John and no one but John, there is another equally clear sense in which they are performed by the XY Corporation. This latter sense, of course, plays an important role in the law. The law imputes these actions to the XY Corporation. Given that these actions constitute wrongful discrimination, the law, by imputing them to the corporation, imputes wrongful discrimination to it. If John's actions did not constitute wrongful discrimination, if they were fair, unbiased, based on the merits of the applicants, the law could still impute them to the corporation, but it would then not be imputing wrongful discrimination to it.

The important thing to note in this paradigmatic case of discrimination in employment is that the wrongness of discrimination is there, so to speak, before the law imputes it to the corporation. In other words, the wrongness is there even if we look at the actions simply as John's actions. When the law imputes these actions to the corporation, it imputes to it something that is wrong independently of the imputation. It is most definitely not the case that the wrongness somehow gets generated in the process of imputing the actions to the corporation.

Let us now compare all this with what goes on in a typical case of sexual harassment. Suppose that Jim makes sexual advances that turn out to be offensive to some of his coworkers at the XY Corporation. Because Jim is a heterosexual, all of the coworkers to whom he addresses the advances are female; he never addresses such advances to males. It can thus be said that Jim, just like John, discriminates on the basis of sex. As in the previous example, the law imputes Jim's actions to the XY Corporation. Given that these actions involve discrimination on the basis of sex, what the law imputes to the corporation is discrimination on the basis of sex.

So far the two cases appear to be parallel. But in John's case we noted not merely that his action was an instance of sex discrimination, but also that it was clearly an instance of *wrongful* sex discrimination. In order for the parallel to be complete, the discrimination in Jim's case would also have to be wrongful. Is it?

Although people often speak as if discrimination on the basis of sex were always wrongful, no one really believes that all instances of such discrimination are wrongful. One clear, often used, example of sex discrimination that is not wrongful is discrimination in favor of male actors in deciding who is to play a male role in a play.

Another obvious example is selection of one's sexual and romantic partners. When looking for such partners heterosexuals discriminate on the basis of sex, in that they tend to select people of the opposite sex, but no one thinks that such discrimination is wrongful. A rapidly increasing number of people also do not think that there is anything wrong with homosexuals selecting sexual and romantic partners of their own sex. Even those who are classified as bisexual are usually not "perfect" bisexuals: they are often dominantly heterosexual or dominantly homosexual, and thus also, to a certain extent, discriminate on the basis of sex in selecting their sexual and romantic partners. No matter how firmly one may be committed to eradication of all forms of wrongful sex discrimination, one is unlikely to seriously think that we are all under obligation to become perfect bisexuals.

The idea that discrimination on the basis of sex in selecting one's sexual and romantic partners is not at all wrongful is certainly a matter of common sense. The Supreme Court gave support to that commonsense idea when, in a decision that gave the state the power to apply antidiscrimination statutes to a wide range of different forms of association, it suggested that the power still does not extend to "intimate association."[70]

The discrimination that people accused of sexual harassment engage in often amounts to nothing more than their being heterosexual or homosexual. As one court has put it, in case of heterosexual harassment:

> The harassment complained of was based upon sex. . . . it is clear that [the alleged harasser] was attracted to plaintiff, and that the motivation for his conduct was his interest as a male in plaintiff as a female[71]

or as another court has put it, in a case of homosexual harassment

> since the evidence established the [alleged harasser's] homosexual proclivities, the harassment to which plaintiff complained was based upon sex.[72]

Why did Jim address his sexual advances, that turned out to be offensive, only to females and never to males? The answer is: because Jim is a heterosexual. Jim directed these problematic advances to females simply because Jim always addresses all his sexual advances to females. He is not sexually interested in males. Insofar as there is, in the terminology of *Williams,* a discriminatory "policy or practice" in Jim's conduct, it is simply the discriminatory "policy or practice" of being a heterosexual.[73] Given that the discrimination inherent in being a heterosexual, as everyone seems to agree, is not wrongful, the discrimination that Jim engaged in was not wrongful, and the same will apply to many other sexual harassment cases.[74]

There is a danger of committing a fallacy in thinking about cases such as Jim's that one should guard against. Showing that an act is an act of discrimination and that it is wrongful does not entail that it is an act of wrongful discrimination. It may well be that the wrongfulness of such an act "resides" in its aspects that are independent of its being an act of discrimination: in that case it would be incorrect to say that the act is an act of wrongful discrimination. Only when the wrongfulness of an act is due to its being an act of discrimination can it be characterized as an act of wrongful discrimination.

Jim's acts may well have been wrongful for various reasons. For example, it may be that Jim was careless as to whether his sexual advances would cause offense. But that feature of his actions is independent of their being acts of discrimination. What makes them discriminatory, namely that Jim prefers to address his sexual advances to females rather than males is, on practically everyone's view on these matters, not wrongful, and it therefore does not contribute to making his actions wrongful. Thus, although Jim's actions may well have been both wrongful and discriminatory, it is still true that they were not acts of wrongful discrimination.

If these actions do not constitute wrongful discrimination when viewed as Jim's actions, then it is not at all clear how they could suddenly come to constitute wrongful discrimination when they are attributed to the XY Corporation. It would seem to be sheer miracle if the wrongfulness of discrimination were to somehow come into being in the process of shifting from looking at the actions as Jim's to looking at them as the corporation's. There is, in fact, no good reason to believe in such miracles. Therefore, there is no good reason to believe that the XY Corporation has committed any wrongful sex discrimination in this case. Nor is there any reason to believe that the employers have committed any wrongful discrimination in thousands of real-life cases that have the same structure as Jim's. A law that treats such cases as instances of sex discrimination on the part of the employer, as the sexual harassment law does, is therefore significantly misguided. In other words, although an employer may rightly be subject to legal sanctions for various failings of its employees, it should not be subject to legal sanctions for the fact that its employees are not bisexual, because not being a bisexual is not a failing.

This argument applies to a great deal of what goes on in the actual operation of the sexual harassment law. It applies to all sexual harassment cases that involve what I have called bona fide sexual advances. No matter how insensitive, gross, vulgar, such advances are, they are not instances of wrongful discrimination because the thing that makes them discriminatory is the heterosexuality or homosexuality of those who make them. The argument also applies to quid pro quo harassment. Such harassment is, everyone will agree, very seriously wrong, but what makes it wrong is that those who engage in it pursue their sexual pleasure through this particular mechanism rather than through, say, ordinary courtship. What makes it wrong is most definitely not that they seek to obtain such pleasure from parties of one sex rather than both, that is, that they discriminate on the basis of sex. The discriminatory aspects of quid pro quo harassment, again, boil down to the heterosexuality or homosexuality of those who engage in it; the aspects that make it wrongful are independent of these discriminatory aspects.

It needs to be acknowledged, however, that the argument of this section does not apply to all of the conduct that is classified as sexual harassment. In particular, it does not apply to many of the deliberate insults of a sexual nature. If, for example, someone directs such insults to females and not to males simply because he dislikes the presence of women in the workplace, and perhaps because he hopes that a persistent campaign of such insults will drive them away, then it seems relatively uncontroversial that he is engaged in wrongful sex discrimination. His case is thus unlike Jim's case and can be readily assimilated to cases like John's. If it is agreed that such deliberate insults constitute wrongful discrimination when viewed as actions of the individual in question, then it is, as in John's case, unproblematic that they can also be regarded as wrongful discrimination when imputed to the individual's employer. But although there are indeed cases of sexual harassment that can thus be assimilated to the paradigmatic instances of sex discrimination in employment, very many cases of it cannot be so assimilated, for reasons outlined in this section. The argument of this section therefore constitutes a powerful objection against the present law.

A Mirror Image of Sexual Harassment

It is in the nature of the notion of discrimination that it does not apply only to active imposition of adverse treatment (such as firing or demotion): simple withholding of benefits (such as promotions or a payrises) can also constitute discrimination. An employer that reduces the salaries of female employees by $1,000, while the salaries of male employees, just because they are male, remain unchanged, clearly discriminates against women, but so does an employer which grants a $1,000 payrise to all of its male employees, just because they are male, while keeping the salaries of its female employees unchanged. These two salary arrangements are, so to speak, mirror images of each other, and it is a feature of the notion of discrimination that, if it applies to something, then it must also apply to such a mirror image of it. This is yet another consequence of the conceptual truth that the wrong of discrimination is a comparative wrong.

This means that, if the creation of "intimidating, hostile, or offensive working environment" for members of one sex, by sexual conduct, is regarded as discrimination, then consistency requires that a failure to create congenial, friendly, or enjoyable working environment, under analogous circumstances, also be regarded as discrimination.

Now imagine that at a particular workplace there is a man who frequently addresses various kinds of flirtations, erotic banter, and sexually charged compliments to his female colleagues, but, because he is heterosexual, never directs such conduct to his male colleagues. Imagine, moreover, that, as is perfectly possible, the women at that particular workplace happen to enjoy this kind of attention. When they go to work, they look forward to these exchanges. Although their interaction with this man may not go beyond flirtations, it makes them feel good about themselves that their sexuality is recognized in that way. They find that, when the demands of their work get particularly stressful, these small sexual pleasantries help them to feel like human beings rather than robots, and thus help them to cope with the pressure. It all makes the workplace feel less cold and impersonal to these women than it would have felt otherwise.

For the purposes of this argument it does not matter how likely this scenario is, nor does it matter why precisely these women would react to this conduct in the way described. It is enough that the scenario is perfectly possible.

It is reasonable to say that, in the scenario described, that man's conduct of a sexual nature makes the women's working environment congenial, friendly, and enjoyable. The man, however, never does anything to make the working environment of the other men working there equally congenial, friendly, or enjoyable. He is perfectly polite to the other men, and does not treat them at all badly; it's just that, being a heterosexual, he doesn't have the slightest inclination to enhance their working environment in the way in which he has, as it happens, enhanced the working environment of his female colleagues.

This scenario is a mirror image of sexual harassment. If one believes that sexual harassment is a form of sex discrimination, and consequently wrong, then one is committed to also believing that the conduct of the man in this example is sex discrimination and consequently wrong. The other men in the example, just because they are male, do not get the benefit of a congenial, friendly, enjoyable working environment that the women get. But for their sex, they would have received the benefit. If the fact that the working environment of one sex is worse than the working environment of the other sex constitutes the reason for regarding sexual harassment as a form of sex discrimination, then it follows that this example is also an instance of sex discrimination, because in it too is the working environment of one sex worse than the working environment of the other sex.

I, of course, expect that most of my readers will find this implication absurd. It is hard to take seriously the idea that the conduct described in this example is sex discrimination. But, if that is so, then this example is a *reductio ad absurdum* of the claim that sexual harassment is a form of sex discrimination. In other words, if one believes that this example is not an instance of sex discrimination, then one cannot consistently believe that sexual harassment is a form of sex discrimination. This example and hostile environment sexual harassment are mirror images of each other and are consequently on a par so far as discrimination is concerned.

One may be tempted to respond to this argument by claiming that the flirtations and pleasantries featured in the example are a purely private matter, and thus have nothing to do with the *working* environment of the women and men in question. This claim has some plausibility, but it does not refute the argument, because it is not any *more* plausible than the claim that sexual harassment is a purely private matter, and not a part of the victim's working environment. One may also try to refute the argument by pointing out that, although the women in the example have had a favorable reaction to the conduct, other women would not have had the same reaction to it. This observation is true, but it does not refute the argument, because it is simply a mirror image of the truth that, in a typical case of sexual harassment, the conduct that offends the victim would not have offended everybody else of the same sex. The observation is thus perfectly compatible with the claim that the example given above is a mirror image of hostile environment sexual harassment, and thus on a par with it so far as discrimination is concerned.

Another possible response to the argument of this section is that the man's conduct cannot be sex discrimination because he is of the same sex as the putative victims. That response has considerable plausibility, but is incompatible with the fact that the law about sexual harassment now treats same-sex harassment as a form of sex discrimination.

Finally, some people may be tempted to respond to the argument of this section by arguing that sexual harassment is wrong while the conduct described in the example is not, on the ground that there is a morally significant difference between subjecting someone to a treatment that is inherently bad, which is what happens in sexual harassment, and merely failing to benefit someone. But if one makes an argumentative move that thus hinges on the *inherent* wrongness of sexual harassment (i.e., on its being wrong independently of how other people are treated), one effectively concedes that sexual harassment is not a comparative wrong. This, in turn, entails that the wrongness of sexual harassment is not captured by classifying it as a form of discrimination.

SAME-SEX HARASSMENT

The preceding sections provide conclusive arguments against the legal doctrine that subsumes sexual harassment under the notion of sex discrimination. Although, from a theoretical viewpoint, no further arguments against the doctrine are necessary, in the remainder of this chapter I still want to boost the case against the doctrine by pointing out how it creates awkwardness in the actual application of the law.

Earlier in the chapter we noted how, in order to subsume the sexual harassment under the notion of sex discrimination, courts had to accept the idea that discrimination on the basis of a "sex plus" criterion constitutes sex discrimination. In the context of sexual harassment opinions, the idea is usually expressed by the courts' saying that, in order to prove that the conduct in question was discriminatory, it only needs to be proven that *but for the alleged victim's sex,* the alleged victim wouldn't have been exposed to the conduct.[75] We also noted in the discussion that this condition is usually easy to satisfy: the simple fact that the alleged harasser is a heterosexual or a homosexual (i.e., anything but a perfect bisexual) is often enough.

A consequence of having such a weak condition for what counts as discrimination is that it can easily be satisfied by the conduct of an alleged harasser who is of the same sex as the alleged victim. Thus, for example, if a male homosexual directs to a male coworker certain sexual advances that turn out to be offensive, it seems true that the second man, *but for his sex* wouldn't have been exposed to such conduct. The courts' acceptance of the but-for-one's-sex criterion of sex discrimination thus commits them to saying that the second man has been discriminated against on the basis of sex.

There are also cases of the same-sex harassment involving conduct other than bona fide sexual advances to which the same reasoning applies. Men sometimes subject to teasing, ridicule and insults of a sexual nature other men whom they perceive as shy, sexually inexperienced, excessively sensitive, or as otherwise not living up to their standards of masculinity. In such cases it is again true that *but for their sex*, the victims of such conduct wouldn't have been subjected to it: they are subjected to it because they are *men* who are perceived as effeminate.[76] Such cases thus also seem to satisfy the condition of discrimination that the courts routinely use in sexual harassment cases and the courts thus appear to be committed to treating them as instances of discrimination on the basis of sex.

On the other hand, however, in practically all other cases of wrongful discrimination, members of one group are discriminated against by members of the other group. Thus, when women are discriminated against, the acts of discrimination are normally carried out by men. There is something inherently odd about regarding same-sex harassment as sex discrimination, given that it consists precisely in acts directed at people of the same sex as those carrying them out.[77]

The courts that are forced to deal with the claims of same-sex harassment thus find themselves in a dilemma which has no easy solution. One option for them is to be faithful to the but-for-one's-sex criterion of discrimination and accept such claims as actionable under antidiscrimination laws, at the cost of the awkwardness inherent in saying that it is possible to discriminate against members of one's own group. The other horn of the dilemma is to avoid that awkwardness by deciding that the conduct at issue in such cases does not amount to sex discrimination, and is thus not prohibited by antidiscrimination laws. This other option, however, comes at the considerable price of creating an awkward clash with the but-for-one's-sex criterion of discrimination.

Until the Supreme Court addressed the issue in 1998, the courts that dealt with such cases were divided. Some took the first option and consequently held that same-sex harassment constituted discrimination on the basis of sex.[78] EEOC has also declared that "[t]he victim does not have to be of the opposite sex from the harasser,"[79] and the lower-level regulations have often explicitly included same-sex harassment within their scope.

Other courts, however, took the position that "same-gender sexual harassment does not and cannot occur, *as a matter of law,* 'because of' the victim's 'sex' " and that it was therefore not covered by the sexual harassment law.[80] In taking such a position, and on that ground rejecting the claim of the male plaintiff, the court in the first and best known of these cases explicitly acknowledged that there was a tension between its decision and the existing body of law, by remarking that

> A wooden application of the verbal formulations created by the courts would salvage [the plaintiff's] sexual-harassment claim. The court, however, chooses instead to adopt a reading of Title VII consistent with the underlying concerns of Congress. . . .[81]

The confidence of this court that it had the accurate insight into "the underlying concerns of Congress" is, however, rather problematic in view of the fact that, as Supreme Court has observed, "we are left with little legislative history to guide us in interpreting the Act's prohibition against discrimination based on 'sex.' "[82]

The split of opinion on same-sex harassment was such that one could even find opposed holdings on the issue within the very same federal district.[83]

There were also cases in which courts expressed the opinion that same-sex harassment could in principle be actionable as sex discrimination, while at the same time suggesting that the threshold that harassing conduct had to cross in order to be actionable was much higher in the same-sex cases than in the more common ones.[84] Some cases made the distinction between same-sex harassment that was homosexual in nature and "sexual teasing"[85] or sexual "locker room antics, joking, or horseplay"[86] between heterosexuals. Two 1996 cases,[87] taken together, thus made it the law within the Fourth Circuit that homosexual harassment was actionable as a form of sexual harassment, while sexual abuse between heterosexuals (or presumed[88] heterosexuals) of the same sex was not, and some district courts elsewhere have pointed in the same direction.[89] While such decisions may, at first sight, appear to provide a sound compromise between the more extreme positions outlined above, they are in fact doubly awkward. Insofar as they allow that same-sex harassment may constitute sex discrimination, they suffer from the awkwardness that it is inherent in saying that it is possible to discriminate against members of one's own group; insofar as they exclude some of it from the coverage of the law, they are at odds with the but-for-one's-sex criterion of discrimination.[90] When people are exposed to sexual teasing and horseplay by others of the same sex, it is typically true that but for their sex they wouldn't have been exposed to it.

From the viewpoint of potential litigants and legal practitioners, all these differences of opinion lost their significance in 1998 when the Supreme Court in *Oncale v. Sundowner Offshore Services, Inc.* held that same-sex sexual harassment is actionable under Title VII.[91] The opinion makes it clear that this includes both homosexual harassment and rough conduct of a sexual nature between heterosexuals of the same sex. From the viewpoint of a theoretician, the history of disagreements about same-sex harassment that was summarized above, however, retains its significance because it points to a problem that is at the very core of the sexual harassment law. These disagreements were due to the fact that every possible way of dealing with such cases generates some kind of theoretical awkwardness, and that is yet another symptom of the underlying awkwardness of placing sexual harassment law under the umbrella of antidiscrimination law.

It needs to be understood that the decision in *Oncale* does not really do anything to remove that awkwardness. The decision does resolve the split that existed between the lower courts, but it does so largely by *fiat*, rather than by producing some powerful argument that would really resolve the conceptual tensions that caused the split. In deciding *Oncale*, the Court had an excellent opportunity to do what it had failed to do in *Meritor* and *Harris*, namely to try to articulate "the doctrinal basis for classifying sexual harassment as sex discrimination."[92] The Court, however, did not really take up that opportunity; instead it simply, in a relatively short opinion, *declared* same-sex harassment to be actionable under Title VII.

To be sure, the Court did state within the *Oncale* opinion that same-sex harassment, just like any other sexual harassment, is actionable under Title VII only insofar as it is discrimination on the basis of sex, and that point got special emphasis in Justice Thomas's one-sentence concurring opinion. Such brief hints that sexual harassment is supposed to be *somehow* related to sex discrimination, however, fall short of a genuine discussion of "the doctrinal basis for classifying sexual harassment as sex discrimination." The reason why the Supreme Court did not really develop in much detail the doctrinal basis for this classification is, I suspect, that it simply cannot be done successfully, because of the insurmountable problems discussed in this chapter.

At the end of this section, it may be worthwhile to note that among the various ways in which the lower courts responded to claims of same-sex harassment before *Oncale*, there exists one which *Oncale* does not seem to affect. Some courts have dealt with claims of what may have appeared to be same-sex sexual harassment by classifying them as claims of harassment on the basis of sexual preference rather than of sexual harassment.[93] Once a claim is classified that way, the issue of whether same-sex harassment is actionable becomes irrelevant, and the plaintiff is bound to lose, because it is generally agreed that Title VII does not cover discrimination on the basis of sexual preference such as homosexuality.[94] These classifications are, however, problematic: in one of the cases, for example, the court has itself said that the plaintiff was harassed because he was a homosexual *male*,[95] which appears to entail that the harassment was, after all, based on sex as well as on sexual preference.[96]

Exasperated by the problematic results of same-sex sexual harassment cases, one author, whose overall view of sexual harassment is very different from mine, has concluded that "[c]ourts should recognize that Title VII encompasses two types of sex discrimination—traditional discrimination and sexual harassment."[97] It is difficult to see how the meaning of these words could amount to anything different from "sexual harassment is not really a form of discrimination, and the courts should not treat it as such, but they should nevertheless keep saying that it is."

SEXUAL FAVORITISM

Suppose a person in a supervisory position enters into a sexual relationship with a subordinate and then chooses, because of that relationship, to grant the subordinate some competitive employment benefit, say a promotion, in spite of the existence of other candidates who are, in fact, better qualified for it. Should those who are passed over have available some kind of a legal remedy?

Most people's immediate response to this question is an unqualified "yes." Most people also intuitively perceive the wrong that needs to be rectified here as closely related to the wrongs committed in the cases that are classified as cases of sexual harassment.[98] Treating sexual harassment as a form of discrimination, however, makes it difficult to deal with such cases of sexual favoritism in a straightforward way.

Let us focus first on the candidates who were passed over as a result of such favoritism and who are of the opposite sex from the person who received the benefit. Suppose, for example, that a male heterosexual in a supervisory position grants a promotion to a female he is sexually involved with, although there are better qualified male candidates. This is certainly a very bad thing, but if the matter is to be dealt with within the antidiscrimination law, its being bad is not enough: it needs to be determined whether there was some discrimination in the case. Were the male candidates discriminated against on the basis of sex?

Here we need to remember that in the very act of subsuming sexual harassment under the notion of sex discrimination, the courts have accepted the idea that discrimination on the basis of a "sex plus" criterion constitutes sex discrimination. Discrimination on the basis of a "sex plus" criterion, we should recall, is discrimination in which being of a particular sex is a necessary but not a sufficient condition for unfavorable treatment. What we have in the present example is in fact a mirror image of "sex plus" discrimination. In this example, being of a particular sex (male) is a sufficient, but not a necessary condition for relatively unfavorable treatment (being passed over for the promotion). It is sufficient because, given that the discriminating supervisor is *ex hypothesi* a heterosexual male, males have no chance whatsoever to obtain his favors. On the other hand, it is not necessary, because not all females can obtain these favors either. Another way of making the same point is to say that in such cases being of a particular sex (in this example female) is a necessary but not a sufficient condition for obtaining *favorable* treatment: the supervisor gives favorable treatment to those candidates who are of a particular sex, plus have some additional features, such as being sexually compliant and found attractive by the supervisor. That is different from the standard cases of sexual harassment in which sex is a necessary but not a sufficient condition for *unfavorable* treatment.

The courts' endorsement of the idea that "sex plus" discrimination of the kind discussed earlier in this chapter constitutes sex discrimination does not logically entail that its mirror image that we find in this example also constitutes sex discrimination. However, the courts' view of "sex plus" discrimination as sex discrimination does create a certain expectation that they will view the conduct of the kind presented in this example as sex discrimination as well. This is so especially if one takes into account that the courts' treatment of "sex plus" discrimination as sex discrimination appears to be motivated by the more basic idea that sex discrimination exists whenever "gender is a factor contributing to the discrimination in a substantial way,"[99] or, in other words, whenever "sex is for no legitimate reason a substantial factor in the discrimination."[100] (It is also that more basic idea that appears to be codified by the provision of the Civil Rights Act of 1991 that "an unlawful employment practice is established when the complaining party demonstrates that . . . sex . . . was a motivating factor for any employment practice, even though other factors also motivated the practice"[101] That provision was, however, enacted after most of the cases I am discussing in this section had been decided.)

In the example at hand it can also be said that "gender is a factor contributing to the discrimination in a substantial way." The promotion went to the particular person because of her sexual involvement with the supervisor, and a significant part of the reason why they were involved was that she was female: had she not been female, the supervisor wouldn't have been involved with her, and thus wouldn't have given her the promotion.

In spite of this, when the Second Circuit, in *DeCintio v. Westchester County Medical Center*, faced an actual case that had the same structure as this hypothetical, it concluded that no sex discrimination had taken place:

> Appellees were not prejudiced because of their status as males; rather, they were discriminated against because [the supervisor] preferred his paramour.[102]

This ignores the important fact that the person promoted wouldn't have been the supervisor's paramour had she not been female. In other words, it is the appellees' being male that disqualified them from becoming the supervisor's paramours, and thus from obtaining the promotion in the same way.

The court goes on to say that acceptance of the appellees' claim would constitute "a distortion of the meaning of the word 'sex' in the context of Title VII,"[103] without providing any discussion of why that would be any more of a distortion than what is involved in subsuming "sex plus" discrimination under the notion of sex discrimination. While discrimination on the basis of criteria that make being of a particular sex a necessary but not sufficient condition for favorable treatment is certainly not the same thing as discrimination on the basis of criteria that make it a necessary but not sufficient condition for unfavorable treatment, the two seem to be, at first sight, equally close to (or equally remote from) the notion of sex discrimination. An argument is needed to show that one is, contrary to the appearances, closer to it than the other, and no such argument has been provided.

The matter is different when one looks at the candidates who were passed over and who are of the same sex as the person who received the benefit because of such favoritism. Thus, keeping all the facts of the example we have been considering exactly the same, let us now focus on the female candidates who were passed over, in spite of being better qualified than the woman who received the benefit. Have they been discriminated against on the basis of their sex? Here the intuitively plausible answer seems "no." It is true that these females lost the benefit as a result of an unjust decision, but the person who gained the benefit is also female, so it seems clear that although the decision was unfair, the females as a group did not lose anything as a result of it.[104] The decision did not result in any fewer females being promoted than would have been the case otherwise.

There are, however, actual cases in which this question was raised and in which the courts managed to reach the conclusion that is exactly the opposite of what seems intuitively plausible. They found that although the person who gained the benefit as a result of favoritism and the person who lost were of the same sex, female, the wrong that was committed in these cases was the wrong of sex discrimination. That unexpected result was reached through an ingenious argument made in *Toscano v. Nimmo*.[105] The crucial trick in that argument is not to treat the promotion itself as the unfairly distributed benefit, but to rather focus on the *condition*, implied by the conduct of the supervisors in such cases, that one provide sexual favors in order to be promoted. Although some women may win promotions by complying with this condition and some may not (because they refuse to comply with it), the argument claims that the condition itself is a burden imposed on both groups of women. It is the imposition of that condition, rather than the denial of promotion itself, that constitutes the relevant unfavorable treatment in such cases, according to the argument. When we focus on the imposition of the condition rather than promotions themselves, we see, the argument claims, that these cases involve sex discrimination, because the condition is imposed on women and not on men.

This argumentative maneuver certainly deserves admiration for its ingenuity, but is it really convincing? There are two responses that can be made to it.

The first is to question the assumption that the argument makes: that the imposition of this condition always constitutes unfavorable treatment. The imposition of the condition is certainly something unfavorable for those women who lose promotions as a result of it, but it is far from obvious that it is something unfavorable for the women who, as a result of it, win promotions they wouldn't have otherwise won. The latter women, it could be argued, gain from the imposition of the condition, and it thus, for them, constitutes favorable treatment. This reasoning brings us back to the original intuitive argument that there is no discrimination in such cases, because those who win and those who lose belong to the same group, and the group as a whole thus does not lose.

The second response to the *Toscano* argument is that it is simply not true that the condition in question is not imposed on men. When a supervisor gives out promotions in exchange for sexual favors, his conduct is more plausibly interpreted as imposing on *all* potential candidates the condition that sexual favors, satisfactory to the supervisor, be provided. The position of male candidates relative to that condition is not that it is not imposed on them, but rather that it *is* imposed on them and that they don't have the slightest chance of satisfying it. Far from the position of men being, as the *Toscano* argument claims, better than the position of women, it is, in fact, worse, because they have less chance than women of satisfying the condition imposed. So we are again brought back to the intuitively plausible point that in such cases women are not discriminated against: if anyone is discriminated against on the basis of sex, it's the male candidates. (In this discussion I am assuming, for the sake of an example, that the supervisor is a heterosexual male, as was the case in *Toscano,* but structurally identical arguments can be made for the cases of homosexual and/or female supervisors.)

In order to avoid a possible misunderstanding, let me emphasize that by making the above objections to the *Toscano* argument, I do not wish to minimize the injustice that is in such cases done to the candidates of the same sex as the person receiving the benefit. Quite the contrary: I do think that the injustice is serious and that precisely out of respect for its seriousness we ought to be clear about its nature. That nature is obscured by trying to squeeze such cases into the sex discrimination mold, as the *Toscano* argument does. The injustice suffered by the female plaintiff in *Toscano* simply did not consist in her having been treated worse than men, but in her having been treated worse than another *woman,* who got the promotion through favoritism.

In *King v. Palmer*[106] the facts were structurally similar to those of *Toscano,* and the district court also held that such facts can amount to sex discrimination.[107] The court then proceeded to find for the defendants on other grounds, but that decision was reversed on appeal. Unfortunately, the specific issues raised on appeal did not give the court of appeals the opportunity to enter into an extended discussion of the fundamental issue of whether such facts can amount to sex discrimination in the first place: both parties agreed that they can, and the court of appeals only summarily endorsed the district court's opinion on that issue.[108] The reasoning of the kind first exemplified in *Toscano* also played a role in a number of other cases at the district court level.[109]

If the way in which the courts dealt with the cases we have considered so far in this section appear messy, the matter gets even messier when one considers *Miller v. Aluminum Company of America.*[110] In that case the person who allegedly received an employment benefit because of a sexual relationship with a supervisor was of the same sex, female, as the plaintiff, who claimed to have suffered a loss as a result. One would thus expect that the court would either follow the *Toscano* reasoning, or that it would reject such reasoning on the basis of some arguments of the kind that has been outlined above. The court, however, did neither, but instead decided to follow *DeCintio,* without commenting on the fact that the case in front of it involved a plaintiff of the same sex as the beneficiary of favoritism, while *DeCintio* involved plaintiffs of the opposite sex from the beneficiary.

These problems with the judicial treatment of sexual favoritism are not confined to the federal level. Within the caselaw of New York one can thus find both a decision that endorses the *Toscano* argument[111] and a *DeCintio*-like decision.[112]

As in the preceding section, my exposing the problems in the way the courts have been dealing with cases of this kind is not an end in itself. Rather I have been discussing the infelicities in these cases, because I believe that they are manifestations of the underlying awkwardness of dealing with sexual harassment as a form of sex discrimination.

Similar infelicities to the ones we have seen in these cases appear in the EEOC Policy Guidance on Employer Liability under Title VII for Sexual Favoritism.[113] The position of the EEOC stated in that document is that whether an instance of sexual favoritism can be legally redressed depends on whether it is isolated or a part of a widespread pattern, and also on whether the sexual relationship that motivated the unfair employment decision was coerced or uncoerced. Thus if the relationship was uncoerced and favoritism isolated, the injustice committed cannot be set right by the law. According to the EEOC legal remedy is available only in cases where favoritism is widespread or where the sexual relationship that motivated the decision involved an element of coercion.

These distinctions strike one as utterly bizarre. If I am the person who, in fact, deserves a certain promotion, and my boss instead gives it to someone he is sexually involved with, then I have suffered an injustice, and the seriousness of *that* injustice is in no way affected by whether my boss's relationship with the other person was coerced or not. To be sure, if the relationship was coerced, then a wrong has also been committed to the person coerced, but that wrong seems to be completely independent from the wrong that was done to me. Similarly, if there is a widespread pattern of favoritism and other people thus suffer similar injustices, then the matter is worse in that more injustices have been committed, but it is again not clear that these injustices in any way affect the particular injustice that was done to me.

Not only does the EEOC Policy Guidance put the boundaries between what is redressable and what is not, at odd places, but even in the cases in which it provides for a legal remedy, it does so for what seem to be wrong reasons. Thus the EEOC's granting of the availability of legal remedy in the cases in which favoritism is widespread is based on its subsuming such cases under the notion of hostile environment harassment. This means that according to the EEOC, when many people at a workplace are denied employment benefits because the benefits go to the supervisors' paramours, it is strictly speaking not the fact that they are denied these benefits that provides the cause of action, but rather the overall workplace *atmosphere* that is created by their being denied the benefits. A consequence of treating the atmosphere as the cause of action is that the people who actually lost specific benefits and the people who were merely discomfited by witnessing someone else's loss of benefits are on a par with respect to the Policy Guidance.

What is implicit in EEOC's granting the possibility of remedy for favoritism when the sexual relationship that led to it involved coercion is again that the unfair loss of benefits is not itself the cause of action. Rather the wrong that is suffered by those who lost a specific benefit because of sexual favoritism is, in these cases, viewed by the EEOC as merely a by-product of the wrong of discriminatorily applied coercion that was inflicted on the person who benefited from favoritism. The EEOC's position thus insists on treating the person who gained a benefit because of favoritism as the primary victim in such cases, and the people who lost the benefit as a result as merely secondary victims. In order to obtain legal relief, the people who lost the benefit thus have to prove that the person who obtained it was coerced into the sexual relationship, which can put them in a rather peculiar position, because that person may not always be willing to cooperate (either because there was, in fact, no coercion, or because the person is more interested in preserving the benefits obtained than in exposing the coercion). In other words, in order to establish their status as secondary victims they need to cast as the primary victim a person who may not be keen to be so cast.[114] An example of bizarre litigation strategies to which this view of sexual favoritism leads can be seen in

Ayers v. American Telephone & Telegraph Co., in which an alleged victim of favoritism claimed that a romantic relationship that eventuated in a marriage was, in fact, coercive.[115]

The EEOC Policy Guidance is a shaky compromise between the moral intuition, which most people have, that those who lose employment benefits because of sexual favoritism deserve a legal remedy, and the doctrinal commitment to dealing with sexual harassment and related problems within antidiscrimination law. If that commitment were given up, the need for odd distinctions and tortuous argumentative maneuvers that we have seen in the way the courts and the EEOC have been dealing with sexual favoritism would disappear.

Discrimination and Stereotypes

I believe that I have by now established that there are serious problems with the legal doctrine that subsumes sexual harassment under the notion of sex discrimination. However, before we fully accept the conclusion that sexual harassment should not be viewed as a form of sex discrimination, there is one more question that needs to be addressed. Someone may accept all the arguments that I have so far made in this chapter and still keep wondering whether there might not perhaps be some *other* way, different from the one that courts actually use, of subsuming sexual harassment under the notion of sex discrimination, that would be immune to these arguments. Perhaps, one may think, there is some entirely different approach to the topic that could still rescue the idea that sexual harassment is a form of sex discrimination.

This question deserves serious consideration because the nonlegal literature on sexual harassment does subsume sexual harassment under the notion of sex discrimination in a way that is different from the one that is operative within the law and that has been discussed in the rest of this chapter. This alternative approach, which is generally pursued outside the law, involves arguing that acts of sexual harassment constitute discrimination because they contribute to a *pattern* of relationships between the sexes in the society as a whole, which pattern discriminates against women. The authors of one empirical study of sexual harassment thus, for example, say that "[s]exual harassment of a woman by a man . . . harms women as a gender group through the reinforcement of a secondary status in a patriarchal culture."[116]

Both ways of subsuming sexual harassment under the notion of sex discrimination have their roots in Catharine MacKinnon's well-known 1979 book on sexual harassment. The way of doing so that ended up forming the core of the caselaw on sexual harassment is what MacKinnon calls the differences approach, while the way of doing it that was embraced in the nonlegal literature corresponds to what she calls the inequality approach. Although she does indicate her special sympathy for the inequality approach,[117] she develops both approaches at considerable length, without, as has already been observed,[118] ever making it really clear how the two approaches are supposed to fit together. One can't help having an impression that MacKinnon included both approaches in her discussion not because they are both parts of a well-structured, unified theory, but rather because of her wishing to play, at the same time, both the role of an influential legal scholar and the role of the leader of a wide political movement: the differences approach had some chance of influencing the courts and thus fitted the former role, while the inequality approach had the rhetorical power suitable for mobilizing wide support for the cause, and thus fitted the latter role. Neither approach would have been suitable for the task of the other: the presuppositions of the inequality approach are too controversial to be taken seriously by any but the most adventurous judges,[119] while the differences approach would have fallen flat as a call for political action.

It should be noted that, according to the reasoning prevalent in the nonlegal literature, the discriminatory character of a particular instance of sexual harassment cannot be appreciated if the case is considered on its own. Rather, what makes a particular case of sexual harassment discriminatory, according to this reasoning, is the way it fits into a larger pattern of social interactions. This is very different from the standard legal argument discussed in the rest of this chapter, which says simply that sexual harassment is discriminatory because in every particular case of it, people of only one sex are exposed to the conduct in question. Most of the authors of the nonlegal literature which is informed by the reasoning outlined here, however, appear to be unaware that their approach to the discriminatory character of sexual harassment is different from the one that is embodied in the law.

Occasionally, this alternative approach to the discriminatory character of sexual harassment does appear in legal literature. One author (who is clearly aware of the differences between these two approaches), for example, argues in a law review that the courts dealing with sexual harassment cases ought to jettison the but-for-one's-sex criterion of discrimination and replace it "with a test which asks whether the victim endured harassment that perpetuated gender stereotypes in the workplace."[120] That would lead them to impose "Title VII liability for harassment that reinforces gender differences and women's subordinate position in society."[121] This amounts to proposing that the courts abandon the theory about the discriminatory character of sexual harassment that is at the heart of the established caselaw and replace it with an account of its discriminatory character of the kind that may currently be found in the nonlegal literature on the topic.

If the sexual harassment law were to be changed in accordance with such a proposal, then many of the arguments developed in this chapter would cease to apply to it. But would a sexual harassment law structured in accordance with this proposal be justifiable, all things considered? I believe that, although such a law would avoid some of the problems that beset the current one, it would still suffer from serious problems that would make it unjustifiable. Here are some of the problems.

First, in order to apply the proposed test to specific cases, the courts would need to determine what the "gender stereotypes" are, which presumably means that they would have to determine which of the widely held views about the differences between men and women are undesirable. That, however, is a highly controversial issue, on which well-informed and thoughtful people differ. Some feminists, for example, believe that there are no significant differences between men and women, that all the differences, other than the obvious anatomical ones, that may be observed between them are superficial, and that any belief to the contrary is a pernicious stereotype. Other feminists, however, believe that there are fundamental differences between the ways in which men and women learn, think, form concepts, and, in general, approach the world around them, and that these differences need to be more widely understood and appreciated. The feminists of the latter kind do not think that their views on the differences between men and women are stereotypes that ought to be eradicated; rather, they think that these views ought to be accepted by everyone. Both kinds of positions have been defended in good faith. Both sides have *prima facie* respectable scientific evidence to support their respective positions. (Needless to say, each of these two kinds of positions has numerous variations, and they are far from exhausting the full spectrum of views that can be, and are, held on the issue.)

If the courts adopted "a test which asks whether the victim endured harassment that perpetuated gender stereotypes in the workplace," they would have to arbitrate between such controversial positions.

Making it incumbent upon courts to do so seems as unwise as it would be to expect them to arbitrate between different religious views.

Second, even if it were somehow agreed what the relevant "gender stereotypes" are, there would remain enormous difficulties with establishing the causal nexus between specific acts of alleged sexual harassment and the stereotypes.[122] Whether the specific acts that are at issue in a particular case, in fact, perpetuate the stereotypes would often turn out to hinge on highly controversial theories. If the acts consist in utterances that explicate the stereotypes (e.g., if what is at issue is someone's saying, in so many words, that women are incapable of being competent police officers), then the causal connection would, perhaps, not be too controversial, but in few cases of what is currently regarded as sexual harassment would the matter be that straightforward.

Some feminists would, for example, argue that complimenting a woman on her physical appearance implies that the principal role of women in the society is to be the source of erotic delight to men, which in turn implies that women's contributions to the industry, arts, professions, and so on, are of limited importance, and thus promotes a stereotype that "reinforces gender differences and women's subordinate position in society." Others would, however, argue that such compliments in no way devalue women's other contributions to the life of the society, or their capacity for such contributions, and that they consequently have nothing to do with any pernicious stereotypes about women. Each side to such an issue can appeal to a well-developed body of theory to support its position. *Mutatis mutandis*, the same can be said of many kinds of sexual jokes and sexual advances.

In view of the controversial character of such issues it is likely that a factfinder's determination whether the specific conduct in question in a particular legal case, in fact, "perpetuated gender stereotypes in the workplace" would largely depend on the idiosyncrasies of the particular factfinder. The overall result of the operation of the sexual harassment law formulated in terms of stereotypes would thus be haphazard and unpredictable.

The above quoted author of the proposal that is under discussion here is unaware of these problems, because she appears to assume that all factfinders would share her specific views on what perpetuates gender stereotypes.[123] That assumption is unfounded because these views are highly controversial.

This brings us to the third and the most fundamental problem with this proposal. Suppose, for the sake of argument, that we all come to agree with some set of feminist views, such as the one assumed by the author of this proposal, according to which most of the conduct that is currently regarded as sexual harassment in fact does contribute to maintaining "gender stereotypes," and thus "reinforces gender differences," and that this is what makes such conduct undesirable. If one believes that these assumptions provide good reasons for legal control of sexual harassment, then one is committed to believing that all conduct that, according to the same set of feminist views, contributes to maintaining "gender stereotypes" and "reinforces gender differences" ought to be legally controlled. That, however, includes a great deal of conduct that no one would want to see legally controlled, including a great deal of conduct that is engaged in by women themselves. A woman whose appearance makes it obvious that she puts a great deal of effort into being erotically appealing, or who declares in a conversation that the only really important thing in her life is being a good mother to her children, contributes to maintaining the "gender stereotypes" at least as much as a man who occasionally tells sexual jokes. If it is plausible to say that a man who openly reads a pornographic magazine during the coffee break thereby "perpetuates gender stereotypes," then it is also plausible to say that a woman who openly reads a magazine devoted to housekeeping topics during the coffee break thereby "perpetuates gender stereotypes." It is incoherent to argue that sexual harassment ought to be legally controlled because it "perpetuates gender stereotypes," if one is not prepared to argue that all the conduct that perpetuates them ought to be legally controlled. My guess is that no one would be prepared to seriously argue that women should be legally prohibited from reading housekeeping magazines.

It will not do to respond to this last point by claiming that women have been "socialized" to behave in the ways outlined in the preceding paragraph, and that they should not be penalized for having been so "socialized." If that argument were accepted, then the same maneuver would be available to men engaging in the conduct now regarded as sexual harassment: they too could equally plausibly claim that they have been "socialized" to behave in such ways.

It should be noted that much of the conduct that, according to the relevant feminist views, "perpetuates gender stereotypes" takes place outside workplaces, educational institutions, or any similar framework. We thus encounter the problem that is analogous to the ones that have been discussed in chapter 1. If one seriously believes that the reason for legal control of sexual harassment is that such conduct "perpetuates gender stereotypes," then one is committed to also believing that all conduct that "perpetuates gender stereotypes" *prima facie* ought to be legally controlled, regardless of whether it occurs within workplaces, educational institutions, and so forth, or not. Whether such conduct occurs within or outside such institutions is irrelevant to its undesirability, especially in view of the fact that the consequences of such conduct may well appear within employment, education, and so on, even if the conduct itself took place outside them. If the line of reasoning that we are considering were followed consistently, it would thus lead one to support a law that would prohibit the conduct that "perpetuates gender stereotypes" regardless of where it occurs. Such a law would be something very different from the sexual harassment law, and it would involve such drastic curtailment of individual liberties that few people would think it justifiable. It would, for example, have to prohibit women from reading housekeeping magazines not only at their workplaces, but also at any other place where they can be seen by others.

Finally, if the wrongness of sexual harassment is understood in terms of the contribution of such conduct to discriminatory stereotypes, then it becomes unclear why the principal legal remedy for it should consist in the award of damages to the individuals directly exposed to the conduct. It is in the nature of stereotypes that the effects of their perpetuation are diffuse. If some conduct is wrong because and insofar as it "perpetuates gender stereotypes," then we should think of all those who are adversely affected by the stereotypes thus perpetuated as the victims of the conduct. We should *not* think of the person to whom the conduct was directed as the only or even primary victim.[124] Thus, if we took seriously the account of sexual harassment in terms of "gender stereotypes," we would not regard the person to whom the conduct was directed as more deserving of compensation than numerous other people who may later be adversely affected by "gender stereotypes" as perpetuated by the conduct.

This view of sexual harassment would be wildly at odds with how most people think about such conduct. When a person has lost a job through quid pro quo harassment or suffered through being exposed to some vicious insults of a sexual nature, most people think that this is bad *in itself,* and not because of some *further* consequences that it might have, such as perpetuation of "gender stereotypes." We think of such a person as *the* victim of the conduct in question and not merely as one member of some large, diffuse class of its victims.

Arguing that sexual harassment is a form of sex discrimination insofar as it contributes to discriminatory stereotypes therefore cannot provide a justification for any kind of law about sexual harassment.[125]

8
Alternatives

The Argument So Far and the Remaining Question

The arguments of the preceding chapters prove that the law about sexual harassment is morally unjustified. Many of these arguments were directed at the essential features of the law, at the features in virtue of which it is the law about sexual harassment, and not about something else. These arguments thus show that the law's being unjustified is not merely a result of some minor mistake that could be easily remedied; they show that the law is beyond repair.

Chapter 7 shows that the subsumption of sexual harassment under the prohibition of discrimination on the basis of sex, which is at the core of the law, is unwarranted. Various alternative justifications of prohibiting sexual harassment that may at first appear to have some plausibility have been considered and rejected in chapter 1. Chapter 5 shows that the law is at odds with the principle of freedom of speech. Chapters 2 and 3 show that the law amounts to a morally unjustified prohibition of all conduct of a sexual nature within workplaces. Chapter 6 shows that, even if the content of the law were significantly changed (say, along the lines suggested in chapter 4), its two-level structure would still result in a morally problematic restriction of individual liberties, as well as in worrisome erosion of the constraints that have, in liberal societies, traditionally governed the relationship between the state and its citizens.

It is impossible to create a law that would avoid all of these problems at the same time, and still, in some recognizable way, *be* sexual harassment law. The conclusion is thus inevitable that the law about sexual harassment ought not to exist.

Much of the conduct that the law about sexual harassment law prohibits is, however, morally wrong, according to any reasonable moral outlook. Some of it is quite seriously wrong, and certainly ought to be illegal. Showing that the law about sexual harassment ought not to exist, therefore, raises the question of what would be the morally justified legal treatments of such conduct. This chapter will briefly sketch an answer to that question.

Once we give up the idea (refuted in chapter 7) that sexual harassment is a species of sex discrimination, there is no reason to think that the sexual harassment that is wrong is all wrong for the same reason.[1] There is thus no reason to think that the kinds of sexually harassing conduct that ought to be illegal should all fit within the same legal category. Giving different kinds of such acts different legal treatment may better reflect the nature of their wrongness than squeezing them all within the same area of the law.[2]

QUID PRO QUO HARASSMENT

The first step in thinking about possible alternatives to sexual harassment law is to sever quid pro quo harassment from the hostile environment harassment so that they can be dealt with separately. These two kinds of conduct are very different, and once we give up the idea that sexual harassment is a species of discrimination, there is no good reason to keep them within the same legal category.

Almost everybody would agree that quid pro quo harassment is fairly seriously wrong. It is, however, a wrong that typically has at least two victims: the person who is subjected to the harassment and the employer. A supervisor who engages in quid pro quo harassment uses the employer's resources for his own private benefit and to the detriment of the employer.[3] For example, if the supervisor dispenses promotions so as to penalize sexual noncompliance or reward sexual compliance, then he is not dispensing them in the way that best advances the employer's business. The person promoted will not be the one who will contribute the most to the productivity of the business. The supervisor's willingness to dispense promotions in that way may also give to all subordinates who come to learn about it an incentive to behave in ways that do not contribute to the productivity of the business. A supervisor's engaging in quid pro quo harassment is thus, in its impact on the employer, on a par with stealing the employer's property.

Because employers are likely to be adversely affected by the conduct currently classified as quid pro quo harassment, they have always had good reasons to strongly discipline supervisors who engage in it, independently of what the law may say about such acts. They had such reasons well before the sexual harassment law came into being, and would continue to have them if the law disappeared. There is thus no reason to fear that such acts would become rampant if they were not illegal. The employers would continue to keep them in check for reasons of their own.

The argument just made, however, needs to be qualified. It is based on the assumption that the disruptions caused by investigating complaints of such misconduct and disciplining those who engage in it affect the productivity *less* than it would to allow the misconduct to continue. This assumption is probably warranted in general, but there are some worrisome exceptions to it. What if, one may ask, the person engaging in quid pro quo harassment is somebody who is extraordinarily valuable to the employer, while the person subjected to it is somebody who is doing some relatively low-level, routine work? In such a case, the employer's overall productivity may be only negligibly affected by the harassment. On the other hand, an attempt to discipline the extraordinarily valuable employee may be quite detrimental to the productivity. In such special cases, the incentives that the employer would have in the absence of a law regulating the matter can easily lead the employer to ignore the complaints of harassment. While it is in such cases still true that the harasser is doing something that is on a par with stealing from the employer, the employer may choose to ignore it, just as it may choose not to scrutinize dubious charges that an extraordinarily valuable employee may be putting on the expense account. Obtaining sexual favors through quid pro quo harassment may thus turn into something like a perquisite of the valuable employee's position, and that would surely be morally wrong. A similar problem may arise when the individual harasser literally *is* the employer.[4]

The existence of such cases makes it desirable to provide legal recourse for victims of quid pro quo harassment. Providing such recourse under the umbrella of antidiscrimination law is, however, awkward, for the reasons presented in the preceding chapter. The area of the law that is much better suited to capturing the wrongness of quid pro quo harassment is the law of contracts. When one accepts a job, one agrees to do whatever the job involves, but one most definitely does not agree to provide sexual favors to supervisors. An employer that tolerates quid pro quo harassment effectively imposes on the employee duties that go beyond those that have been agreed upon. It is true that in many cases, the duties that one contracts to perform when one takes a job are quite vague, especially when there is no written employment contract, but no matter how vague they are, it will be clear in all but the most unusual cases that they do not include providing sexual favors to supervisors. It can thus be argued, with considerable plausibility, that practically every employment contract (including merely oral ones) implies that the employee shall not be subjected to quid pro quo harassment. That entails that an employer that tolerates such harassment is in breach of the employment contract.

Most employees in the United States are, however, employed "at will," which means that their employment is not contractually guaranteed to go on for any particular length of time: the employment relationship can be broken at any point. The employer could thus respond to the above argument by claiming that a quid pro quo threat should be treated as a termination of the original employment contract, which termination is legal at any time if the employment was at will. This would imply that the supervisor's carrying out the threat is not a breach of the original contract, because that contract is not in force any more. Changing an employment contract in this way can, however, easily be characterized as acting in bad faith, and there already exists a body of law that imposes on employers the obligation to act in good faith in exercising the privileges of employment at will.

In fact, a couple of years before the emergence of the sexual harassment law, the Supreme Court of New Hampshire, in *Monge v. Beebe Rubber Company*,[5] endorsed an argument that treated (what we now call) quid pro quo harassment as a breach of contract, notwithstanding that the victim was employed at will. The *Monge* case was not very influential (probably because of the appearance of the sexual harassment law), but if the sexual harassment law went out of existence, such contracts-based arguments could be developed further, and chances are that they would be widely accepted. The body of law that would be developed around such arguments would provide the victims of quid pro quo harassment with needed legal protection, without the doctrinal awkwardness of dealing with such conduct within the antidiscrimination law.

There are several noteworthy differences between this contracts-based line of argument about quid pro quo harassment and the way in which it is treated within antidiscrimination law. First, the sexual character of the conduct in question is not central to the contracts-based argument. Analogous arguments could be made about the cases in which a supervisor exacts nonsexual favors (that are similarly removed from the operation of the employer's business and solely aimed at the supervisor's private benefit) from a subordinate, by threatening to withdraw some employment-related benefit. That is a salutary feature of this approach, as the moral wrongness of at least some nonsexual cases is indeed comparable to the wrongness of the sexual cases, and there is no good reason for the legal system to treat them differently. Second, the line of reasoning outlined above is available not only to the victims of quid pro quo harassment, but also, and with the same degree of plausibility, to those who are not directly exposed to it, but who still miss out on some competitive employment benefit because the supervisor has chosen to grant it to his (willing) "paramour." In the preceding chapter we have seen that it is one of the weaknesses of the sexual harassment law that it cannot deal with such cases of sexual favoritism in the same way in which it deals with quid pro quo harassment. The contracts-based approach to quid pro quo harassment also fits the intuition that each instance of such harassment is wrong independently of how other people are treated, unlike the approach embodied in the antidiscrimination law, according to which the most salient feature of such conduct is that its victims are treated worse than employees of the opposite sex. In other words, the contracts-based approach fits the intuition that quid pro quo harassment is a noncomparative wrong, unlike the wrong of discrimination, which is essentially comparative.

Once we accept the idea that what is wrong with quid pro quo harassment is that it is at odds with what the employee has agreed to in accepting the job, it may also be possible to advocate, in some cases, the legal approach that treats the harassing supervisor as tortiously interfering with the contractual relationship between the employer and the employee. Unlike the preceding approach which involves suing the employer, this one involves suing the harasser as an individual. Like the preceding approach, this one is available to victims of sexual favoritism as well as quid pro quo harassment, it does not treat the sexual character of the conduct as essential, and it captures the noncomparative character of the wrong.

A different ground for regarding quid pro quo harassment as illegal, even if there were no sexual harassment law, has been outlined in the 1984 Eighth Circuit decision *Lucas v. Brown & Root, Inc.*[6] According to that decision, an employee's fulfillment of a supervisor's quid pro quo sexual request would effectively amount to prostitution. This implies that, by rejecting such a request, the employee is simply refusing to do what the law forbids. As people should not be penalized by their employers for refusing to do what the law forbids, the court concluded that an employee who was fired for rejecting her supervisor's sexual request has a legally actionable claim against the employer, one that is independent of the antidiscrimination law. This approach to quid pro quo harassment, however, has a somewhat more limited appeal than the ones considered above, as it cannot be wholeheartedly embraced by those who are, for independent reasons, fighting for the legalization of prostitution.

If the sexual harassment law went out of existence, there would thus still be sufficient ways to combat quid pro quo harassment, and these alternative ways would capture the wrongness of such conduct better than the sexual harassment law does.

HOSTILE ENVIRONMENT HARASSMENT IN THE CRIMINAL LAW AND THE LAW OF TORTS

The next step in thinking about the alternatives to sexual harassment law is to observe that some of the acts that are currently classified as sexual harassment also fit the legal definitions of assault, battery, and even rape (or of their more recent variants, such as sexual assault). This probably includes the most egregious instances of sexual harassment. If the sexual harassment law disappeared completely, these acts would still remain clearly illegal. They constitute crimes, and can be prosecuted as such. Their victims can also sue the perpetrators under the traditional law of torts. Certain cases of severe hostile environment harassment can also (like quid pro quo harassment) be handled as cases of tortious interference with the contractual relationship between the employer and the employee.

Furthermore, some sexual harassment fits the criteria for the tort of intentional infliction of emotional distress, and can be handled as such. Handling these cases in such a way, again, captures the nature of their wrongness far better than the law about sexual harassment does. Inflicting significant emotional distress on a person is a very bad thing independently of whether similar distress is also inflicted on people of the opposite sex. Treating such cases as torts recognizes this noncomparative nature of the wrong. Furthermore, when such cases are treated as torts of intentional infliction of emotional distress, the sexual character of the conduct is relevant only insofar as it contributes to the distress: it is not a defining feature of this tort that the conduct in question is sexual. Treating the sexual nature of the conduct as of only limited significance is, again, salutary, as it fits the moral intuition that inflicting emotional distress is something wrong independently of the means by which it is inflicted. The most salient feature of such cases is that distress *has been* inflicted, not *how* it has been inflicted.

In fact, the attorneys for plaintiffs in sexual harassment cases nowadays occasionally, as a matter of litigation strategy, add claims of intentional infliction of emotional distress to the claims of sexual harassment under the antidiscrimination law. In such cases, it often happens that the claims of sexual harassment succeed, while the claims of intentional infliction of emotional distress, based on the same conduct, do not.[7] The threshold that the conduct needs to cross in order to be legally classified as intentional infliction of emotional distress is much higher than the threshold that it needs to cross in order to constitute sexual harassment. The threshold for the tort typically requires that the conduct be "extreme and outrageous," and that the distress caused by it be severe. Much of the conduct that constitutes sexual harassment in virtue of creating an offensive working environment is not extreme and outrageous, and consequently does not constitute the tort. Moreover, the tort is partially defined in terms of the mental states of the tortfeasor: the emotional distress, in general, needs to be inflicted intentionally or recklessly in order to constitute the tort. Such matters are, on the other hand, almost completely irrelevant in the sexual harassment law. Thus, while the tort of intentional infliction of emotional distress captures very well the wrongness of some cases of sexual harassment, it does not come anywhere near covering all of the hostile environment sexual harassment.

Finally, there are cases of sexual harassment that can be argued to constitute the tort of intrusion, which is one of species of tortious invasion of privacy.[8] The legal category of intrusion has traditionally been defined in terms of physical intrusion at a place of seclusion, and in that traditional form could not be straightforwardly applied to sexual harassment, given that workplaces are almost never places of seclusion. There is nevertheless caselaw on intrusion according to which "[o]ne's emotional sanctum is certainly due the same expectations of privacy as one's physical environment,"[9] and which thus extends the tort to the acts that intrude into one's private affairs, even if these acts take place in a public physical location. So extended, the notion of intrusion can be applied to at least some of the conduct that one finds in the cases of sexual harassment, and in fact has been so applied.[10]

Treating sexual harassment as intrusion, again, captures well the noncomparative character of the wrong, and thus avoids the problems of the current law that were discussed in chapter 7. Moreover, because the tort of intrusion is not defined in terms of the sexual character of the conduct, handling sexual harassment as intrusion encourages comparison with nonsexual intrusions, which can help to ensure that sexual harassment is treated neither more nor less severely than comparable nonsexual misconduct. That is in sharp contrast with the current sexual harassment law, which treats sexual harassment as sui generis, and in which such comparisons therefore rarely get made. On the other hand, although handling cases of sexual harassment as intrusions would not treat their sexual character as significant *in itself,* it would not treat it as entirely insignificant either: it would treat it as significant *insofar as* most people are specially keen to preserve the privacy of the manifestations of their sexuality.

The fact that the tort of intrusion is not defined in terms of the sexual character of the conduct means that, to the extent to which that tort covers speech, it covers it in a content-neutral way. The consequence of that is that treating cases of sexual harassment as instances of intrusion would avoid the conflict with the principle of freedom of speech, which was discussed in chapter 5. Restricting speech in a content-neutral way, in order to protect privacy, fits the established First Amendment jurisprudence well.

The standard definition of the tort of intrusion requires that the conduct be "highly offensive to a reasonable person," and that may, at first, seem to reopen some of the problems discussed earlier in this book. There is, however, an important difference between the offensiveness of the intruding character of the conduct in question, which is relevant here, and the offensiveness of its sexual content, which is relevant in the sexual harassment law: there is convergence among people's views about the former that does not exist among their views about the latter. Because of that convergence, the use of the notion of offensiveness in the context of intrusion is not subject to the problems discussed in chapter 2, nor is the use of the notion of reasonableness in this context subject to the problems discussed in chapter 3. The concept of intrusion (like most other legal concepts) admittedly has fuzzy edges, and there is thus room for debate about its precise contours, but it does not suffer from the much deeper demarcation problem from which the concept of sexual harassment suffers.

The concept of intrusion, like the concepts of assault, battery, rape, and intentional infliction of emotional distress, does not differentiate between the conduct that takes place within employment, education, and so forth, and similar conduct that takes place elsewhere. That is a salutary aspect of the concept, as the moral significance of intrusive conduct does not depend on where it takes place. Thinking about such conduct in terms of privacy does, however, explain why many people are specially concerned about harassment at workplaces, in schools, and in other similar settings. When one is at such a place, one does not have at one's disposal certain simple, informal ways of protecting the privacy of one's affairs that are readily available in many other settings: at a workplace or in an educational institution, one generally cannot walk away from the source of intrusion or otherwise ignore it. One's being an employee or a student almost always requires that one be at a particular physical location and that one engage in interaction with other people. Because of that, people's privacy interests are specially vulnerable in such settings.

HOSTILE ENVIRONMENT HARASSMENT AND CONTRACTS

While the legal mechanisms outlined in the preceding section can handle a great deal of the conduct that is currently classified as hostile environment sexual harassment, there still remain quite a few cases of such conduct that are not covered by any of them. Even the concept of intrusion, which can arguably cover a wide range of sexually harassing acts, can, in general, be applied only to the conduct that is *highly* offensive, unlike the concept of sexual harassment, which also encompasses conduct that is less than highly offensive. There thus remain some acts, which are illegal under the sexual harassment law, that would cease to be illegal if the law about sexual harassment went out of existence. We thus now need to examine whether it would be a bad thing if these remaining cases of sexual harassment (the cases that do not fit any of the legal categories outlined above) ceased to be illegal.

Some of these remaining cases are cases of sexual conduct that is worthwhile (in the sense that was elucidated in chapter 4), and whose legalization should, other things being equal, be welcomed. There are, however, also some cases of conduct that is currently classified as sexual harassment that are neither worthwhile in that sense, nor sufficiently severe to fit the legal categories of the preceding section. Examples may be sexual comments that are gross and crude, but not outrageously so. Our question in this section is whether, taking into account both the cases that are worthwhile and the cases that are not, it would be a good or a bad thing if all sexual harassment that does not fit other legal categories ceased to be illegal.

In answering that question, it is important to bear in mind that, if such conduct ceased to be prohibited by law, it would not thereby become immune to all forms of control. First, in most social circles, such conduct has always been regulated by informal social mechanisms: those who discuss sexual topics in crude, vulgar terms, or who make insensitively persistent sexual advances, or who make demeaning comments about the differences between the sexes, have always been subject to informal censure and ostracism and would continue to be subject to such sanctions, even if the law about sexual harassment completely disappeared.[11] Second, it would, in the absence of the law about sexual harassment, still be possible for an employer and its employees to voluntarily enter into a contract that would regulate conduct of a sexual nature within the workplace. In fact, that wouldn't be something entirely new: well before anybody thought of the concept of sexual harassment, many businesses implicitly prohibited a great deal of the conduct that is now so classified by their general rules about employee conduct.

Regulation of sexual conduct within employment by contracts that are created freely, without upper-level pressure, would have significant advantages over its regulation by the sexual harassment law.[12] The crude push toward high restrictiveness that is, as has been shown in chapter 6, generated by the two-level structure of the law, would disappear. As all employees at a particular workplace would be parties to such a contract, the content of the contract would, in the absence of upper-level pressure, have to be the result of balancing all of their relevant interests (in a way similar to what has been outlined in chapter 4). The employees' interest in not being subjected to unwanted sexual conduct would thus be taken into account in the drafting of these contracts, but so would be the interests that are currently ignored: the interest that people have in the opportunities for fulfilling sexual interaction and the interest that they have in being treated fairly if they should be accused of some sexual misconduct.

The removal of the upper-level constraints would also make it possible for each employer to tailor its regulation of sexual conduct to the character of the workplace and to the profile of its employees (or perhaps to the profile of potential employees that it is hoping to attract). At some workplaces, it may be important to maintain a certain kind of decorum and that may give rise to significant restrictions on sexually colored interaction. At other workplaces, it may be more important to make possible free-flowing, spontaneous, unselfconscious communication among the employees; in order to make it possible, the employers and employees at such places may prefer not to have any official rules that would constrain the communication. If the sexual harassment law disappeared, the businesses would probably differ in the extent to which they regulate sexual conduct, just as they now differ in the extent to which they regulate other aspects of their employees' conduct (some businesses, for example require their employees to follow strict, conservative dress codes, others require them to wear uniforms, yet others permit or even encourage casual dressing, and so forth). Such diversity of regulation of sexual conduct among workplaces would probably produce more satisfaction overall than the present "one size fits all" law. If such diversity existed, people would have better opportunities to work under the conditions that they find congenial. For example, those who find the prospect of hearing sexual jokes disturbing would aim their job-seeking efforts at the workplaces where such jokes are prohibited, while those who enjoy exchanging such jokes would be able to look for work at the places where the prohibitions do not exist. Those for whom flirting is a waste of time would be able to seek work at the places where the rules make it unlikely that their time will be wasted by their coworkers' attempts at flirting, while those for whom flirting is one of the things that make life worth living would aim their job-seeking efforts at the places where it is possible to engage in flirting without fear of disciplinary sanctions.

The rules of sexual conduct that would be created without upper-level pressure would also be better integrated into overall regulation of workplace conduct. Currently, the fact that sexual harassment is governed by the law forces employers to give it the significance that overrides the significance of any workplace problem that is not governed by law. It also pushes them to have special sets of rules about sexual conduct rather than apply to sexual conduct some more general rules that govern both sexual and nonsexual conduct. If the law about sexual harassment went out of existence, the decisions about how the problems of sexual conduct are to be dealt with would probably be based on comparing them to other workplace problems. The undesirable sexual conduct would get neither more nor less attention than comparable nonsexual conduct. Many employers would probably also choose to deal with undesirable sexual conduct by applying to it general rules of workplace conduct, rather than have special rules about it. These would all be salutary developments, as they would create the mechanisms of dealing with such conduct that better reflect the nature of its wrongness (insofar as it is wrong).

There are thus good reasons to think that freely created contracts would, on the whole, generate the optimal level of control of sexual harassment that does not fit the legal categories discussed in the preceding two sections.

Notes

1. Sexual Harassment and Other Problems

1. *Williams v. Saxbe,* 413 F. Supp. 654 (D.D.C. 1976), reversed on other grounds *sub nom. Williams v. Bell,* 587 F. 2d 1240 (D.C. Cir. 1978).

2. *Meritor Savings Bank v. Vinson,* 477 U.S. 57 (1986). It has been observed that "[w]hat made this case noteworthy to the high court is somewhat of a mystery" (William L. Woerner and Sharon L. Oswald, "Sexual Harassment in the Workplace: A View through the Eyes of the Courts," 41 *Labor Law Journal* 786, 789 [1990]).

Incidentally, this book uses a format of referencing that is a hybrid between the format that is customary in the humanities and the one customary in legal scholarship. The format should be self-explanatory, except that the readers who are unfamiliar with legal writing need to be alerted to the fact that, in the references to scholarly periodicals, the volume number always precedes the name of the periodical, and that the name of the periodical is followed by the number of the first page of the article in question, which is then, if applicable, followed by the number of the specific page referred to. Thus "41 *Labor Law Journal* 786, 789" is a reference to page 789 in the article that begins on page 786, of volume 41 of *Labor Law Journal.*

3. Jan Crosthwaite and Christine Swanton, "On the Nature of Sexual Harassment," 64. Supp. *Australasian Journal of Philosophy* 91 (1986); Susan M. Dodds et al., "Sexual Harassment," 14 *Social Theory and Practice* 111 (1988); Anita M. Superson, "A Feminist Definition of Sexual Harassment," 24.1 *Journal of Social Philosophy* 46 (1993); Jan Crosthwaite and Graham Priest, "The Definition of Sexual Harassment," 74 *Australasian Journal of Philosophy* 66 (1996); Debra A. DeBruin, "A Critique of Superson's Feminist Definition of Sexual Harassment," 29.1 *Journal of Social Philosophy* 49 (1998); Vrinda Dalmiya, "Why Is Sexual Harassment Wrong?" 30 *Journal of Social Philosophy* 46 (1999).

4. This is what the articles referred to in the preceding footnote have effectively done, in spite of Crosthwaite and Priest's calling their definition of sexual harassment a "real definition" (Crosthwaite and Priest, "The Definition of Sexual Harassment," 66).

5. Dodds et al., "Sexual Harassment," 111–12.

6. This criticism does not apply to Superson and DeBruin, but it does apply to the other philosophers referred to above.

7. Cf. Crosthwaite and Priest, "The Definition of Sexual Harassment," 69–71.

8. Louise F. Fitzgerald, "Sexual Harassment: The Definition and Measurement of a Construct," in *Ivory Power: Sexual Harassment on Campus,* ed. Michele A. Paludi (Albany: State University of New York Press, 1990), 24.

9. That this is so may be acknowledged by the empirical researchers, but in a way that obscures the significance of the acknowledgment: "The data support the view

that working women are increasingly familiar with the term sexual harassment and are willing to use it. However, the multi-faceted approach employed here to examine elements of consciousness about sexual harassment indicates the conditional and *subjective nature of the naming process itself*" (Beth E. Schneider, "Consciousness about Sexual Harassment among Heterosexual and Lesbian Women Workers," 38.4 *Journal of Social Issues* 75, 95 [1982], italics added).

10. See, for example, Richard Wasserstrom, "Is Adultery Immoral?" and Frederick Elliston, "In Defense of Promiscuity," in *Philosophy and Sex*, ed. Robert Baker and Frederick Elliston (Buffalo: Prometheus Books, 1975), 207–21, 222–43. Wasserstom's article has been reprinted in several other anthologies.

11. See, for example, Catharine A. MacKinnon, *Sexual Harassment of Working Women: A Case of Sex Discrimination* (New Haven: Yale University Press, 1979), 172–73.

12. One manifestation of the merging of sexual harassment and promiscuity in the minds of people can be found in one empirical study, in which the subjects were presented with brief descriptions of a man directing some conduct of a sexual nature to a woman, and then asked to what extent such conduct constituted sexual harassment. The subjects regarded the conduct as more harassing if the description said that the man had frequently directed similar conduct to other women than if it said that he had never done so (John B. Pryor, "The Lay Person's Understanding of Sexual Harassment," 13 *Sex Roles* 273, 280–81 [1985]).

13. Barbara A. Gutek, *Sex and the Workplace: The Impact of Sexual Behavior and Harassment on Women, Men, and Organizations* (San Francisco: Jossey-Bass, 1985), 160.

14. Billie Wright Dziech and Linda Weiner, *The Lecherous Professor: Sexual Harassment on Campus*, 2nd ed. (Urbana: University of Illinois Press, 1990), 76.

15. Peggy Crull, "The Impact of Sexual Harassment on the Job: A Profile of the Experiences of Ninety-Two Women," in *Sexuality in Organizations: Romantic and Coercive Behaviors at Work*, ed. Dail Ann Neugarten and Jay M. Shafritz (Oak Park, IL: Moore Publishing, 1980), 68.

16. Jill. L. Sherer, "Sexually Harassed," 69.2 *Hospitals and Health Networks* 54, 56 (1995); Dorraine A. Larison and Mary E. Olk, "Sexual Harassment Awareness Training: It's Not the Boogie Monster," 72 *North Dakota Law Review* 387, 392 (1996); Daryl Strickland, "Board Game Helps Workers Learn Do's, Don'ts of Sexual Harassment," *The Seattle Times*, 1 March 1996.

17. It is tempting to think of that trend as a completely new, twentieth-century phenomenon, but the history is, in fact, repeating itself in it. Blackstone records how in seventeenth-century England, adultery and fornication were decriminalized because "it was not thought proper to renew a law of such unfashionable rigour" (*Commentaries on the Laws of England*, IV, 64).

18. For example, a statute which is still technically valid makes adultery in the state of Massachusetts punishable by imprisonment of up to three years or a fine of up to $500 (Mass. Ann. Laws ch. 272, § 14), and fornication by imprisonment of up to three months or a fine of up to $30 (Mass. Ann. Laws ch. 272, § 18).

19. *Toscano v. Nimmo*, 570 F.Supp. 1197, 1200 (D. Del. 1983). One lawyer who represents plaintiffs in sexual harassment cases goes as far as to suggest that "the plaintiff should consider seeking discovery . . . on . . . whether [the alleged harasser] reads or goes to see pornography" (Barbara S. Bryant, "Evidentiary Issues in Sexual Harassment Cases, Part II: Broadening Access to the Defendant's Sexual/Personal History," 1994 *California Employment Law Reporter* 171, 176).

20. Criticism of this aspect of the law is one of the central themes of Jeffrey Rosen's book *The Unwanted Gaze: The Destruction of Privacy in America* (New York: Random House, 2000). Rosen's criticism specially focuses on the role that the 1994

changes to the Federal Rules of Evidence have played in reducing the constraints on such scrutiny of the alleged harasser's background (*Unwanted Gaze,* 129–38).

21. Groupe d'aide et d'information sur le harcèlement sexuel au travail, *Ça fait pas partie d'la job,* (Montréal: La pleine lune, 1989).

22. Cf. Jan Narveson, *The Libertarian Idea* (Philadelphia: Temple University Press, 1988), 317.

23. Lin Farley's book on sexual harassment, published in the seventies, provided several examples of job advertisements from that time that actually indicated that the applicants were expected to accept sexual interaction at work, e.g. "I am offering a job to a female as a receptionist, who must be open-minded and a swinging chick" (Lin Farley, *Sexual Shakedown: The Sexual Harassment of Women on the Job* [New York: McGraw-Hill, 1978], 148). Farley presented these examples as yet another manifestation of the problem that her book was about; she clearly did not think that openly announcing such expectations in a job advertisement made the expectations acceptable.

24. In making these responses, I will take it for granted that sexual harassment does, in fact, decrease productivity, and will set aside the special problems that are raised by businesses in which sexual harassment seems to be positively correlated with productivity. (In a certain kind of establishment, for example, a customer's harassment of a waitress may well put him in the mood to buy more drinks and, if tolerated, increase the likelihood of his being a regular customer.)

25. Cf. Kingsley R. Browne, "Title VII as Censorship: Hostile-Environment Harassment and the First Amendment," 52 *Ohio State Law Journal* 481, 491 n. 60 (1991).

26. Nancy Tuana, "Sexual Harassment: Offers and Coercion," 19.2 *Journal of Social Philosophy* 30 (1988); cf. Thomas A. Mappes, "Sexual Morality and the Concept of Using Another Person," in *Social Ethics: Morality and Social Policy,* 5th ed., ed. Thomas A. Mappes and Jane S. Zembaty (New York: McGraw-Hill, 1997), 171–72; John C. Hughes and Larry May, "Sexual Harassment," 6 *Social Theory and Practice* 249, 252–56 (1980).

27. See, for example, the staged photographs on the front and back cover of the paperback edition of Lin Farley, *Sexual Shakedown: The Sexual Harassment of Women on the Job* (New York: Warner Books, 1980).

28. Vita C. Rabinowitz, "Coping with Sexual Harassment," in *Ivory Power,* ed. Paludi, 112–13.

29. Dziech and Weiner, *The Lecherous Professor,* 75.

2. The Demarcation Problem

1. See, for example, Susan Estrich, "Sex at Work," 43 *Stanford Law Review* 813, 860 (1991).

2. A small number of employers do, in fact, have explicit policies against all dating (or "fraternization") between employees. Some institutions of higher education have policies against dating between faculty and students, which have been the subject of debate in both popular ("New Rules about Sex on Campus," *Harper's,* September 1993) and scholarly literature (Sherry Young, "Getting to Yes: The Case against Banning Consensual Relationships in Higher Education," 4 *Journal of Gender and the Law* 269 [1996]; M. Cynara Stites, "University Consensual Relationship Policies," in *Sexual Harassment on College Campuses: Abusing the Ivory Power,* ed. Michele A. Paludi [Albany: State University of New York Press, 1996], 153–75). These policies

are, however, typically limited to dating between faculty and the students who are currently enrolled in their courses.

3. *Wilson v. Taylor,* 733 F. 2d 1539, 1544 (11th Cir. 1984).

4. For example, Constance Backhouse and Leah Cohen, *Sexual Harassment on the Job: How to Avoid the Working Woman's Nightmare* (Englewood Cliffs, N.J.: Prentice-Hall, 1981), 187–88; Rosemarie Tong, *Women, Sex, and the Law* (Totowa, N.J.: Rowman and Allanheld, 1984), 78; Dorene Ludwig, *But It Was Just a Joke . . . !: Theater Scenes and Monologues for Eliminating Sexual Harassment* (Los Angeles: The Center for Labor Research and Education, Institute of Industrial Relations, University of California, 1991), 160–61.

5. Margaret Mead, "A Proposal: We Need Taboos on Sex at Work," *Redbook,* April 1978, 33.

6. Cf. "The story, perhaps apocryphal, that the headmaster of a new English public school announced that, as from the beginning of the next term, it would be a tradition of the school that senior boys should wear a certain dress, depends for its comic effect wholly on the logical incompatibility of the notion of a tradition with that of deliberate enactment and choice" (H. L. A. Hart, *The Concept of Law* [Oxford: Clarendon Press, 1961], 172).

7. Mead herself observes this ("A Proposal," 33), but does not realize that it unravels her argument.

8. Billie Wright Dziech and Linda Weiner, *The Lecherous Professor: Sexual Harassment on Campus,* 2nd ed. (Urbana: University of Illinois Press, 1990), 25.

9. Dziech and Weiner, *The Lecherous Professor,* 25, italics added. Cf. Edmund Wall, "The Definition of Sexual Harassment," in *Sexual Harassment: Confrontations and Decisions,* ed. Edmund Wall (Buffalo: Prometheus Books, 1992), 73; Groupe d'aide et d'information sur le harcèlement sexuel au travail, *Ça fait pas partie d'la job,* (Montréal: La pleine lune, 1989), 32.

10. Lin Farley, *Sexual Shakedown: The Sexual Harassment of Women on the Job* (New York: McGraw-Hill, 1978), 144.

11. Jan C. Leventer, "Sexual Harassment and Title VII: EEOC Guidelines, Conditions Litigation, and the United States Supreme Court," 10 *Capital University Law Review* 481, 495 (1981).

12. "'[V]oluntariness' in the sense of consent is not a defense to such a claim" (*Meritor Savings Bank v. Vinson,* 477 U.S. 57, 69 [1986]).

13. Mary F. Radford, "By Invitation Only: The Proof of Welcomeness in Sexual Harassment Cases," 72 *North Carolina Law Review* 499, 505 (1994).

14. U.S. Office of Personnel Management, Memorandum to Heads of Departments and Independent Agencies of 12 December 1979, reprinted in *Sexuality in Organizations: Romantic and Coercive Behaviors at Work,* ed. Dail Ann Neugarten and Jay M. Shafritz (Oak Park, IL: Moore Publishing Co., 1980), 98–99.

15. *Meritor Savings Bank v. Vinson,* 477 U.S. 57, 68.

16. "Guidelines on Sexual Harassment" is the name that is generally used for what is, strictly speaking, the section on sexual harassment (29 C.F.R. § 1604.11) of the document entitled "Guidelines on Discrimination Because of Sex."

17. See, for example, Nancy Dodd McCann and Thomas A. McGinn, *Harassed: 100 Women Define Inappropriate Behavior in the Workplace* (Homewood, IL: Business One Irwin, 1992), 67.

18. *Vinson v. Taylor,* 760 F. 2d 1330, 1332 n. 6 (D.C. Cir. 1985, dissent from denial of rehearing *en banc*).

19. *General Elec. Co. v. Gilbert,* 429 U.S. 125 (1976), quoted in *Henson v. City of Dundee,* 682 F. 2d 897, 903 n. 7 (11th Cir. 1982).

20. See, for example, Michigan Elliott-Larsen Civil Rights Act, M.C.L. §37.2103(i), and Minnesota Human Rights Act, Minn. Stat. § 363.01, subd. 41.

21. Employment Relations Act, 2000 (N.Z.), s. 108(1)(b).

22. Cf. Deborah Epstein, "Can a 'Dumb Ass Woman' Achieve Equality in the Workplace? Running the Gauntlet of Hostile Environment Harassing Speech," 84 *The Georgetown Law Journal* 399, 419 (1996).

23. See, for example, *Chamberlin v. 101 Realty, Inc.*, 915 F. 2d 777, 784 (1st Cir. 1990); *Brassfield v. Jack McLendon Furniture, Inc.*, 953 F. Supp. 1438, 1449–50 (M.D. Ala. 1996); Commission of the European Communities, *Commission Recommendation of 27 November 1991 on the Protection of the Dignity of Women and Men at Work (92/131/EEC)*, 1992 OJ L 49, Article 1.

24. Arjun P. Aggarwal, *Sexual Harassment: A Guide for Understanding and Prevention* (Toronto: Butterworths, 1992), 22

25. This has been acknowledged in the initial panel opinion in *Ellerth v. Burlington Industries, Inc.*, 102 F. 3d 848, 855 (7th Cir. 1996). (This case, which was reheard *en banc*, 123 F. 3d 490 [7th Cir. 1997] and eventually proceeded to the Supreme Court, 524 U.S. 742 [1998] is discussed further in chapter 7.) Cf. Eugene Scalia, "The Strange Career of *Quid pro Quo* Sexual Harassment," 21 *Harvard Journal of Law and Public Policy* 307 (1998).

26. *Janzen v. Platy Enterprises, Ltd.*, 59 D.L.R. 4th 352, 375 (1989).

27. 59 D.L.R. 4th 352, 375.

28. *Burlington Industries, Inc. v. Ellerth*, 524 U.S. 742, 751.

29. *Burns v. McGregor Electronic Industries, Inc.*, 989 F. 2d 959, 962 (8th Cir. 1993), paraphrasing *Burns v. McGregor Electronic Industries, Inc.*, 955 F. 2d 559, 565 (8th Cir. 1992).

30. *Moylan v. Maries County*, 792 F. 2d 746, 749 (8th Cir. 1986), quoted in *Hall v. Gus Construction Co., Inc.*, 842 F. 2d 1010, 1014 (8th Cir. 1988), italics added.

31. 682 F. 2d 897, 903. The wording of *Henson*, however has "incite" instead of "invite."

32. *Burns v. McGregor Electronic Industries, Inc.*, 989 F. 2d 959, 962, italics added.

33. Sexual conduct that is not directed at anybody in particular can also create an offensive working environment for those who witness it, hear about it, or are otherwise exposed to its consequences. Indeed, in its *amicus curiae* brief to the Eleventh Circuit in *Robinson v. Jacksonville Shipyards, Inc.* (No. 91–3655), EEOC has argued that "[a]ny attempt to separate out directed from non-directed conduct . . . would unravel the hostile environment theory" (reprinted in 533 PLI/Lit 715, 733).

34. *Broderick v. Ruder*, 685 F. Supp. 1269 (D.D.C. 1988); *Spencer v. General Electric Co.*, 697 F. Supp. 204 (E.D. Va. 1988); cf. *Vinson v. Taylor*, 753 F. 2d 141, 146 (D.C. Cir. 1985). (The last reference is to the appellate level decision in the case that later became famous as the first sexual harassment case to reach the Supreme Court.) The harassing conduct in *Faragher v. City of Boca Raton*, 524 U.S. 775, 782 (1998), also included comments made "[w]ithin earshot of" the victims, and apparently not directed *to* them, but these comments do not seem to have played a crucial role in how the case was decided.

35. Richard Bernstein, "Guilty If Charged," *The New York Review of Books*, 13 January 1994, 12.

36. Cheryl Gomez-Preston with Randi Reisfeld, *When No Means No: A Guide to Sexual Harassment* (New York: Carol Publishing Group, 1993), 29.

37. I am not implying here anything as to whether adulterous affairs can ever be worthwhile or not. The point made here is merely that the immorality of adultery cannot be invoked in interpreting the *legal* prohibition of sexual harassment, with-

out turning the law into a vehicle of legal moralism, which would make it vulnerable to the arguments of the kind considered in chapter 1.

38. Commission of the European Communities, *Commission Recommendation of 27 November 1991 on the Protection of the Dignity of Women and Men at Work (92/131/EEC)*, 1992 OJ L 49, Annex, section 2.

39. Cf. "Because it is difficult to know whether sexual joking and banter is offending someone in the group, it is best not to engage in such behavior in the work environment" (U.S. Army, *The Issue is Respect—Leader's Guide*, quoted in Joan S. Weiner, "Understanding Unwelcomeness in Sexual Harassment Law: Its History and a Proposal for Reform," 72 *Notre Dame Law Review* 621, 648 [1997]).

40. The argument developed in the last two sections has in a highly condensed, two-sentence form been independently made by F. M. Christensen, " 'Sexual Harassment' Must Be Eliminated," 8 *Public Affairs Quarterly* 1, 5 (1994).

41. 51 F. 3d 591, 593 (5th Cir. 1995), *cert.* denied, 516 U.S. 974 (1995).

42. 477 U.S. 57.

43. See the dissenting opinion in *State v. Wal-Mart Stores, Inc.*, 621 N.Y.S. 2d 158, 160 (A.D. 3 Dept. 1995) for a discussion of the same problem in a different context.

44. *Meritor Savings Bank v. Vinson*, 477 U.S. 57, 67, italics added.

45. 682 F. 2d 897, 904 (11th Cir. 1982).

46. 682 F. 2d 897, 904., italics added.

47. 895 F. 2d 1469, 1482 (3d Cir. 1990).

48. This problem has been noted in *Lehmann v. Toys 'R' Us, Inc.*, 626 A.2d 445, 455 (N.J. 1993).

49. *King v. Board of Regents*, 898 F. 2d 533, 537 (7th Cir. 1990); *Ellison v. Brady*, 924 F. 2d 872, 878 (9th Cir. 1991); *Lehmann v. Toys 'R' Us, Inc.*, 626 A.2d 445, 455.

50. E.g., in *Smith v. Sheahan*, 189 F. 3d 529, 533–34 (7th Cir. 1999), and in *Radtke v. Everett*, 501 N.W. 2d 155, 168 (Mich. 1993), decided under a state statute. A single incident has also been found to constitute sexual harassment by a tribunal in Great Britain: *Insitu Cleaning Co. Ltd. v. Heads*, [1995] IRLR 4.

51. Wendy Pollack, "Sexual Harassment: Women's Experience vs. Legal Definitions," 13 *Harvard Women's Law Journal* 35, 59 (1990); cf. Toni Lester, "The Reasonable Woman Test in Sexual Harassment Law—Will it Really Make a Difference?" 26 *Indiana Law Review* 227, 239 (1993). But see *Ellison v. Brady*, 924 F. 2d 872, 877.

52. *Rabidue v. Osceola Refining Co.*, 805 F. 2d 611, 620 (6th Cir. 1986), *cert.* denied, 481 U.S. 1041 (1987).

53. See *Haynes v. Williams*, 88 F. 3d 898 (10th Cir. 1996); *Williams v. Bannings*, 72 F. 3d 552 (7th Cir. 1995); *Tomka v. Seiler Corp.*, 66 F. 3d 1295, 1313–16 (2d. Cir. 1995); *Gary v. Long*, 59 F. 3d 1391, 1399 (D.C. Cir. 1995); *Grant v. Lone Star Co.*, 21 F. 3d 649, 651–53 (5th Cir. 1994); *Sauers v. Salt Lake County*, 1 F. 3d 1122, 1125 (10th Cir. 1993); *Miller v. Maxwell's International, Inc.*, 991 F. 2d 583, 587–88 (9th Cir. 1993), *cert.* denied, 510 U.S. 1109 (1994); *Grissom v. Waterloo Industries, Inc.*, 902 F. Supp. 867 (E.D. Ark. 1995).

54. See *Paroline v. Unisys Corp.*, 879 F. 2d 100, 104, 106 (4th Cir. 1989), aff'd in relevant part, 900 F. 2d 27 (4th Cir. 1989) (*en banc*); Phillip L. Lamberson, "Personal Liability for Violations of Title VII: Thirty Years of Indecision," 46 *Baylor Law Review* 419 (1994); John A. Bourdeau, "Individual Liability of Supervisors, Managers, or Officers for Discriminatory Actions—Cases Postdating The Civil Rights Act of 1991," 131 A.L.R. Fed. 221 (1996). Although *Paroline* is routinely cited as having held that supervisors can be sued in their individual capacities, its text is not entirely unambiguous, and admits of an alternative reading: see *Williams v. Banning*, 72 F. 3d 552, 554 n. 3.

55. *Monell v. Department of Social Services of the City of New York*, 436 U.S. 658, 690 n. 55 (1978).

56. Gomez-Preston, *When No Means No*, 95.

57. Cf. Eugene Volokh, "What Speech Does 'Hostile Work Environment' Harassment Law Restrict?" 85 *The Georgetown Law Journal* 627 (1997); Eugene Volokh, "Freedom of Speech and Workplace Harassment," 39 *UCLA Law Review* 1791, 1811–14 (1992); Kingsley R. Browne, "Title VII as Censorship: Hostile-Environment Harassment and the First Amendment," 52 *Ohio State Law Journal* 481, 504–8 (1991); Eugene Volokh, "How Harassment Law Restricts Free Speech," 47 *Rutgers Law Review* 563, 567–69 (1995); Kingsley R. Browne, "Workplace Censorship: A Response to Professor Sangree," 47 *Rutgers Law Review* 579, 583 (1995); Michael S. Greve, "Civil Rights and Uncivil Speech," 1994 *The Public Interest Law Review* 1, 14. (Greve, unfortunately, seems to forget the observation he made there in his later article "Sexual Harassment: Telling the Other Victims' Story," 23 *Northern Kentucky University Law Review* 523, 525–26 [1996].)

58. This unlikely possibility should not be confused with the fact that a person whom the employer finds guilty of sexual harassment and then fires because of that, may occasionally be successful in suing the employer on the ground that the sexual harassment was merely a pretext and that the firing was in fact motivated by something else. The cases of the latter kind do not really show anything about the sexual harassment law itself. For an example see *Valdez v. Church's Fried Chicken, Inc.*, 683 F. Supp. 596, 622–37 (W.D. Tex. 1988).

59. 875 F. 2d 468 (5th Cir. 1989).

60. Cf. Volokh, "What Speech Does 'Hostile Work Environment" Harassment Law Restrict?" 638, 643, 646.

61. The sexual harassment policy of the Yale University School of Medicine, quoted in Robert O. Riggs, Patricia H. Murrell, and JoAnn C. Cutting, *Sexual Harassment in Higher Education: From Conflict to Community* (Washington: The George Washington University School of Education and Human Development, 1993), 36. It should be noted that the policy does not say that "a single episode" has to be severe. A Denver law firm recommends that employers state that "[s]exual harassment includes *all* unwelcome sexual advances" ("Sexual Harassment Policy Statement," 10.4 *Preventive Law Reporter* 32 [1991], italics added), which has the same implication. Cf. Dziech and Weiner, *The Lecherous Professor*, 21.

62. Nat Hentoff, "When a Bad Joke Is Harassment, Free Speech Is in Peril," *The Los Angeles Daily Journal*, 19 June 1992.

63. Greg Krikorian, "A Rare Look inside Files on Sex Harassment in LAPD," *Los Angeles Times*, 27 March 1994. The department's "women's coordinator" is quoted within the same article as saying: "we certainly want to nip [inappropriate words and actions] in the bud before they rise to harassment."

3. Demarcation and Reasonableness

1. *Rabidue v. Osceola Refining Co.*, 805 F. 2d. 611, 620 (6th Cir. 1986), *cert.* denied, 481 U.S. 1041 (1987).

2. Lynn McLain, "The EEOC Sexual Harassment Guidelines: Welcome Advances under Title VII?" 10 *University of Baltimore Law Review* 275, 312 (1981).

3. Equal Opportunity Act, 1984 (South Australia), s. 87(11).

4. See Stacy J. Cooper, "Sexual Harassment and the Swedish Bikini Team: A Reevaluation of the 'Hostile Environment' Doctrine," 26 *Columbia Journal of Law and Social Problems* 387, 413 (1993).

5. 1993 WL 302216, 4–6, 8, 32.

6. John B. Pryor and Nora J. Whalen, "A Typology of Sexual Harassment: Characteristics of Harassers and the Social Circumstances under which Sexual Harassment Occurs," in *Sexual Harassment: Theory, Research, and Treatment,* ed. William O'Donohue (Boston: Allyn and Bacon, 1997), 134, summarizing J. B. Pryor, "The Phenomenology of Sexual Harassment" (paper presented at the meeting of the American Psychological Association, Los Angeles, 1994).

7. Barbara Amiel, "U.S.A.: A Nation Being Stripped of Its Sexuality—Judge Clarence Thomas," *Sunday Times,* 13 October 1991.

8. *Roth v. United States,* 354 U.S. 476 (1957).

9. *Miller v. California,* 413 U.S. 15 (1973).

10. 524 F. 2d 320 (8th Cir. 1975).

11. 524 F. 2d 320, 322.

12. 524 F. 2d 320, 323.

13. 805 F. 2d 611, 626–27.

14. *Vermett v. Hough,* 627 F. Supp. 587, 607 (W.D. Mich. 1986); *Lipsett v. Rive-Mora,* 669 F. Supp. 1188, 1199 (D.P.R. 1987), rev'd on other grounds, 864 F. 2d 881 (1st Cir. 1988).

15. *Spencer v. General Electric Co.,* 697 F. Supp. 204, 218 (E.D. Va. 1988), aff'd 894 F. 2d 651 (4th Cir. 1990).

16. Within the very same paragraph in which it invokes "a reasonable female employee," the *Spencer* court speaks simply of "a reasonable employee," and there is no suggestion that the former phrase is intended to mean something different from the latter (697 F. Supp. 204, 219).

17. 895 F. 2d 1469, 1482 (3d Cir. 1990).

18. 924 F. 2d. 872 (9th Cir. 1991).

19. 924 F. 2d. 872, 879 n. 11.

20. Kathleen A. Kenealy, "Sexual Harassment and the Reasonable Woman Standard," 8 *The Labor Lawyer* 203, 203 n. 4 (1992); Jessica M. Karner, "Political Speech, Sexual Harassment, and a Captive Workforce," 83 *California Law Review* 637, 643 (1995); Titus E. Aaron with Judith A. Isaksen, *Sexual Harassment in the Workplace: A Guide to the Law and a Research Overview for Employers and Employees* (Jefferson, N.C.: McFarland, 1993), 72.

21. 819 F. 2d 630 (6th Cir. 1987).

22. 924 F. 2d. 872, 878, 879.

23. 760 F. Supp. 1486 (M.D. Fla. 1991).

24. See, for example, *Smolsky v. Consolidated Rail Corp.,* 780 F. Supp. 283, 294–95 (E.D. Pa. 1991); *Burns v. McGregor Electronic Industries, Inc.,* 989 F. 2d 959, 965 (8th Cir. 1993); *Lehmann v. Toys 'R' Us, Inc.,* 626 A.2d 445, 457–59 (N.J. 1993).

25. 765 F. Supp. 1509 (D. Me. 1991), vacated in part (not pertinent to this point), 765 F. Supp. 1529 (D. Me. 1991).

26. 765 F. Supp. 1509, 1515–16.

27. 510 U.S. 17 (1993).

28. 510 U.S. 17, 21.

29. *DeAngelis v. El Paso Municipal Police Officers Association,* 51 F. 3d 591, 594 (5th Cir. 1995), *cert.* denied, 516 U.S 974 (1995).

30. *Gillming v. Simmons Industries,* 91 F. 3d 1168, 1172 (8th Cir. 1996). Mary Anne Weiss reads more into this opinion than is in the actual text, when she says that,

according to it, "the reasonable person standard, not that of the reasonable women, should apply after *Harris*" ("Ninth Circuit Broadens Reasonableness Standard for Hostile Work Environment Sexual Harassment: *Fuller v. City of Oakland*," 31 *University of San Francisco Law Review* 665, 693 [1997]).

31. *Radtke v. Everett*, 501 N.W. 2d 155, 165–67 (Mich. 1993).

32. *Nichols v. Frank*, 42 F. 3d 503, 512 (9th Cir. 1994), italics added. It needs to be acknowledged that the quotation comes from an opinion of only one judge with whom other members of the panel concurred only in the result.

33. *Fuller v. City of Oakland, California*, 47 F. 3d 1522, 1527 (9th Cir. 1995).

34. *Crowe v. Wiltel Communications Systems*, 103 F. 3d 897, 900 (9th Cir. 1996).

35. Cf. Tracy L. Treger, "The Reasonable Woman? Unreasonable!!! *Ellison v. Brady*," 14 *Whittier Law Review* 675, 683 (1993).

36. 924 F. 2d. 872, 879.

37. See Sarah A. DeCosse, "Simply Unbelievable: Reasonable Women and Hostile Environment Sexual Harassment," 10 *Law and Inequality* 285, 286, 309 (1992).

38. *Rabidue v. Osceola Refining Co.*, 805 F. 2d 611, 620.

39. *Bennett v. Corroon & Black Corp.*, 845 F. 2d. 104, 106 (5th Cir. 1988), italics added.

40. Cf. *Radtke v. Everett*, 501 N.W. 2d 155, 166; Treger, "The Reasonable Woman?" 683, 687.

41. 12 N.W. 155 (Mich. 1882).

42. Cf. Cheryl L. Dragel, "Hostile Environment Sexual Harassment: Should the Ninth Circuit's 'Reasonable Woman' Standard Be Adopted?" 11 *Journal of Law and Commerce* 237, 253 (1992).

43. Jane L. Dolkart, "Hostile Environment Harassment: Equality, Objectivity, and the Shaping of Legal Standards," 43 *Emory Law Journal* 151, 218–21 (1994).

44. Cf. Richard L. Weiner, "Social Analytic Jurisprudence in Sexual Harassment Litigation: The Role of Social Framework and Social Fact," 51.1 *Journal of Social Issues* 167 (1995).

45. Paul B. Johnson, "The Reasonable Woman in Sexual Harassment Law: Progress or Illusion?," 28 *Wake Forest Law Review* 619, 645–52 (1993); Robert Unikel "'Reasonable' Doubts: A Critique of the Reasonable Woman Standard in American Jurisprudence," 87 *Northwestern University Law Review* 326, 366–70 (1992); Saba Ashraf, "The Reasonableness of the 'Reasonable Woman' Standard: An Evaluation of Its Use in Hostile Environment Sexual Harassment Claims under Title VII of the Civil Rights Act," 21 *Hofstra Law Review* 483, 500 (1992); Anita Bernstein, "Treating Sexual Harassment with Respect," 111 *Harvard Law Review* 445, 474 (1997). Cf. David I. Gedrose, "Workplace Sexual Harassment: The Ninth Circuit's Reasonable Woman Standard and Employer Remedial Actions in Hostile Environment Claims Following *Ellison v. Brady*," 28 *Willamette Law Review* 151, 169–70 (1991); Jeffrey A. Gettle, "Sexual Harassment and the Reasonable Woman Standard: Is It a Viable Solution?" 31 *Duquesne Law Review* 841, 856 (1993); DeCosse, "Simply Unbelievable," 298.

46. Cf. Treger, "The Reasonable Woman?" 685.

47. 924 F. 2d 872, 880.

48. Cf. Johnson, "The Reasonable Woman," 658.

49. 924 F. 2d 872, 880, italics added.

50. 924 F. 2d 872, 879, italics added. In paraphrasing the *Ellison* decision, one commentator used the words "*the* reasonable woman would consider the behavior . . . as harassment" (DeCosse, "Simply Unbelievable," 300, italics added). Replacing "a" with "the" is noteworthy, because it smuggles in an unwarranted

assumption that there is a uniformity in the reactions of reasonable women to such conduct.

51. One district court has, however, interpreted the formulation as expressing (1') rather than (2'). Immediately after quoting it, that court said: "*Thus*, under *Ellison*, . . . this Court will grant summary judgment to Defendants only if *no* reasonable woman would find Defendants' conduct sufficiently severe or pervasive to have caused a hostile working environment" (*Canada v. Boyd Group, Inc.*, 809 F. Supp. 771, 776 [D. Nev. 1992], italics added).

52. *Tindall v. Housing Authority*, 762 F. Supp. 259, 263 (W.D. Ark. 1991).

53. 542 F. Supp. 123, 128 (W.D. Tenn. 1981), aff'd *sub nom. Sones-Morgan v. Hertz Corp.*, 725 F. 2d 1070 (6th Cir. 1984).

54. 865 F. Supp. 1430, 1435 (C.D. Cal. 1994).

55. 865 F. Supp. 1430, 1435.

56. Helen Gurley Brown, "At Work, Sexual Electricity Sparks Creativity," *The Wall Street Journal*, 29 October 1991.

57. Diane Baroni and Betty Kelly, *How to Get Him Back from the Other Woman if You Still Want Him* (New York: St. Martin's Press, 1992), 121. It may be worth noting that the authors grant this dispensation only to *cute* hardhats. Cf. pp. 79–80 above.

58. Barbara A. Gutek, *Sex and the Workplace: The Impact of Sexual Behavior and Harassment on Women, Men, and Organizations* (San Francisco: Jossey-Bass, 1985), 84.

59. Nancy Dodd McCann and Thomas A. McGinn, *Harassed: 100 Women Define Inappropriate Behavior in the Workplace* (Homewood, IL: Business One Irwin, 1992).

60. McCann and McGinn, *Harassed*, xv. In claiming that, they themselves put the phrase "reasonable women" in quotation marks, for reasons that they don't make clear.

61. McCann and McGinn, *Harassed*, scenarios 2, 34, and 48.

62. McCann and McGinn, *Harassed*, scenarios 8, 12, and 34.

63. Although the authors of this study were relatively casual about their methodology, the study does have an important advantage over most of the other, more formally structured research about sexual harassment. Most of the more formal research involves presenting to the subjects descriptions of various kinds of conduct and then asking, for each kind of conduct, whether it, in the subjects' opinion, constitutes sexual harassment. The term "sexual harassment" is, however, as has been pointed out in chapter 1, a technical term of the law, and it is, however infelicitously, defined in the law. What people *think* constitutes sexual harassment is, therefore, irrelevant to the application of the existing law. The empirical questions that are relevant to the application of the law and appreciating its implications are questions about whether people's reactions to various kinds of conduct have the characteristics in terms of which the law defines sexual harassment (such as being offended). This study, problematic as it is in many ways, at least asks its subject the right kind of questions. That much of the empirical research on sexual harassment might be asking the wrong question has been, albeit in an oblique way, acknowledged by one of the leading empirical researchers in the field (Barbara A. Gutek, "How Subjective Is Sexual Harassment?: An Examination of Rater Effects," 17 *Basic and Applied Social Psychology* 447, 463–64 [1995]).

64. 805 F. 2d 611, 627.

65. 805 F. 2d 611, 627. Similarly, Martha Chamallas interprets, with apparent approval, the perspective of the reasonable woman invoked in *Robinson v. Jacksonville Shipyards* "as the perspective that might reasonably be taken by women consciously interested in *improving* their status in the workplace" ("Feminist Constructions of

Objectivity: Multiple Perspectives in Sexual and Racial Harassment Litigation," 1 *Texas Journal of Women and the Law* 95, 135 [1992], italics added).

66. What I say in this paragraph constitutes an answer to Andrew Altman's criticism ("Making Sense of Sexual Harassment Law," 25 *Philosophy and Public Affairs* 36, 60 n. 39 [1996]) of an earlier, shorter version of my argument about reasonableness (Mane Hajdin, "Sexual Harassment in the Law: The Demarcation Problem," 25.3 *Journal of Social Philosophy* 102, 113–18 [1994]).

67. Dolkart, "Hostile Environment Harassment," 200.

68. DeCosse, "Simply Unbelievable," 298. (I am assuming that the phrase "sexual orientation" is used in this remark in the sense that it has acquired in the recent political rhetoric, namely for one's position on the heterosexuality-bisexuality-homosexuality spectrum.) Cf. Dragel, "Hostile Environment Sexual Harassment," 253; Treger, "The Reasonable Woman?" 690–91.

69. Cf. Suzanne Sangree, "A Reply to Professors Volokh and Browne," 47 *Rutgers Law Review* 595, 595 (1995). Some people are so firmly convinced that complaints of sexual harassment are never made about trivial incidents, that upon hearing that a complaint has been made, they immediately proceed to the conclusion that the incident must have been serious, even if they don't know the details: see the comments of Bernice R. Sandler quoted in Edward Walsh, "Sexual Ethics in the Seminary: A Professor's Biblical Discourse Collides with Correctness," *The Washington Post*, 13 May 1994.

70. Complaints of sexual harassment have been made about such arguably minor matters as man's keeping on his desk a 5" x 7" photograph of his wife wearing a bikini: Nat Hentoff, "A 'Pinup' of His Wife," *The Washington Post*, 5 June 1993 (the same syndicated column appeared in other papers as well).

71. Incidentally, the *whole* of the sexual harassment law at the federal level is technically a judicial interpretation of a statue that does not say anything explicit about sexual harassment. The connection between the law and the statute on which it purports to be based will be explored in chapter 7.

72. Cf. Johnson, "The Reasonable Woman," 667; Bernstein, "Treating Sexual Harassment with Respect," 507–8.

73. The criterion considered here is, in fact, similar to the criterion that appears in the Ontario Human Rights Code, R.S.O. 1990, c. H. 19, s. 10(1).

74. I am here simply assuming, for the sake of argument, that it is clear that X has, in fact, made *n* advances and that Y has unambiguously rejected all *n* of them. Given that human sexual interaction is often deliberately ambiguous, it will, in real-life cases, often be debatable what counts as an advance, what counts as a distinct advance, and what counts as a rejection. (If X says "We should have a drink sometime," without being any more specific, does that count as an advance? If Y then changes the topic, has Y politely rejected the advance or simply not responded to it at all? If Y's reaction is interpreted the first way, then X's saying the next day "How about a drink this afternoon?" will probably be counted as a new, distinct advance, but if Y's reaction is interpreted as no response at all, then X's question the next day may be regarded as a continuation of the same advance, that merely makes the advance more specific.)

75. In speaking about a change of mind here, I am assuming, for the sake of argument, that Y's rejections of the prior advances were sincere. The argument I am making here thus does not depend on the possibility that Y's resistance to X's advances may have been mere token resistance.

76. Gutek, *Sex and the Workplace*, 187.

77. Carol Botwin, "Are *You* Having an Office Affair?: *Woman*'s Stunning Survey Results," *Woman*, April 1990, 58.

78. Botwin, "Are *You* Having an Office Affair?" 57.

79. Botwin, "Are *You* Having an Office Affair?" 56.

80. See, for example, *Sexual Harassment Manual for Managers and Supervisors: How to Prevent and Resolve Sexual Harassment Complaints in the Workplace* (Chicago: Commerce Clearing House, 1991), 8, 14; Mary P. Rowe, "Dealing with Harassment: A Systems Approach," in *Sexual Harassment in the Workplace: Perspectives, Frontiers, and Response Strategies*, ed. Margaret S. Stockdale (Thousand Oaks, CA: Sage Publications, 1996), 264.

81. The criterion of harassment in the Ontario Human Rights Code, which is, as noted above, similar to (4), does not seem to have this narrowing effect, because it is, in its application, probably not taken at face value. Although the Code defines harassment as the "conduct that is known or ought reasonably to be known to be unwelcome," the Policy Statement on Sexual Harassment and Inappropriate Gender Related Comments and Conduct of the Ontario Human Rights Commission interprets that definition as making relevant the knowledge of "how such behaviour *might* generally be received" (italics added), which transforms the definition into something like (5), discussed below.

82. Whether it is possible to bring the notion of a reasonable person into the law in a way that would avoid the dilemma between (5) and (4) is something we will explore in chapter 4.

83. *Coates v. Cincinnati*, 402 U.S. 611, 614 (1971). Cf. the dissenting opinion of Justice Douglas in *Miller v. California*, 413 U.S. 15, 46.

4. How Much Is Too Much?

1. J. Clay Smith, Jr., "Prologue to the EEOC Guidelines on Sexual Harassment," 10 *Capital University Law Review* 471, 473 (1981).

2. *Hall v. Guss Construction Co., Inc.*, 842 F. 2d 1010,1012 (8th Cir. 1988).

3. Louise F. Fitzgerald, "Science v. Myth: The Failure of Reason in the Clarence Thomas Hearings," 65 *Southern California Law Review* 1399, 1399 (1992). Cf. Joan Vermeulen, "Employer Liability under Title VII for Sexual Harassment by Supervisory Employees," 10 *Capital University Law Review* 499, 501 (1981); Judy Trent Ellis, "Sexual Harassment and Race: A Legal Analysis of Discrimination," 8 *Journal of Legislation* 30, 31 (1981); Kathleen A. Kenealy, "Sexual Harassment and the Reasonable Woman Standard," 8 *The Labor Lawyer* 203, 204 (1992); Arjun P. Aggarwal, *Sexual Harassment: A Guide for Understanding and Prevention* (Toronto: Butterworths, 1992), 37; Cheryl Gomez-Preston with Randi Reisfeld, *When No Means No: A Guide to Sexual Harassment* (New York: Carol Publishing Group, 1993), 33; Joseph Posner, "Attacking a Stone Wall—Examination of the Alleged Sexual Harasser," in *Litigating the Sexual Harassment Case: A Guide for Plaintiff and Defense Attorneys*, ed. Juanita B. Luis (Chicago: Tort and Insurance Practice Section, American Bar Association, 1994), 242.

4. Kerry Segrave, *The Sexual Harassment of Women in the Workplace, 1600 to 1993* (Jefferson, NC: McFarland, 1994), 2.

5. Larry May, *Masculinity and Morality* (Ithaca, NY: Cornell University Press, 1998), 106.

6. *Ellison v. Brady*, 924 F. 2d 872, 874 (9th Cir. 1991).

7. 924 F. 2d 872, 874.

8. Mary F. Radford, "By Invitation Only: The Proof of Welcomeness in Sexual Harassment Cases," 72 *North Carolina Law Review* 499, 526 (1994).

9. In one empirical study, 16.8% of female respondents said that they would be flattered if an opposite-sex worker asked them to have sex (Barbara A. Gutek, *Sex and the Workplace: The Impact of Sexual Behavior and Harassment on Women, Men, and Organizations* [San Francisco; Jossey-Bass, 1985], 96), and that result is widely quoted throughout the literature as if it supported the legal prohibition of sexual harassment. The assumption behind such reasoning seems to be that, if only 16.8% of female workers have a certain interest, then that interest may be ignored. Whether this percentage deserves to be taken at face value is debatable, but assuming, for the sake of argument, that it does, there are more than ten million people in the United States in that group. That is hardly a group whose interests can be simply ignored.

10. I use "harm" here in a broad sense, in which "offense" is a species of harm (unlike many theoreticians who use it in a narrower sense, which is such that offense does not even count as harm).

11. It is, in fact, debatable whether the harms that go against the interests of the second kind should be counted in favor of the legal prohibition, against it, or neither. On the one side, they *are* harms, and it thus seems that they should be counted in favor of the prohibition. Counting them in its favor is, however, paternalistic, and thus vulnerable to the general objections to paternalism. Moreover, it can be said that the interests of the second kind themselves function as disincentives against making the advances, which reduces the need for legal intervention. Which of these ways of dealing with the interests of the second kind we adopt, however, does not significantly affect the general direction of the argument I am making in this section.

12. *United States v. Carroll Towing Co.*, 159 F. 2d 169, 173 (2d Cir. 1947).

13. Cf. Paul B. Johnson, "The Reasonable Woman in Sexual Harassment Law: Progress or Illusion?" 28 *Wake Forest Law Review* 619, 665–67 (1993).

14. Guido Calabresi and A. Douglas Melamed, "Property Rules, Liability Rules, and Inalienability: One View of the Cathedral," 85 *Harvard Law Review* 1089 (1972).

15. This is corroborated by the fact that, in the popular literature, sexual harassment is sometimes described as a "crime" or as "criminal." See, for example, Jane Gallop, *Feminist Accused of Sexual Harassment* (Durham: Duke University Press, 1997), 9, 10, 21.

16. That this is so has been effectively acknowledged by a federal court which found that a charge of sexual harassment implicated the alleged harasser's "liberty interests in his good name and reputation because the charge of sexual harassment and the subsequent sanctions . . . 'might seriously damage his standing and associations in his community' " (*Silva v. University of New Hampshire,* 888 F. Supp. 293, 317 [D.N.H. 1994], quoting *Board of Regents v. Roth,* 408 U.S. 564, 573 [1972]; see also *Huff v. County of Butler,* 524 F. Supp. 751, 753 [W.D. Pa. 1981]).

5. Sexual Harassment and Freedom of Speech

1. The statutory definitions of sexual harassment in some states, with apparent redundancy, even add "communication" to the wording taken over from the federal EEOC Guidelines, and thus speak of "verbal or physical conduct or communication" (Elliott-Larsen Civil Rights Act [Michigan], M.C.L. § 37.2103[i]; Minnesota Human Rights Act, Minn. Stat. § 363.01, subd. 41).

2. Kingsley R. Browne, "Title VII as Censorship: Hostile-Environment Harassment and the First Amendment," 52 *Ohio State Law Journal* 481 (1991).

3. Jules B. Gerard, "The First Amendment in a Hostile Environment: A Primer on Free Speech and Sexual Harassment," 68 *Notre Dame Law Review* 1003 (1993). In "Political Speech, Sexual Harassment, and a Captive Workforce," 83 *California Law Review* 637 (1995), Jessica M. Karner replicates many of the results of Browne's article, but then makes an argumentative turn that leads to a very different conclusion. For a popular, semihumorous account of the topic, inspired by Browne's article, see Richard Dooling, *Blue Streak: Swearing, Free Speech, and Sexual Harassment* (New York: Random House, 1996), 84–111.

4. Nadine Strossen, "Regulating Workplace Sexual Harassment and Upholding the First Amendment—Avoiding a Collision," 37 *Villanova Law Review* 757 (1992).

5. Strossen, "Regulating Workplace Sexual Harassment," 770.

6. Catharine A. MacKinnon, *Only Words* (Cambridge, MA: Harvard University Press, 1993).

7. MacKinnon, *Only Words*, 46.

8. MacKinnon, *Only Words*, 49.

9. Suzanne Sangree, "A Reply to Professors Volokh and Browne," 602–3; Deborah Epstein, "Free Speech at Work: Verbal Harassment as Gender-Based Discriminatory (Mis)treatment," 85 *The Georgetown Law Journal* 649, 656–57 (1997); cf. Amy Horton, "Of Supervision, Centerfolds, and Censorship: Sexual Harassment, the First Amendment, and the Contours of Title VII," 46 *University of Miami Law Review* 403, 428–32 (1991).

10. Cf. Karner, "Political Speech," 649.

11. See, for example, *Lipsett v. University of Puerto Rico*, 864 F. 2d 881, 887 (1st Cir. 1988); *Spencer v. General Electric Co.*, 697 F. Supp. 204, 213 (E.D. Va. 1988), aff'd 894 F. 2d 651 (4th Cir. 1990); *Bowersox v. P. H. Glatfelter Co.*, 677 F. Supp. 307, 308 (M.D. Pa. 1988); *Arnold v. City of Seminole, Okl.*, 614 F. Supp. 853, 862–63 (E.D. Okl. 1985); *Harris v. Forklift Systems, Inc.*, 510 U.S. 17, 19 (1993).

12. Jessica Karner has argued that this problem could be solved by simply stipulating that the sexual harassment law does not apply to political speech (Karner, "Political Speech," 686–89; cf. Richard H. Fallon, Jr., "Sexual Harassment, Content Neutrality, and the First Amendment Dog that Didn't Bark," 1994 *The Supreme Court Review* 1, 47). A law creating such an exception would, however, be exceedingly difficult to apply, because it is very difficult to ascertain where the boundaries between political and nonpolitical speech lie: much of the speech that is not overtly political could be argued to have political implications. (Under such a law, feminist arguments that broaden the concept of the political could, ironically, be used for aims of which their authors would not approve.)

13. That this possibility is not merely speculative is indicated by the fact that the student bookstore at the University of Minnesota was (in the name of combating sexual harassment, although not by way of direct operation of the law) "forced to stop selling a mug that read: 'Sexual harassment is not a problem around here; it's one of the benefits.' " (Anne T. Truax, "Sexual Harassment in Higher Education: What We've Learned," in *Combating Sexual Harassment in Higher Education,* ed. Bernice Lott and Mary Ellen Reilly [Washington: National Education Association, 1996], 73). The message on the mug can be regarded as, at least partially, a humorous expression of opposition to the sexual harassment law, and thus eminently political.

14. At least one court opinion suggests that, when one person complains of sexual harassment by another, and third parties who are coworkers of both express their disapproval of the complaint by giving the complainant "cold-shoulder treatment," these third parties may be regarded as engaging in sexual harassment, even though

there is nothing explicitly sexual about their conduct (*Campbell v. Florida Steel Corporation*, 919 S.W. 2d 26 [Tenn. 1996]).

15. *Chaplinsky v. New Hampshire*, 315 U.S. 568, 572 (1942).

16. Gerard, "The First Amendment in a Hostile Environment," 1020.

17. *NAACP v. Claiborne Hardware Co.*, 458 U.S. 886, 927 (1982).

18. Browne, "Title VII as Censorship," 527–28; cf. Marcy Strauss, "Sexist Speech in the Workplace," 25 *Harvard Civil Rights-Civil Liberties Law Review* 1, 18–19 (1990).

19. *FCC v. Pacifica Foundation*, 438 U.S. 726, 745 (1978).

20. *NAACP v. Clairborne Hardware Co.*, 458 U.S. 886, 910.

21. *Members of the City Council v. Taxpayers for Vincent*, 466 U.S. 789, 804 (1984).

22. *Lehman v. City of Shaker Heights*, 418 U.S. 298 (1974).

23. *Greer v. Spock*, 424 U.S. 828, 838–39 (1976).

24. *Young v. American Mini Theatres, Inc.*, 427 U.S. 50, 70 (1976).

25. Geoffrey R. Stone, "Restrictions of Speech Because of its Content: The Peculiar Case of Subject-Matter Restrictions," 46 *The University of Chicago Law Review* 81, esp. 99 (1978); cf. Gerard, "The First Amendment in a Hostile Environment," 1008–9.

26. The cases that make that commitment particularly clear are *R. A. V. v. City of St. Paul, Minnesota*, 505 U.S. 377 (1992), which is discussed below, and *Rosenberger v. Rector and Visitors of University of Virginia*, 515 U.S. 819 (1995).

27. Cf. *Rowan v. United States Post Office Department*, 397 U.S. 728 (1970). Deborah Epstein's characterization of *Rowan* as an exception to the requirement of viewpoint neutrality ("Can a 'Dumb Ass Woman' Achieve Equality in the Workplace? Running the Gauntlet of Hostile Environment Harassing Speech," 84 *The Georgetown Law Journal* 399, 434 [1996]) is misleading, because *Rowan* does not leave the selection of viewpoints whose expression is to be restricted in the hands of the government.

28. David M. Jaffe completely ignores this central argument of Browne's article, in spite of referring to Browne several times in his "Walking the Constitutional Tightrope: Balancing Title VII Hostile Environment Sexual Harassment Claims with Free Speech Defenses," 80 *Minnesota Law Review* 979 (1996). Browne's argument, properly understood precludes the possibility of such balancing. Shannon Mcauliffe "deals" with Browne's article in a similar way in her "Speak No Evil: The First Amendment Offers No Protection for Sexual Harassers," 29 *Suffolk University Law Review* 233 (1995): Browne is referred to there, but the substance of his arguments is ignored. Cynthia L. Estlund attempts to avoid the problem by making the declaration, whose implausibility borders on self-contradiction, that, in many cases, the offensivenss of speech *on the basis of sex* should not be regarded as a consequence of the viewpoint expressed, but as a feature of the *manner* of speaking ("Freedom of Expression in the Workplace and the Problem of Discriminatory Harassment," 75 *Texas Law Review* 687, 751 [1997]).

29. 760 F. Supp. 1486 (M.D. Fla. 1991).

30. 760 F. Supp. 1486, 1534.

31. Browne, "Title VII as Censorship," 512 n.188.

32. Strauss, "Sexist Speech in the Workplace," 38–41; cf. Karner, "Political Speech," 687.

33. 760 F. Supp. 1486, 1535.

34. *Roberts v. United States Jaycees*, 468 U.S. 609, 628 (1984).

35. Horton, "Of Supervision, Centerfolds, and Censorship," 435.

36. 760 F. Supp. 1486, 1498.

37. MacKinnon, *Only Words*, 49.

38. *Texas v. Johnson,* 491 U.S. 397, 412 (1989), quoting *Boos v. Barry,* 485 U.S. 312, 321 (1988).

39. *U.S. v. Lee,* 6 F. 3d 1297 (8th Cir. 1993, *en banc*), *cert.* denied, 511 U.S. 1035 (1994).

40. 760 F. Supp. 1486,1535.

41. 760 F. Supp. 1486,1535.

42. 760 F. Supp. 1486, 1535–36.

43. Eugene Volokh, "Freedom of Speech and Workplace Harassment," 39 *UCLA Law Review* 1791, 1838–40 (1992); Eugene Volokh, "How Harassment Law Restricts Free Speech," 47 *Rutgers Law Review* 563, 571 (1995).

44. 760 F. Supp. 1486, 1536.

45. See Kingsley R. Browne, "Workplace Censorship: A Response to Professor Sangree," 47 *Rutgers Law Review* 579, 586 (1995), for a criticism of the tendency to engage in such balancing in a manner does not treat the First Amendment "as a real constraint on policy choices."

46. Browne, "Title VII as Censorship," 539–40.

47. 760 F. Supp. 1486,1536.

48. *Waters v. Churchill,* 511 U.S. 661, 671–75 (1994). See also *Pickering v. Board of Education,* 391 U.S. 563, 568 (1968); *Rankin v. McPherson,* 483 U.S. 378, 384 (1987).

49. Cf. Browne, "Title VII as Censorship," 511 n. 180; Volokh, "Freedom of Speech," 1821 n. 130.

50. Supreme Court docket number 92-1168; p. 16 of the brief.

51. 771 F. 2d 323 (7th Cir. 1985), sum. aff'd, 475 U.S. 1001 (1986).

52. 760 F. Supp. 1486, 1536.

53. I am grateful to Professor Franklyn Haiman for providing me with this explanation of why the appellate decision has never been made.

54. For examples of their influence within the caselaw see *Aguilar v. Avis Rent a Car System, Inc.,* 21 Cal. 4th 121, 142 (1999) (see also the concurring opinion by Justice Werdegar at p. 163), *cert.* denied (with a dissenting statement by Justice Thomas), 529 U.S. 1138 (2000); *Berman v. Washington Times Corp.,* 1994 WL 750274 3 n. 4 (D.D.C.). Because of the publicity it has received, the *Robinson* case is also likely to be exercising considerable influence at the lower level of the operation of the law: see Nat Hentoff, "Trivializing Sexual Harassment," *The Washington Post,* 11 January 1992.

55. 172 F. 3d 1232, 1246–47 (10th Cir. 1999).The Supreme Court was not petitioned for a review of this decision.

56. 857 F. Supp. 1540, 1549 (M.D. Ala. 1994), aff'd without opinion, 56 F. 3d 1391 (11th Cir. 1995).

57. *Connick v. Meyers,* 461 U.S. 138, 146 (1983).

58. 888 F. Supp 293 (D.N.H. 1994).

59. 888 F. Supp 293, 317.

60. 888 F. Supp 293, 312–17.

61. 888 F. Supp 293, 314.

62. Michael S. Greve, "Sexual Harassment: Telling the Other Victims' Story," 23 *Northern Kentucky University Law Review* 523, 524 (1996).

63. 933 F. Supp. 1425 (C.D. Ill. 1996).

64. 933 F. Supp. 1425, 1441.

65. 933 F. Supp. 1425, 1440.

66. 933 F. Supp. 1425, 1449.

67. 865 F. Supp. 1430 (C.D. Cal. 1994).

68. 865 F. Supp. 1430, 1440.

69. 747 F. Supp. 951, 954, 958–59 (S.D.N.Y. 1990).
70. 865 F. Supp. 1430, 1436.
71. 865 F. Supp. 1430, 1440. The significance of such qualifications in the *Johnson* opinion is made particularly vivid by *O'Rourke v. City of Providence*, 235 F. 3d 713 (1st Cir. 2001). That case also involved the use of pornography in a fire station, but the pornography appears to have been different from *Playboy*, and its use more extensive than in *Johnson*; the court regarded the case as not analogous to *Johnson* (235 F. 3d 713, 719, 722, 735). (The use of pornography was, however, only a minor aspect of the issue in *O'Rourke*, and the court therefore does not discuss it in much detail.)
72. 865 F. Supp. 1430, 1438.
73. 865 F. Supp. 1430, 1441.
74. *Davis v. Monsanto Chemical Co.*, 858 F. 2d 345, 350 (6th Cir. 1988); criticized in Browne, "Title VII as Censorship," 549.
75. 51 F. 3d 591 (5th Cir. 1995), *cert.* denied, 516 U.S. 974.
76. 51 F. 3d 591, 596–97.
77. 420 Mass. 517 (1995).
78. "Sex-Harassment Ruling," *The Wall Street Journal*, 14 June 1995.
79. 420 Mass. 517, 519 n. 4.
80. *Heller v. Bowman*, 516 U.S. 1032 (1995).
81. 92 F. 3d 968 (9th Cir. 1996), *cert.* denied, 520 U.S. 1140 (1996).
82. 92 F. 3d 968, 972. The wording of the college's policy of which the court suggests that it could be made "clearer and more precise" closely follows the wording of the EEOC Guidelines.
83. *Booher v. Board of Regents, Northern Kentucky University*, 1998 U.S.Dist. LEXIS 11404 (E.D. Ky.), appeals dismissed, 163 F. 3d 395 (6th Cir. 1998).
84. 1998 U.S.Dist. LEXIS 11404, 29 n. 18, cf. 33.
85. 505 U.S. 377 (1992).
86. 505 U.S. 377, 386.
87. 505 U.S. 377, 390.
88. 505 U.S. 377, 391–92.
89. 505 U.S. 377, 389–90, citations omitted.
90. Cf. *DeAngelis v. El Paso Municipal Police Officers Association*, 51 F. 3d 591, 597 and n. 7; *Saxe v. State College Area School District*, 240 F. 3d 200, 207–9 (3d Cir. 2001). In spite of the plausibility of the interpretation that gives the remarks that the Court has made in *R. A. V.* about harassment a very narrow application, they have been invoked in support of a very broad restriction of racially harassing speech in *Aguilar v. Avis Rent a Car System, Inc.*, 21 Cal. 4th 121, 135–37. The decision in *Aguilar* was, however, accompanied by three dissenting opinions. The strongly worded opinion by Justice Brown is particularly noteworthy for arguing that *R.A.V.* implies that "Title VII is unconstitutional because it is a content-based regulation of speech not limited to fighting words" (21 Cal. 4th 121, 192).
91. 505 U.S. 377, 409–10.
92. Supreme Court docket number 92-1168.
93. 526 U.S. 629, 667, 682, 683 (1999).
94. Another encouragement to such litigation can be found in *Saxe v. State College Area School District*, in which the Third Circuit declared unconstitutional a general antiharassment policy of a school district. The policy in question covered much more than sexual harassment and the court's opinion mostly focused on its aspects other than those that concerned sexual harassment. Nevertheless, the opinion is noteworthy in the present context for its energetic insistence that various rules

created in the name of combating different kinds of harassment need to be carefully scrutinized by the courts for their compatibility with the First Amendment.

95. *Hurley v. Irish-American Gay, Lesbian and Bisexual Group of Boston, Inc.*, 515 U.S. 557, 575 (1995).

96. *Hurley v. Irish-American Gay, Lesbian and Bisexual Group of Boston, Inc.*, 515 U.S. 557, 575; *West Virginia State Board of Education v. Barnette*, 319 U.S. 624, 633–34, 645 (1943); *Wooley v. Maynard*, 430 U.S. 705, 714 (1977).

97. 29 C.F.R. § 1604.11(f); cf. *Ellison v. Brady*, 924 F. 2d 872, 880 (9th Cir. 1991).

6. A Tale of Two Levels

1. An article on sexual harassment in an internal industrial relations newsletter thus warns the managers that "[o]ur defense is stronger if the [potentially offensive] pictures are not there at all than to argue that they are in an area where the employee shouldn't have been." This piece of advice is quoted in *Robinson v. Jacksonville Shipyards, Inc.*, 760 F. Supp. 1486, 1518 (M.D. Fla. 1991), in a manner that suggests that the court believes that it would have been wise for the defendant to have followed such advice.

2. An employer's interest in having a very wide margin of safety against "possible claims of sexual harassment" has been recognized as legitimate by an appellate court in California which regarded a prohibition of "fraternization" (romantic relationships) between employees as justifiable by that interest (*Crosier v. United Parcel Service, Inc.*, 150 Cal. App. 3d 1132, 1140 [1983]).

3. Cf. Kingsley R. Browne, "Title VII as Censorship: Hostile-Environment Harassment and the First Amendment," 52 *Ohio State Law Journal* 481, 504–8 (1991); Eugene Volokh, "Freedom of Speech and Workplace Harassment," 39 *UCLA Law Review* 1791, 1809–14 (1992); Eugene Volokh, "What Speech Does 'Hostile Work Environment' Law Restrict?" 85 *The Georgetown Law Journal* 627 (1997); Eugene Volokh, "How Harassment Law Restricts Free Speech," 47 *Rutgers Law Review* 563, 567–69 (1995); Kingsley R. Browne, "Workplace Censorship: A Response to Professor Sangree," 47 *Rutgers Law Review* 579, 581–85 (1995); Michael S. Greve, "Civil Rights and Uncivil Speech," 1994 *The Public Interest Law Review* 1, 14; Robert S. Adler and Ellen R. Peirce, "The Legal, Ethical, and Social Implications of the 'Reasonable Woman' Standard in Sexual Harassment Cases," 61 *Fordham Law Review* 773, 818–19 (1993). Browne's, Volokh's and Greve's arguments are made in the context of their discussions of the conflict between the sexual harassment law and freedom of speech: they argue that the interplay between what I have called the two levels of the law amplifies the law's restriction of freedom of speech. The argument that I am making here is broader: it concerns how the law affects individual freedoms in general. Adler and Peirce argue that the adoption of the reasonable woman standard may lead employers to enact highly restrictive workplace regulations; my argument, on the other hand, is that the two-level operation tends to lead to highly restrictive lower-level regulations *independently* of what standard is adopted at the upper level.

4. Stephen J. Schulhofer, *Unwanted Sex: The Culture of Intimidation and the Failure of Law* (Cambridge, MA: Harvard University Press, 1998), 41, 176–79.

5. *Horn v. Duke Homes, Division of Windsor Mobile Homes Inc.*, 755 F. 2d 599, 605 (7th Cir. 1985).

6. For an example of how the informal proceedings control individual conduct, see Howard Gadlin, "Mediating Sexual Harassment," in *Sexual Harassment on*

Campus: A Guide for Administrators, Faculty, and Students, ed. Bernice R. Sandler and Robert J. Shoop (Boston: Allyn and Bacon, 1997), 194–99, which describes at length the case of a professor who was subjected to "mediation" for having expressed exactly *once* that he was attracted to a student who was not at the time enrolled in any of his courses. According to the student's own account, he did that politely and without any physical contact. It is obvious that the purpose of the "mediation" was to impress it upon him, in a way that will carry an air of formal authority, that he ought not to express, even only once and politely, his attraction to any student.

7. See Rita Risser, "Sexual Harassment Training: Truth and Consequences," 52.8 *Training and Development* 21 (1999).

8. The argument that sexual harassment proceedings of a private employer should be regarded as state action has been considered and rejected in *Logan v. Bennington College Corp.*, 72 F. 3d 1017, 1027–28 (2d Cir. 1995), *cert.* denied, 519 U.S. 822 (1996).

9. The state itself when it acts as an employer is also subject to less stringent due process standards than it is when it acts through its judicial system. See *Cleveland Board of Education v. Loudermill,* 470 U.S. 532 (1985); *Kennedy v. Marion Correctional Institution,* 630 N.E. 2d 324 (Ohio 1994).

10. James J. Oh, "Internal Sexual Harassment Complaints: Investigating to Win," 18 *Employee Relations Law Journal* 227, 235 (1992).

11. Kirstin Downey Grimsley, "Sexual Harassment Evokes Wide Range of Responses," *The Washington Post,* 23 December 1996.

12. *Erickson v. Marsh & McLennan Co.*, 569 A. 2d 793, 803–4 (N.J. 1990).

13. Cf. Benjamin A. Holden, "Hilton Hotels Loses $ 5 Million Verdict in Tailhook Case," *The Wall Street Journal,* 1 November 1994.

14. Mary Braid, "College Clams Up on 'Unfair' Disciplinary System," *Independent,* 20 October 1993.

15. Anthea Hall, "Sex and the Single Student: Not All Men Are Rapists," *Sunday Telegraph,* 24 October 1993.

16. Numerous examples of the operation of such "kangaroo courts" within the U.S. institutions of higher education can be found in Alan Charles Kors and Harvey A. Silverglate, *The Shadow University: The Betrayal of Liberty on America's Campuses* (New York: The Free Press, 1998).

17. It is true that some employers are, usually as a result of collective bargaining, bound by employment contracts that can be construed as implying that a relatively stringent standard of proof will be used in disciplinary proceeding against employees. When an employer bound by such a contract encounters a case of sexual harassment, it will find itself with an irresolvable problem: the use of a more stringent standard will expose it to the risk of upper-level liability for sexual harassment, while the use of a less stringent one will likely trigger a well-founded grievance by the alleged harasser. See Estelle D. Franklin, "Maneuvering through the Labyrinth: The Employers' Paradox in Responding to Hostile Environment Sexual Harassment—A Proposed Way Out," 67 *Fordham Law Review* 1517, 1579–82 (1999). Employers that are prudent enough to consider the possibility of such problems ahead of their occurrence will realize that there is exactly one way to avoid them. The law about sexual harassment is a *law,* and thus inescapable, while contracts are, by definition, voluntary. Therefore, the one way to avoid the problems is to simply not enter into the contracts that may require the use of more stringent standards (or, if the employer is already bound by them, to not reenter them).

18. See *Cotran v. Rollins Hudig Hall International, Inc.*, 17 Cal. 4th 93 (1998). The California Supreme Court in *Cotran,* interestingly, based its decision not to

grant the alleged harasser the right to having the facts ascertained in a court of law partially on "the jury's relative remoteness from the everyday reality of the workplace" (17 Cal. 4th 93, 106). It is clearly inconsistent for a court to treat the jury's remoteness from the workplace as an obstacle to its reexamining the facts of alleged harassment when such a reexamination is sought by the alleged harasser, and not to so regard it when the reexamination is sought by the alleged victim.

19. An example of such weighing of evidence is the decision of LAPD about the incident that the complainants characterized as intentional touching, while the accused and the two witnesses characterized it as stumbling: the decision accepts the complainants' version on the ground that to do otherwise "would be to indict [the complainants'] own judgment and integrity" (Greg Krikorian, "A Rare Look inside Files on Sex Harassment in LAPD," *Los Angeles Times*, 27 March 1994). As any choice between such conflicting testimonies is bound to "indict" somebody's judgment and integrity, the reasoning supports the decision only under the assumption that the complainants' judgment and integrity is somehow inherently worthier than the judgment and integrity of the accused and his witnesses.

20. Ruth Shalit, "On the Hill: Caught in the Act," *New Republic*, 12 July 1993, quoted in Christina Hoff Sommers, *Who Stole Feminism?* (New York: Simon & Schuster, 1994), 224.

21. Violence Against Women Act of 1994, Pub. L. No. 103-322, § 40302, 108 Stat. 1902, 1941–42 (1994). The Supreme Court eventually declared the law unconstitutional, on the basis of federalism, in *United States v. Morrison*, 529 U.S. 598 (2000).

22. Jo Backer Laird, "Conducting a Discrimination or Harassment Investigation," SB36 *ALI-ABA* 1257, 1261 (1997).

23. Cf. Helen Remick et al., "Investigating Complaints of Sexual Harassment," in *Sexual Harassment on College Campuses: Abusing the Ivory Power*, ed. Michele A. Paludi (Albany: State University of New York Press, 1996), 242–43.

24. Laird, "Conducting a Discrimination or Harassment Investigation," SB36 *ALI-ABA* 1257, 1261.

25. See, for example, Louise F. Fitzgerald et al., "The Incidence and Dimensions of Sexual Harassment in Academia and the Workplace," 32 *Journal of Vocational Behavior* 152 (1988); Shmuel Ellis, Azy Barak, and Adaya Pinto, "Moderating Effects of Personal Cognitions on Experienced and Perceived Sexual Harassment of Women at the Workplace," 21 *Journal of Applied Social Psychology* 1320 (1991); Margaret S. Stockdale and Alan Vaux, "What Sexual Harassment Experiences Lead Respondents to Acknowledge Being Sexually Harassed? A Secondary Analysis of a University Survey," 43 *Journal of Vocational Behavior* 221 (1993); Sharon Toffey Shepela and Laurie L. Levesque, "Poisoned Waters: Sexual Harassment and the College Climate," 38 *Sex Roles* 589 (1998).

26. Edward Lafontaine and Leslie Tredeau, "The Frequency, Sources, and Correlates of Sexual Harassment among Women in Traditional Male Occupations," 15 *Sex Roles* 433, 435 (1986).

27. Shepela and Levesque, "Poisoned Waters," 607.

28. Cf. Michael S. Greve, "Sexual Harassment: Telling the Other Victims' Story," 23 *Northern Kentucky Law Review* 523, 530–33 (1996).

29. See, for example, Daphne Patai, *Heterophobia: Sexual Harassment and the Future of Feminism* (Lanham, MD: Rowman and Littlefield, 1998).

30. Titus E. Aaron with Judith A. Isaksen, *Sexual Harassment in the Workplace: A Guide to the Law and a Research Overview for Employers and Employees* (Jefferson, NC: McFarland, 1993), 83.

31. Another source of advice for employers encourages them to *require* their employees to report all sexual harassment, even if they are not directly affected by it: "Discipline may be appropriate not only for the harasser, but for employees who witnessed it and did not report it" ("Sexual Harassment: Addressing the New Realities of the 1990s," a report published by BNA Communications, reprinted, under the title "Preventing Harassment: What Employers Can and Should Do," in 82 *Business and Society Review* 32, 33 [1992]). Such a result of the two-level operation of the law is at odds with the legal tradition that otherwise seems to abhor any requirements that citizens spy on each other, and thus generally does not require them to report the illegal acts of others (including even the most heinous crimes). It should be noted that a prudent employee who is subject to such a requirement will report not only all actual sexual harassment, but all conduct that may appear to be sexual harassment. The requirement is thus likely to result, again, in a large-scale invasion of privacy.

32. Oh, "Internal Sexual Harassment Complaints," 240. It is symptomatic that the author refers to a person who has been exonerated of the charge as a "perpetrator."

33. *Sexual Harassment Manual for Managers and Supervisors: How to Prevent and Resolve Sexual Harassment Complaints in the Workplace* (Chicago: Commerce Clearing House, 1991), 16.

34. Ellen J. Wagner, *Sexual Harassment in the Workplace: How to Prevent, Investigate, and Resolve Problems in Your Organization* (New York: Amacom, 1992), 96.

35. Bernice Resnick Sandler, "Elements of a Good Policy," in *Sexual Harassment on Campus*, ed. Sandler and Shoop, 117.

36. As we shall see in the next chapter, the sexual harassment law is partially based on the principle that employers are liable for the consequences of negligent *hiring* or supervision of their employees.

37. John B. Pryor, Christine M. LaVite, and Lynnette M. Stoller "A Social Psychological Analysis of Sexual Harassment: The Person/Situation Interaction," 42 *Journal of Vocational Behavior* 68, 80 (1993), referring to a conference paper by M. A Moorman and D. Mankin.

7. SEXUAL HARASSMENT AND DISCRIMINATION

1. Title VII of the Civil Rights Act of 1964 (usually referred to simply as "Title VII" in the literature about employment law) continues to be the principal statutory basis for the federal law about sexual harassment, but cases of sexual harassment are occasionally also litigated in federal courts under an antidiscrimination statute (42 U.S.C. § 1983 and 42 U.S.C. § 1985[3]) that was enacted in the nineteenth century to enforce the Fourteenth Amendment of the Constitution.

2. 413 F. Supp. 654 (D.D.C. 1976), reversed on other grounds *sub nom. Williams v. Bell*, 587 F. 2d 1240 (D.C.Cir. 1978). (The district court eventually tried the case *de novo* as *Williams v. Civiletti*, 487 F. Supp. 1387 [D.D.C. 1980], and found for the plaintiff.)

3. Richard A. Epstein, *Forbidden Grounds: The Case against Employment Discrimination Laws* (Cambridge, MA: Harvard University Press, 1992).

4. 390 F. Supp. 161 (D. Ariz. 1975).

5. 390 F. Supp. 161, 163. While it is now settled law that a court dealing with the claims of an alleged victim cannot dismiss sexual harassment as merely "satisfying a personal urge," it is interesting that a court can dismiss it in almost the same words

(as "motivated by [the harasser's] own desire for sexual excitement") when deciding about the rights of a harasser who claimed that he suffered psychic injury because of the coworkers' treatment after he had been disciplined for sexual harassment (*Martone v. State of Rhode Island/Registry of Motor Vehicles*, 611 A. 2d 384, 388 [R.I. 1992]).

6. 390 F. Supp. 161, 163.

7. 390 F. Supp. 161, 163. Cf. Ellen Frankel Paul, "Sexual Harassment as Sex Discrimination: A Defective Paradigm," 8 *Yale Law and Policy Review* 333, 356 (1990).

8. 418 F. Supp. 233 (N.D. Cal. 1976).

9. 13 FEP Cases 123 (D.D.C. 1974).

10. *Miller v. Bank of America*, 600 F. 2d 211 (9th Cir. 1979); *Barnes v. Costle*, 561 F. 2d 983 (D.C.Cir. 1977). The decision in *Corne* was vacated without opinion: 562 F. 2d 55 (9th Cir. 1977).

11. 413 F. Supp. 654.

12. 413 F.Supp 654, 660.

13. *Meritor Savings Bank v. Vinson*, 477 U.S. 57, 72 (1986).

14. *Horn v. Duke Homes, Division of Windsor Mobile Homes, Inc.*, 755 F. 2d 599, 605 (7th Cir. 1985); *Martin v. Cavalier Hotel Corp.*, 48 F. 3d 1343, 1351–52 (4th Cir. 1995); and the initial panel opinion in *Ellerth v. Burlington Industries, Inc.*, 102 F. 3d 848, 857–60 (7th Cir. 1996). When *Ellerth* was reheard *en banc*, 123 F. 3d 490 (7th Cir. 1997), Judge Diane P. Wood (joined by Judges Easterbrook and Rovner) continued to defend the claim that the harassing conduct at issue was within the scope of employment, but the other members of the court disagreed. *Ellerth* eventually proceeded to the Supreme Court, as discussed below.

15. Restatement (Second) of Agency § 235. (The initial panel opinion in *Ellerth v. Burlington Industries, Inc.*, 102 F. 3d 848, 858, does mention that provision of the Restatement, but proceeds as if it did not imply that practically all sexual harassment is outside the scope of employment.) See also Restatement (Second) of Agency § 229(2) for the test of whether an act is "incidental" to the tasks one is employed to carry out: it would be very rare for sexual harassment to satisfy that test.

16. Cf. *Hicks v. Gates Rubber Co.*, 833 F. 2d 1406, 1417–18 (10th Cir. 1987).

17. Restatement (Second) of Agency § 219(2). Most of the discussion of these issues relies on the Restatement as the formulation of the relevant law of agency. That reliance has been strongly criticized in Judge Posner's opinion in *Ellerth* (decided together with *Jansen v. Packaging Corporation of America*), 123 F. 3d 490, 506–10. In view of the Supreme Court's decision in the same case, 524 U.S. 742 (1998), Judge Posner's criticism has no formal authority, but it is of considerable theoretical interest.

18. See *Sparks v. Pilot Freight Carriers, Inc.*, 830 F. 2d 1554, 1559–60 (11th Cir. 1987); *Hicks v. Gates Rubber Co.*, 833 F. 2d 1406, 1418; *Henson v. City of Dundee*, 682 F. 2d 897, 911 n. 21 (11th Cir. 1982).

19. *Rauh v. Coyne*, 744 F. Supp. 1186, 1190 (D.D.C. 1990).

20. See Restatement (Second) of Agency § 213.

21. See *Hicks v. Gates Rubber Co.*, 833 F. 2d 1406, 1418; cf. *Hall v. Gus Construction Co., Inc.*, 842 F. 2d 1010, 1015–16 (8th Cir. 1988).

22. 524 U.S. 742.

23. 524 U.S. 775 (1998).

24. In the same week as these two cases, the Supreme Court decided *Gebser v. Lago Vista Independent School District*, 524 U.S. 274 (1998), in which it held that this kind of reasoning does not apply to sexual harassment in education. According to that decision, the correct basis for imputing sexual harassment of students to edu-

cational institutions is not the law of agency, but rather something like a contract between educational institutions and the federal government, which is created by the institutions' acceptance of federal funding. A consequence of that decision is that the responsibility of educational institutions for sexual harassment of students is somewhat less extensive than the responsibility of employers for sexual harassment of employees. (*Davis v. Monroe County Board of Education,* 526 U.S. 629 (1999), decided a year later, seems to imply, however, that the responsibility is not much less extensive.)

25. The Court also specified that the harasser cannot be regarded as aided in accomplishing the harassment by the existence of the agency relationship on the sole ground that the employment relationship afforded him "proximity and regular contact" with the victim (*Burlington Industries, Inc. v. Ellerth,* 524 U.S. 742, 760).

26. While these two decisions provided a satisfactory answer to the general, theoretically significant question as to how the law of agency is related to sexual harassment, it is debatable whether they provided clear enough criteria for distinguishing the cases in which the harasser was aided by the agency relationship from the cases in which the employer was negligent or reckless: see the dissenting opinion in *Burlington Industries.* That distinction can be of considerable importance to the lower courts and potential litigants, because classifying the harasser as aided by the agency relationship implies that the plaintiff does not need to prove the employer's negligence or recklessness.

27. The argument has also been influential outside the United States: the Commission of the European Communities has, for example, declared that "Sexual Harassment is sex discrimination because the gender of the recipient is the determining factor in who is harassed" (Commission of the European Communities, *Commission Recommendation of 27 November 1991 on the Protection of the Dignity of Women and Men at Work [92/131/EEC],* 1992 OJ L 49, Annex, section 3).

28. *Meritor Savings Bank v. Vinson,* 477 U.S. 57.

29. *Harris v. Forklift Systems, Inc.,* 510 U.S. 17 (1993).

30. *Hopkins v. Baltimore Gas & Electric Co.,* 871 F. Supp. 822, 832 (D. Md. 1994).

31. 523 U.S. 75 (1998).

32. One commentator (Lynn McLain, "The EEOC Harassment Guidelines: Welcome Advances under Title VII?" 10 *University of Baltimore Law Review* 275, 290 [1981]) speculated that in promulgating the Guidelines, the EEOC confused two distinct meanings of the word "sex": the quality of being male or female (which is what Title VII is about), and sexual activities (which are what the Guidelines are about, but not what Title VII is about).

33. Vrinda Dalmiya claims, in the context of offering an analysis of the wrongness of sexual harassment, that when a man whistles at a woman, he is reacting to her as "a mere example or token of" the class of women, thus making her lose her individuality and treating her as "replaceable by other particulars or tokens of that" class ("Why Is Sexual Harassment Wrong?" 30 *Journal of Social Philosophy* 46, 54 [1999]). Larry May similarly asserts that "[t]he type of behavior characteristic of sexual harassment rarely relates to the differences of individual women" (*Masculinity and Morality* [Ithaca, N.Y.: Cornell University Press, 1998], 106). While this might be true of some cases of sexual harassment, it is most definitely not true of sexual harassment in general. A typical harasser does not treat all people of the relevant sex as interchangeable. In fact, victims of sexual harassment often complain that they felt "singled out" by the harassment, that is, that they did not feel as merely tokens of a class.

34. Catharine A. MacKinnon, *Sexual Harassment of Working Women: A Case of Sex Discrimination* (New Haven, CT: Yale University Press, 1979), 190.

35. 42 U.S.C. § 2000e-2(a).

36. *Phillips v. Martin Marietta Corp.*, 400 U.S. 542 (1971), discussed in *Williams* at pp. 658–59.

37. *Sprogis v. United Air Lines, Inc.*, 444 F. 2d 1194 (7th Cir. 1971); discussed in *Williams* at p. 659.

38. The actual facts of *Sprogis* made the comparison less than straightforward: see the dissenting opinion of Judge Stevens, 444 F. 2d, 1194, 1202–6.

39. 429 U.S. 125 (1976).

40. Pub. L. No. 95–555, 92 Stat. 2076 (1978), codified as 42 U.S.C. § 2000e(k).

41. Civil Rights Act of 1991, Pub. L. No. 102-166, § 107(a), 105 Stat. 1071, 1075 (1991), codified as 42 U.S.C. § 2000e-2(m).

42. *Price Waterhouse v. Hopkins*, 490 U.S. 228, 241 (1989).

43. 506 U.S. 263, 271–73 (1993); see, however, the dissenting opinion of Justice Stevens, joined by Justice Blackmun, 506 U.S. 263, 322–31.

44. 42 U.S.C. § 1985(3).

45. Paul, "Sexual Harassment as Sex Discrimination," 350.

46. For an example of such an attempt, see Robert L. Holmes, "Sexual Harassment and the University," 79 *The Monist* 499, 502–6 (1996).

47. 716 F. 2d 1167 (7th Cir. 1983).

48. 716 F. 2d 1167, 1172.

49. *Volk v. Coler*, 845 F. 2d 1422, 1433 (7th Cir. 1988).

50. 898 F. 2d 533, 538 (7th Cir. 1990).

51. 898 F. 2d 533, 542.

52. *Trautvetter v. Quick*, 916 F. 2d 1140 (7th Cir. 1990).

53. 916 F. 2d 1140, 1152, quoting *Bohen v. City of East Chicago*, 799 F. 2d 1180, 1188 (7th Cir. 1986), which, in turn, quotes the district court's opinion, 622 F. Supp. 1234, 1240 (N.D. Ind. 1985).

54. *Neal v. Evitts*, 55 FEP Cases 473, 474 (E.D. Ky. 1991).

55. 390 F. Supp. 161, 163.

56. 760 F. 2d 1330, 1333 n. 7 (D.C.Cir. 1985). This is an opinion of three judges who all later became very famous, albeit in very different ways. They were Robert Bork, Antonin Scalia, and Kenneth Starr.

57. *Barnes v. Costle*, 561 F. 2d 983, 990 n. 55; *Henson v. City of Dundee*, 682 F. 2d 897, 904; *Rabidue v. Osceola Refining Co.*, 805 F. 2d 611, 620 (6th Cir. 1986) *cert.* denied, 481 U.S. 1041 (1987); *Prescott v. Independent Life and Accident Insurance Co.*, 878 F. Supp. 1545, 1551 (M.D. Ala. 1995); "Note: Sexual Harassment and Title VII: The Foundation for the Elimination of Sexual Cooperation as an Employment Condition," 76 *Michigan Law Review* 1007, 1020 n. 99 (1978).

58. Until recently, such cases of bisexual harassers figured only in hypothetical examples. However, in *Holman v. Indiana,* 211 F. 3d 399 (7th Cir. 2000), *cert.* denied, 531 U.S. 880 (2000) two real-life plaintiffs, a man and a woman, had their claims of sexual harassment dismissed because they alleged that the same person harassed both of them in similar ways. See also *Ryczek v. Guest Services, Inc.*, 877 F. Supp. 754 (D.D.C. 1995) in which the court came close (at pp. 761–62) to having to deal with the allegation that the harasser was, in fact, bisexual.

59. *Bundy v. Jackson*, 641 F. 2d 934, 942 n. 7 (D.C.Cir. 1981); *Jones v. Flagship International*, 793 F. 2d 714, 720 n. 5 (5th Cir. 1986), *cert.* denied, 479 U.S. 1065 (1987); *Saulpaugh v. Monroe Community Hospital*, 4 F. 3d 134, 141 (2d Cir. 1993), *cert.* denied, 510 U.S. 1164 (1994); MacKinnon, *Sexual Harassment of Working Women*,

203; "Comment: Employment Discrimination—Sexual Harassment and Title VII," 51 *New York University Law Review* 148, 152 (1976); Lucinda M. Finley, "Transcending Equality Theory: A Way out of the Maternity and the Workplace Debate," 86 *Columbia Law Review* 1118, 1143 n. 110 (1986); John J. Donohue III, "Advocacy versus Analysis in Assessing Employment Discrimination Law," 44 *Stanford Law Review* 1583, 1611 (1992); Dale Carpenter, "Same-Sex Sexual Harassment under Title VII," 37 *South Texas Law Review* 699, 716 (1996).

60. A similar misunderstanding of the character of the objection permeates Deborah N. McFarland's reasoning in "Beyond Sex Discrimination: A Proposal for Federal Sexual Harassment Legislation," 65 *Fordham Law Review* 493 (1996). McFarland treats the objection as if it posed a merely practical problem that could be solved by adding a suitable piece of legislation to the existing body of sexual harassment law, rather than as casting doubt on the justifiability of treating sexual harassment as a species of sex discrimination, and thus on the very root of the existing law.

61. Dodds et al., unlike the authors referred to above, understand the "logic" of the bisexual objection well, but do not appreciate its significance, because they are completely unaware that the law about sexual harassment is *based* on subsuming sexual harassment under the notion of discrimination (Susan M. Dodds et al., "Sexual Harassment," 14 *Social Theory and Practice* 111, 113–14 [1988]).

62. *McDonnell v. Cisneros*, 84 F. 3d 256, 260 (7th Cir. 1996).

63. 25 F. 3d 1459 (9th Cir. 1994), *cert.* denied, 513 U.S. 1082 (1995).

64. 25 F. 3d 1459, 1463.

65. 25 F. 3d 1459, 1463; cf. *Chiapuzio v. BLT Operating Corp.*, 826 F.Supp 1334, 1337–38 (D. Wyo. 1993). It has been remarked that the reasoning in *Chiapuzio* "appears contrived to engineer a fair outcome" (McFarland, "Beyond Sex Discrimination," 526).

66. 25 F. 3d 1459, 1464. Cf. *Cardin v. Via Tropical Fruits, Inc.*, 1993 U.S.Dist. LEXIS 16302, 46 (S.D. Fla.).

67. MacKinnon, *Sexual Harassment of Working Women*, 203.

68. See pp. 83–92 above.

69. One empirical study, for example, claims to have found that "the male and female respondents did *not* differ in the manner by which they were psychologically traumatized by sexual harassment" (Rebecca A. Thacker and Stephan F. Gohmann, "Emotional and Psychological Consequences of Sexual Harassment: A Descriptive Study," 130 *The Journal of Psychology* 429, 440 [1996], italics added). That study, however, does not really settle the issue of whether the male and female responses differ, because both the harassing conduct and its effects were characterized in very general terms. Upon careful reading, the study thus leaves it open whether *the same* specific conduct traumatizes males and females to *the same* extent.

70. *Roberts v. United States Jaycees*, 468 U.S. 609, 618 (1984).

71. *Stewart v. Cartessa Corp.*, 771 F. Supp. 876, 880 (S.D. Ohio 1990).

72. *Joyner v. AAA Cooper Transportation*, 597 F. Supp. 537, 542 (M.D. Ala. 1983).

73. Cf. Katherine M. Franke, "What's Wrong with Sexual Harassment?" 49 *Stanford Law Review* 691, 733 (1997).

74. Cf. F. M. Christensen, "'Sexual Harassment' Must Be Eliminated," 8 *Public Affairs Quarterly* 1, 8–9 (1994).

75. *Barnes v. Costle*, 561 F. 2d 983, 990 n. 55; *Henson v. City of Dundee*, 682 F. 2d 897, 904.

76. Cf. Franke, "What's Wrong with Sexual Harassment?" 749; *pace* Michelle Ridgeway Peirce, "Sexual Harassment and Title VII—A Better Solution," 30 *Boston College Law Review* 1071, 1099 (1989).

77. Cf. Paul, "Sexual Harassment as Sex Discrimination," 352; Peirce, "Sexual Harassment and Title VII," 1095.

78. See, for example, *Wright v. Methodist Youth Services, Inc.*, 511 F. Supp. 307, 309–10 (N.D. Ill. 1981); *Joyner v. AAA Cooper Transportation*, 597 F. Supp. 537, 541–42, aff'd without opinion, 749 F. 2d 732 (11th Cir. 1984); *Quick v. Donaldson Co., Inc.*, 90 F. 3d 1372 (8th Cir. 1996); *Mogilefsky v. Superior Court*, 20 Cal. App. 4th 1409 (1993); *McCoy v. Johnson Controls World Services Inc.*, 878 F. Supp. 229, 231–32 (S.D. Ga. 1995); *Prescott v. Independent Life and Accident Insurance Co.*, 878 F. Supp. 1545, 1549–51; *King v. M.R. Brown, Inc.*, 911 F. Supp. 161, 166–67 (E.D. Pa. 1995); *Sardinia v. Dellwood Foods*, 69 FEP Cases 705 (S.D.N.Y. 1995); *Tanner v. Prima Donna Resorts, Inc.*, 919 F. Supp. 351, 354–56 (D. Nev. 1996); *Johnson v. Community Nursing Services*, 932 F. Supp. 269 (D. Utah 1996); *Peric v. Board of Trustees of the University of Illinois*, 71 FEP Cases 1760 (N.D. Ill. 1996).

79. EEOC Compliance Manual § 615.2(b)(3).

80. *Schoiber v. Emro Marketing Co.*, 941 F. Supp. 730, 738 (N.D. Ill. 1996), italics added. The identical wording can be found in *Torres v. National Precision Blanking*, 943 F. Supp. 952, 959 (N.D. Ill. 1996). See also, for example, *Goluszek v. Smith*, 697 F. Supp. 1452 (N.D. Ill. 1988); *Giddens v. Shell Oil Co.*, 67 FEP Cases 576 (5th Cir. 1993), *cert.* denied, 513 U.S. 925 (1994); *Garcia v. Elf Atochem North America*, 28 F. 3d 446, 451–52 (5th Cir. 1994); *Oncale v. Sundowner Offshore Services, Inc.*, 83 F. 3d 118 (5th Cir. 1996), rev'd, 523 U.S. 75; *Fleenor v. Hewitt Soap Co.*, 67 FEP Cases 1625 (S.D. Ohio 1994); *Myers v. City of El Paso*, 874 F. Supp. 1546, 1548 (W.D. Tex. 1995); *Ashworth v. RoundUp Co.*, 897 F. Supp. 489, 492–94 (W.D. Wash. 1995). The *Giddens* court, which made the first appellate-level decision on the issue, seemed completely unaware that it was ruling on a difficult and potentially controversial matter: the opinion is short, contains practically no argument, and was not even designated for publication by the court. It appeared in print only after it had been referred to in *Garcia*, and after *Garcia* had proven to be influential.

81. *Goluszek v. Smith*, 697 F. Supp. 1452, 1456.

82. *Meritor Savings Bank v. Vinson*, 477 U.S. 57, 64.

83. See the cases of the Northern District of Illinois cited above.

84. *Easton v. Crossland Mortgage Corp.*, 905 F. Supp. 1368, 1378–80, 1381–84 (C.D. Cal. 1995); *Blozis v. Mike Raisor Ford, Inc.*, 896 F. Supp. 805 (N.D. Ind. 1995); cf. *Vandeventer v. Wabash National Corporation*, 887 F. Supp. 1178 (N.D. Ind. 1995), qualifying, on reconsideration, the apparently much stronger position on same-sex harassment expressed in the initial decision in 867 F. Supp. 790, 796 (N.D. Ind. 1994).

85. *EEOC v. Walden Book Co., Inc.*, 885 F. Supp. 1100, 1102 (M.D. Tenn. 1995).

86. *Tietgen v. Brown's Westminster Motors, Inc.*, 921 F. Supp. 1495, 1501 (E.D. Va. 1996).

87. *Wrightson v. Pizza Hut of America*, 99 F. 3d 138 (4th Cir. 1996); *McWilliams v. Fairfax County Board of Supervisors*, 72 F. 3d 1191, 1195–96 (4th Cir. 1996), *cert.* denied, 519 U.S. 819 (1996).

88. See the dissenting opinion in *McWilliams v. Fairfax County Board of Supervisors*, 72 F. 3d 1191, 1198–99.

89. *EEOC v. Walden Book Co., Inc.*, 885 F. Supp. 1100, 1102; *Martin v. Norfolk Southern Railway Co.*, 926 F. Supp. 1044, 1049–50 (N.D. Ala. 1996).

90. This has been misunderstood by Pamela J. Papish, "Homosexual Harassment or Heterosexual Horseplay? The False Dichotomy of Same-Sex Sexual Harassment Law," 28 *Columbia Human Rights Law Review* 201 (1996). Papish is critical of the trend exemplified by such cases, and blames the but-for-one's-sex criterion for it,

not realizing that a strict and consistent application of the criterion to such cases would have generally produced the results she favors.

91. 523 U.S. 75.

92. *Hopkins v. Baltimore Gas & Electric Co.*, 871 F. Supp. 822, 832.

93. *Carreno v. Local Union No. 226, International Brotherhood of Electrical Workers*, 54 FEP Cases 81 (D. Kan. 1990); *Dillon v. Frank*, 1992 WL 5436 (6th Cir.).

94. See *DeSantis v. Pacific Telephone & Telegraph Co., Inc.*, 608 F. 2d 327 (9th Cir. 1979). Interestingly, although it is generally agreed that discrimination on the basis of *actual* homosexuality is not covered by Title VII, and although the *Dillon* court has interpreted that to apply to discrimination on the basis of *perceived* homosexuality, at least one other court was of the opinion that *falsely* calling someone a lesbian may be a part of sexual harassment that is actionable under Title VII: *Saville v. Houston County Healthcare Authority*, 852 F. Supp. 1512, 1526 (M.D. Ala 1994).

95. *Carreno v. Local Union No. 226, Int'l Brotherhood of Elec. Workers*, 54 FEP Cases 81, 82–83.

96. Cf. Samuel A. Marcosson, "Harassment on the Basis of Sexual Orientation: A Claim of Sex Discrimination under Title VII," 81 *The Georgetown Law Journal* 1 (1992); Sandra Levitsky, "Footnote 55: Closing the 'Bisexual Defense' Loophole in Title VII Sexual Harassment Cases," 80 *Minnesota Law Review* 1013, 1035–36 (1996).

97. Amy Shahan, "Determining Whether Title VII Provides a Cause of Action for Same-Sex Sexual Harassment," 48 *Baylor Law Review* 507, 526 (1996); cf. Gabriel A. Terrasa, "Fitting a Square Peg into a Round Hole: 'Same-Sex' Sexual Harassment and the 'Because of . . . Sex' Requirement in Hostile Environment Claims," 67 *Revista Jurídica Universidad de Puerto Rico* 163, 196 (1998).

98. Cf. Martha Chamallas, "Consent, Equality, and the Legal Control of Sexual Conduct," 61 *Southern California Law Review* 777, 849 (1988).

99. *Barnes v. Costle*, 561 F. 2d 983, 990.

100. *Bundy v. Jackson*, 641 F. 2d 934, 942.

101. 42 U.S.C. § 2000e-2(m).

102. *DeCintio v. Westchester County Medical Center*, 807 F. 2d 304, 308 (2d Cir. 1986), *cert.* denied, 484 U.S. 825 (1987). See also *Becerra v. Dalton*, 94 F. 3d 145 (4th Cir. 1996), *cert.* denied, 519 U.S. 115 (1997); *Womack v. Runyon*, 147 F. 3d 1298 (11th Cir. 1998).

103. 807 F. 2d 304, 308.

104. Cf. McLain, "The EEOC Harassment Guidelines," 297.

105. 570 F. Supp. 1197, 1199 (D. Del. 1983).

106. 598 F. Supp. 65 (D.D.C. 1984); 778 F. 2d 878 (D.C. Cir. 1985).

107. 598 F. Supp. 65, 66–67.

108. 778 F. 2d 878, 880, cf. 883.

109. *Priest v. Rotary*, 634 F. Supp. 571, 581–82 (N.D. Cal. 1986), *Broderick v. Ruder*, 685 F. Supp. 1269 (D.D.C. 1988); *Piech v. Arthur Andersen & Co., S.C.*, 841 F. Supp. 825, 829–30 (N.D. Ill. 1994); Dirksen v. City of Springfield, 842 F. Supp. 1117, 1122 (C.D. Ill. 1994).

110. 679 F. Supp. 495, 501 (W.D. Pa. 1988), aff'd without opinion, 856 F. 2d 184 (3d Cir. 1988). The fact that the court of appeals affirmed this decision *without opinion* is noteworthy in view of the fact that the district court that made the decision and the district court that decided *Toscano* are both within the same appellate circuit. (An appellate court normally publishes an opinion when dealing with a matter on which the courts below appear to be in disharmony.) For another case with the same structure and the same result as *Miller*, see *Harvey v. Chevron U.S.A., Inc.*, 961 F. Supp. 1017, 1029–30 (S.D. Tex. 1997).

111. *Kersul v. Skulls Angels, Inc.*, 495 N.Y.S. 2d 886, 888–89 (Sup. 1985).

112. *Nicolo v. Citibank New York State, N.A.*, 554 N.Y.S. 2d 795 (Sup. 1990); cf. *Erickson v. Marsh & McLennan Co., Inc.*, 569 A.2d 793, 800–3 (N.J. 1990); *Duet v. Martin Marietta Corp.*, 720 So. 2d 1290, 1291–92 (La. Ct. App. 1998).

113. EEOC Notice No. N-915-048 (12 January 1990).

114. Cf. Joan E. Van Tol, "Eros Gone Awry: Liability under Title VII for Workplace Sexual Favoritism," 13 *Industrial Relations Law Journal* 153, 179 (1991).

115. 826 F. Supp. 443 (S.D. Fla. 1993).

116. Sharon Toffey Shepela and Laurie L. Levesque, "Poisoned Waters: Sexual Harassment and the College Climate," 38 *Sex Roles* 589, 608 (1998), citing a communication from A. Johnson.

117. See MacKinnon, *Sexual Harassment of Working Women*, 119.

118. Andrew Altman, "Making Sense of Sexual Harassment Law," 25 *Philosophy and Public Affairs* 36, 39–40 (1996).

119. Cf. Altman, "Making Sense of Sexual Harassment Law," 40–41.

120. Levitsky, "Closing the 'Bisexual Defense' Loophole," 1038. Cf. Franke, "What's Wrong with Sexual Harassment?"; Anita M. Superson, "A Feminist Definition of Sexual Harassment," 24.1 *Journal of Social Philosophy* 46 (1993); John C. Hughes and Larry May, "Sexual Harassment," 6 *Social Theory and Practice* 249, 263–68 (1980); Dalmiya, "Why Is Sexual Harassment Wrong?" 57–59.

121. Levitsky, "Closing the 'Bisexual Defense' Loophole," 1038.

122. Cf. Hughes and May, "Sexual Harassment," 266–67.

123. See Levitsky, "Closing the 'Bisexual Defense' Loophole," 1042–43.

124. Cf. Superson, "A Feminist Definition of Sexual Harassment," 49, 52; MacKinnon, *Sexual Harassment of Working Women*, 172.

125. Some further discussion of the idea that sexual harassment is a form of sex discrimination can be found in my "Why the Fight against Sexual Harassment is Misguided," in Linda LeMoncheck and Mane Hajdin, *Sexual Harassment: A Debate* (Lanham, MD: Rowman and Littlefield, 1997), 130–40.

8. ALTERNATIVES

1. Cf. Alan Vaux, "Paradigmatic Assumptions in Sexual Harassment Research: Being Guided without Being Misled," 42 *Journal of Vocational Behavior* 116, 127 (1993): "the construct sexual harassment . . . needs to be broken down."

2. Interestingly, the existence of most of the alternatives to the sexual harassment law that will be discussed in this chapter has been acknowledged by the most famous defender of the law, Catharine MacKinnon (*Sexual Harassment of Working Women: A Case of Sex Discrimination* [New Haven, Conn.: Yale University Press, 1979], 158–59). She does not regard that acknowledgment as significantly affecting her argument in favor of the law, because she is convinced that sexual harassment is a form of sex discrimination, and that handling it under the umbrella of antidiscrimination law consequently captures the nature of its wrongness better than any of these alternative mechanisms. We have, however, seen in chapter 7 that thinking of sexual harassment as a form of discrimination is misguided.

3. Cf. Ellen Frankel Paul, "Sexual Harassment as Sex Discrimination: A Defective Paradigm," 8 *Yale Law and Policy Review* 333, 356 (1990).

4. This is only very rarely the case, as the overwhelming majority of employed people nowadays work for corporate employers (which is why I have, throughout this

book, been referring to an employer as "it"). The rarity of such cases is, however, obscured by the peculiar terminology of the Civil Rights Act, in which the word "employer" refers not only to employers in the usual sense of the word, but also to supervisors.

5. 316 A. 2d 549 (N.H. 1974).

6. 736 F. 2d 1202 (8th Cir. 1984).

7. See, for example, *Andrews v. City of Philadelphia*, 895 F. 2d 1469 (3d Cir. 1990).

8. Cf. Jeffrey Rosen, *The Unwanted Gaze: The Destruction of Privacy in America* (New York: Random House, 2000), esp. 115–22.

9. *Phillips v. Smalley Maintenance Services*, 435 So. 2d 705, 711 (Ala. 1983).

10. *Phillips v. Smalley Maintenance Services*, 435 So. 2d 705, 711; *Busby v. Truswal Systems Corp.*, 551 So. 2d 322, 324 (Ala. 1989); *Van Jelgerhuis v. Mercury Finance Co.*, 940 F. Supp. 1344, 1368 (S.D. Ind. 1996).

11. One court has observed, in a different context, that "[o]ur distaste for legal recognition of breaches of etiquette does not in the least diminish the importance of etiquette. Quite the contrary: Etiquette governs things that are more important to people than most of the things for which courts do offer redress" (*Keyes v. Keyes*, 392 S.E. 2d 693, 696 [W.Va. 1990]).

12. Richard A. Epstein, *Forbidden Grounds: The Case against Employment Discrimination Laws* (Cambridge, MA: Harvard University Press, 1992), 356.

Bibliography

Aaron, Titus E., with Judith A. Isaksen. *Sexual Harassment in the Workplace: A Guide to the Law and a Research Overview for Employers and Employees.* Jefferson, NC: McFarland, 1993.

Adler, Robert S., and Ellen R. Peirce. "The Legal, Ethical, and Social Implications of the 'Reasonable Woman' Standard in Sexual Harassment Cases." 61 *Fordham Law Review* 773 (1993).

Aggarwal, Arjun P. *Sexual Harassment: A Guide for Understanding and Prevention.* Toronto: Butterworths, 1992.

Altman, Andrew. "Making Sense of Sexual Harassment Law." 25 *Philosophy and Public Affairs* 36 (1996).

Ashraf, Saba. "The Reasonableness of the 'Reasonable Woman' Standard: An Evaluation of Its Use in Hostile Environment Sexual Harassment Claims under Title VII of the Civil Rights Act." 21 *Hofstra Law Review* 483 (1992).

Backhouse, Constance, and Leah Cohen. *Sexual Harassment on the Job: How to Avoid the Working Woman's Nightmare.* Englewood Cliffs, NJ: Prentice-Hall, 1981.

Bernstein, Anita. "Treating Sexual Harassment with Respect." 111 *Harvard Law Review* 445 (1997).

Browne, Kingsley R. "Title VII as Censorship: Hostile-Environment Harassment and the First Amendment." 52 *Ohio State Law Journal* 481 (1991).

——. "Workplace Censorship: A Response to Professor Sangree." 47 *Rutgers Law Review* 579 (1995).

Bryant, Barbara S. "Evidentiary Issues in Sexual Harassment Cases, Part II: Broadening Access to the Defendant's Sexual/Personal History." 1994 *California Employment Law Reporter* 171.

Carpenter, Dale. "Same-Sex Sexual Harassment under Title VII." 37 *South Texas Law Review* 699 (1996).

Chamallas, Martha. "Consent, Equality, and the Legal Control of Sexual Conduct." 61 *Southern California Law Review* 777 (1988).

——. "Feminist Constructions of Objectivity: Multiple Perspectives in Sexual and Racial Harassment Litigation." 1 *Texas Journal of Women and the Law* 95 (1992).

Christensen, F. M. "'Sexual Harassment' Must Be Eliminated." 8 *Public Affairs Quarterly* 1 (1994).

Cooper, Stacy J. "Sexual Harassment and the Swedish Bikini Team: A Reevaluation of the 'Hostile Environment' Doctrine." 26 *Columbia Journal of Law and Social Problems* 387 (1993).

Crosthwaite, Jan, and Christine Swanton. "On the Nature of Sexual Harassment." 64. Supp. *Australasian Journal of Philosophy* 91 (1986).

Crosthwaite, Jan, and Graham Priest. "The Definition of Sexual Harassment." 74 *Australasian Journal of Philosophy* 66 (1996).

Dalmiya, Vrinda. "Why Is Sexual Harassment Wrong?" 30 *Journal of Social Philosophy* 46 (1999).

DeBruin, Debra A. "A Critique of Superson's Feminist Definition of Sexual Harassment." 29.1 *Journal of Social Philosophy* 49 (1998).

DeCosse, Sarah A. "Simply Unbelievable: Reasonable Women and Hostile Environment Sexual Harassment." 10 *Law and Inequality* 285 (1992).

Dodds, Susan M., et al. "Sexual Harassment." 14 *Social Theory and Practice* 111 (1988).

Dolkart, Jane L. "Hostile Environment Harassment: Equality, Objectivity, and the Shaping of Legal Standards." 43 *Emory Law Journal* 151 (1994).

Donohue, John J., III. "Advocacy Versus Analysis in Assessing Employment Discrimination Law." 44 *Stanford Law Review* 1583 (1992).

Dragel, Cheryl L. "Hostile Environment Sexual Harassment: Should the Ninth Circuit's 'Reasonable Woman' Standard Be Adopted?" 11 *Journal of Law and Commerce* 237 (1992).

Dziech, Billie Wright, and Linda Weiner. *The Lecherous Professor: Sexual Harassment on Campus*, 2d ed. Urbana: University of Illinois Press, 1990.

Ellis, Shmuel, Azy Barak, and Adaya Pinto. "Moderating Effects of Personal Cognitions on Experienced and Perceived Sexual Harassment of Women at the Workplace." 21 *Journal of Applied Social Psychology* 1320 (1991).

Ellis, Judy Trent. "Sexual Harassment and Race: A Legal Analysis of Discrimination." 8 *Journal of Legislation* 30 (1981).

"Employment Discrimination—Sexual Harassment and Title VII." 51 *New York University Law Review* 148 (1976).

Epstein, Deborah. "Can a 'Dumb Ass Woman' Achieve Equality in the Workplace? Running the Gauntlet of Hostile Environment Harassing Speech." 84 *The Georgetown Law Journal* 399 (1996).

——. "Free Speech at Work: Verbal Harassment as Gender-Based Discriminatory (Mis)treatment." 85 *The Georgetown Law Journal* 649 (1997).

Epstein, Richard A. *Forbidden Grounds: The Case against Employment Discrimination Laws.* Cambridge, MA: Harvard University Press, 1992.

Estlund, Cynthia L. "Freedom of Expression in the Workplace and the Problem of Discriminatory Harassment." 75 *Texas Law Review* 687 (1997).

Estrich, Susan. "Sex at Work." 43 *Stanford Law Review* 813 (1991).

Fallon, Richard H., Jr. "Sexual Harassment, Content Neutrality, and the First Amendment Dog that Didn't Bark." 1994 *The Supreme Court Review* 1.

Farley, Lin. *Sexual Shakedown: The Sexual Harassment of Women on the Job.* New York: McGraw-Hill, 1978.

Finley, Lucinda M. "Transcending Equality Theory: A Way out of the Maternity and the Workplace Debate." 86 *Columbia Law Review* 1118 (1986).

Fitzgerald, Louise F. "Science v. Myth: The Failure of Reason in the Clarence Thomas Hearings." 65 *Southern California Law Review* 1399 (1992).

Fitzgerald, Louise F., et al., "The Incidence and Dimensions of Sexual Harassment in Academia and the Workplace." 32 *Journal of Vocational Behavior* 152 (1988).

Franke, Katherine M. "What's Wrong with Sexual Harassment?" 49 *Stanford Law Review* 691 (1997).

Franklin, Estelle D. "Maneuvering through the Labyrinth: The Employers' Paradox in Responding to Hostile Environment Sexual Harassment—A Proposed Way Out." 67 *Fordham Law Review* 1517 (1999).

Gallop, Jane. *Feminist Accused of Sexual Harassment.* Durham: Duke University Press, 1997.

Gedrose, David I. "Workplace Sexual Harassment: The Ninth Circuit's Reasonable Woman Standard and Employer Remedial Actions in Hostile Environment Claims Following *Ellison v. Brady.*" 28 *Willamette Law Review* 151 (1991).

Gerard, Jules B. "The First Amendment in a Hostile Environment: A Primer on Free Speech and Sexual Harassment." 68 *Notre Dame Law Review* 1003 (1993).

Gettle, Jeffrey A. "Sexual Harassment and the Reasonable Woman Standard: Is It a Viable Solution?" 31 *Duquesne Law Review* 841 (1993).

Gomez-Preston, Cheryl, with Randi Reisfeld. *When No Means No: A Guide to Sexual Harassment.* New York: Carol Publishing Group, 1993.

Greve, Michael S. "Civil Rights and Uncivil Speech." 1994 *The Public Interest Law Review* 1.

——. "Sexual Harassment: Telling the Other Victims' Story." 23 *Northern Kentucky University Law Review* 523 (1996).

Gutek, Barbara A. "How Subjective Is Sexual Harassment?: An Examination of Rater Effects." 17 *Basic and Applied Social Psychology* 447 (1995).

——. *Sex and the Workplace: The Impact of Sexual Behavior and Harassment on Women, Men, and Organizations.* San Francisco: Jossey-Bass, 1985.

Holmes, Robert L. "Sexual Harassment and the University." 79 *The Monist* 499 (1996).

Horton, Amy. "Of Supervision, Centerfolds, and Censorship: Sexual Harassment, the First Amendment, and the Contours of Title VII." 46 *University of Miami Law Review* 403 (1991).

Hughes, John C., and Larry May, "Sexual Harassment." 6 *Social Theory and Practice* 249 (1980).

Jaffe, David M. "Walking the Constitutional Tightrope: Balancing Title VII Hostile Environment Sexual Harassment Claims with Free Speech Defenses." 80 *Minnesota Law Review* 979 (1996).

Johnson, Paul B. "The Reasonable Woman in Sexual Harassment Law: Progress or Illusion?" 28 *Wake Forest Law Review* 619 (1993).

Karner, Jessica M. "Political Speech, Sexual Harassment, and a Captive Workforce." 83 *California Law Review* 637 (1995).

Kenealy, Kathleen A. "Sexual Harassment and the Reasonable Woman Standard." 8 *The Labor Lawyer* 203 (1992).

Kors, Alan Charles, and Harvey A. Silverglate. *The Shadow University: The Betrayal of Liberty on America's Campuses.* New York: The Free Press, 1998.

Lafontaine, Edward, and Leslie Tredeau. "The Frequency, Sources, and Correlates of Sexual Harassment among Women in Traditional Male Occupations." 15 *Sex Roles* 433 (1986).

Laird, Jo Backer. "Conducting a Discrimination or Harassment Investigation." SB36 *ALI-ABA* 1257 (1997).

Lamberson, Phillip L. "Personal Liability for Violations of Title VII: Thirty Years of Indecision." 46 *Baylor Law Review* 419 (1994).

Larison, Dorraine A., and Mary E. Olk. "Sexual Harassment Awareness Training: It's Not the Boogie Monster." 72 *North Dakota Law Review* 387 (1996).

LeMoncheck, Linda, and Mane Hajdin. *Sexual Harassment: A Debate.* Lanham, MD: Rowman and Littlefield, 1997.

Lester, Toni. "The Reasonable Woman Test in Sexual Harassment Law—Will It Really Make a Difference?" 26 *Indiana Law Review* 227 (1993).

Leventer, Jan C. "Sexual Harassment and Title VII: EEOC Guidelines, Conditions Litigation, and the United States Supreme Court." 10 *Capital University Law Review* 481 (1981).

Levitsky, Sandra. "Footnote 55: Closing the 'Bisexual Defense' Loophole in Title VII Sexual Harassment Cases." 80 *Minnesota Law Review* 1013 (1996).

Lott, Bernice, and Mary Ellen Reilly, eds. *Combating Sexual Harassment in Higher Education.* Washington: National Education Association, 1996.

Luis, Juanita B., ed. *Litigating the Sexual Harassment Case: A Guide for Plaintiff and Defense Attorneys.* Chicago: Tort and Insurance Practice Section, American Bar Association, 1994.

MacKinnon, Catharine A. *Only Words.* Cambridge, MA: Harvard University Press, 1993.

——. *Sexual Harassment of Working Women: A Case of Sex Discrimination.* New Haven: Yale University Press, 1979.

Mappes, Thomas A. "Sexual Morality and the Concept of Using Another Person." In *Social Ethics: Morality and Social Policy,* 5th ed., ed. Thomas A. Mappes and Jane S. Zembaty. New York: McGraw-Hill, 1997.

Marcosson, Samuel A. "Harassment on the Basis of Sexual Orientation: A Claim of Sex Discrimination under Title VII." 81 *The Georgetown Law Journal* 1 (1992).

May, Larry. *Masculinity and Morality.* Ithaca, N.Y.: Cornell University Press, 1998.

Mcauliffe, Shannon. "Speak No Evil: The First Amendment Offers No Protection for Sexual Harassers." 29 *Suffolk University Law Review* 233 (1995).

McCann, Nancy Dodd, and Thomas A. McGinn, *Harassed: 100 Women Define Inappropriate Behavior in the Workplace.* Homewood, IL: Business One Irwin, 1992.

McFarland, Deborah N. "Beyond Sex Discrimination: A Proposal for Federal Sexual Harassment Legislation." 65 *Fordham Law Review* 493 (1996).

McLain, Lynn. "The EEOC Sexual Harassment Guidelines: Welcome Advances under Title VII?" 10 *University of Baltimore Law Review* 275, 312 (1981).

Mead, Margaret. "A Proposal: We Need Taboos on Sex at Work." *Redbook,* April 1978.

Neugarten, Dail Ann, and Jay M. Shafritz, eds. *Sexuality in Organizations: Romantic and Coercive Behaviors at Work.* Oak Park, IL: Moore Publishing, 1980.

O'Donohue, William, ed. *Sexual Harassment: Theory, Research, and Treatment.* Boston: Allyn and Bacon, 1997.

Oh, James J. "Internal Sexual Harassment Complaints: Investigating to Win." 18 *Employee Relations Law Journal* 227 (1992).

Paludi, Michele A., ed. *Ivory Power: Sexual Harassment on Campus.* Albany: State University of New York Press, 1990.

——, ed. *Sexual Harassment on College Campuses: Abusing the Ivory Power.* Albany: State University of New York Press, 1996.

Papish, Pamela J. "Homosexual Harassment or Heterosexual Horseplay? The False Dichotomy of Same-Sex Sexual Harassment Law." 28 *Columbia Human Rights Law Review* 201 (1996).

Patai, Daphne. *Heterophobia: Sexual Harassment and the Future of Feminism.* Lanham, MD: Rowman and Littlefield, 1998.

Paul, Ellen Frankel. "Sexual Harassment as Sex Discrimination: A Defective Paradigm." 8 *Yale Law and Policy Review* 333 (1990).

Peirce, Michelle Ridgeway. "Sexual Harassment and Title VII—A Better Solution." 30 *Boston College Law Review* 1071 (1989).

Pollack, Wendy. "Sexual Harassment: Women's Experience vs. Legal Definitions." 13 *Harvard Women's Law Journal* 35 (1990).

Pryor, John B. "The Lay Person's Understanding of Sexual Harassment." 13 *Sex Roles* 273 (1985).

Pryor, John B., Christine M. LaVite, and Lynnette M. Stoller. "A Social Psychological Analysis of Sexual Harassment: The Person/Situation Interaction." 42 *Journal of Vocational Behavior* 68 (1993).

Radford, Mary F. "By Invitation Only: The Proof of Welcomeness in Sexual Harassment Cases." 72 *North Carolina Law Review* 499 (1994).

Riggs, Robert O., Patricia H. Murrell, and JoAnn C. Cutting. *Sexual Harassment in Higher Education: From Conflict to Community.* Washington: The George Washington University School of Education and Human Development, 1993.

Risser, Rita. "Sexual Harassment Training: Truth and Consequences." 52.8 *Training and Development* 21 (1999).

Rosen, Jeffrey. *The Unwanted Gaze: The Destruction of Privacy in America.* New York: Random House, 2000.

Sandler, Bernice R., and Robert J. Shoop, eds. *Sexual Harassment on Campus: A Guide for Administrators, Faculty, and Students.* Boston: Allyn and Bacon, 1997.

Sangree, Suzanne. "A Reply to Professors Volokh and Browne." 47 Rutgers Law Review 595 (1995).

Scalia, Eugene. "The Strange Career of *Quid pro Quo* Sexual Harassment." 21 *Harvard Journal of Law and Public Policy* 307 (1998).

Schneider, Beth E. "Consciousness about Sexual Harassment among Heterosexual and Lesbian Women Workers." 38.4 *Journal of Social Issues* 75 (1982).

Schulhofer, Stephen J. *Unwanted Sex: The Culture of Intimidation and the Failure of Law.* Cambridge, MA: Harvard University Press, 1998.

Segrave, Kerry. *The Sexual Harassment of Women in the Workplace, 1600 to 1993.* Jefferson, NC: McFarland, 1994.

"Sexual Harassment and Title VII: The Foundation for the Elimination of Sexual Cooperation as an Employment Condition." 76 *Michigan Law Review* 1007 (1978).

Sexual Harassment Manual for Managers and Supervisors: How to Prevent and Resolve Sexual Harassment Complaints in the Workplace. Chicago: Commerce Clearing House, 1991.

Shahan, Amy. "Determining Whether Title VII Provides a Cause of Action for Same-Sex Sexual Harassment." 48 *Baylor Law Review* 507 (1996).

Shepela, Sharon Toffey, and Laurie L. Levesque. "Poisoned Waters: Sexual Harassment and the College Climate." 38 *Sex Roles* 589 (1998).

Sherer, Jill. L. "Sexually Harassed." 69.2 *Hospitals and Health Networks* 54 (1995).

Smith, J. Clay, Jr. "Prologue to the EEOC Guidelines on Sexual Harassment." 10 *Capital University Law Review* 471 (1981).

Stockdale, Margaret S., ed. *Sexual Harassment in the Workplace: Perspectives, Frontiers, and Response Strategies*, Thousand Oaks, CA: Sage Publications, 1996.

Stockdale, Margaret S., and Alan Vaux, "What Sexual Harassment Experiences Lead Respondents to Acknowledge Being Sexually Harassed? A Secondary Analysis of a University Survey." 43 *Journal of Vocational Behavior* 221 (1993).

Stone, Geoffrey R. "Restrictions of Speech Because of Its Content: The Peculiar Case of Subject-Matter Restrictions." 46 *The University of Chicago Law Review* 81 (1978).

Strauss, Marcy. "Sexist Speech in the Workplace." 25 *Harvard Civil Rights-Civil Liberties Law Review* 1 (1990).

Strossen, Nadine. "Regulating Workplace Sexual Harassment and Upholding the First Amendment—Avoiding a Collision." 37 *Villanova Law Review* 757 (1992).

Superson, Anita M. "A Feminist Definition of Sexual Harassment." 24.1 *Journal of Social Philosophy* 46 (1993).

Terrasa, Gabriel A. "Fitting a Square Peg into a Round Hole: 'Same-Sex' Sexual Harassment and the 'Because of . . . Sex' Requirement in Hostile Environment Claims." 67 *Revista Jurídica Universidad de Puerto Rico* 163 (1998).

Thacker, Rebecca A., and Stephan F. Gohmann. "Emotional and Psychological Consequences of Sexual Harassment: A Descriptive Study." 130 *The Journal of Psychology* 429 (1996).

Tol, Joan E. Van. "Eros Gone Awry: Liability under Title VII for Workplace Sexual Favoritism." 13 *Industrial Relations Law Journal* 153 (1991).

Tong, Rosemarie. *Women, Sex, and the Law.* Totowa, NJ: Rowman and Allanheld, 1984.

Treger, Tracy L. "The Reasonable Woman? Unreasonable!!! *Ellison v. Brady.*" 14 *Whittier Law Review* 675 (1993).

Tuana, Nancy. "Sexual Harassment: Offers and Coercion." 19.2 *Journal of Social Philosophy* 30 (1988).

Unikel, Robert. "'Reasonable' Doubts: A Critique of the Reasonable Woman Standard in American Jurisprudence." 87 *Northwestern University Law Review* 326 (1992).

Vaux, Alan. "Paradigmatic Assumptions in Sexual Harassment Research: Being Guided without Being Misled." 42 *Journal of Vocational Behavior* 116 (1993).

Vermeulen, Joan. "Employer Liability under Title VII for Sexual Harassment by Supervisory Employees." 10 *Capital University Law Review* 499 (1981).

Volokh, Eugene. "Freedom of Speech and Workplace Harassment." 39 *UCLA Law Review* 1791 (1992).

——. "How Harassment Law Restricts Free Speech." 47 *Rutgers Law Review* 563 (1995).

——. "What Speech Does 'Hostile Work Environment' Harassment Law Restrict?" 85 *The Georgetown Law Journal* 627 (1997).

Wagner, Ellen J. *Sexual Harassment in the Workplace: How to Prevent, Investigate, and Resolve Problems in Your Organization.* New York: Amacom, 1992.

Wall, Edmund, ed. *Sexual Harassment: Confrontations and Decisions.* Buffalo: Prometheus Books, 1992.

Weiner, Joan S. "Understanding Unwelcomeness in Sexual Harassment Law: Its History and a Proposal for Reform." 72 *Notre Dame Law Review* 621 (1997).

Weiner, Richard L. "Social Analytic Jurisprudence in Sexual Harassment Litigation: The Role of Social Framework and Social Fact." 51.1 *Journal of Social Issues* 167 (1995).

Weiss, Mary Anne. "Ninth Circuit Broadens Reasonableness Standard for Hostile Work Environment Sexual Harassment: *Fuller v. City of Oakland.*" 31 *University of San Francisco Law Review* 665 (1997).

Woerner, William L., and Sharon L. Oswald. "Sexual Harassment in the Workplace: A View through the Eyes of the Courts." 41 *Labor Law Journal* 786 (1990).

Young, Sherry. "Getting to Yes: The Case against Banning Consensual Relationships in Higher Education." 4 *Journal of Gender and the Law* 269 (1996).

General Index

Aaron, Titus E., 232, 244
Adler, Robert S., 242
adultery, 13, 20–23, 40, 61, 127, 226, 229
agency, law of, 175–76, 246–47
Aggarwal, Arjun P., 229, 236
Altman, Andrew, 235, 252
American Civil Liberties Union, 132, 141, 150, 168
American Jewish Congress, 141, 150
antidiscrimination laws. *See* discrimination
Ashraf, Saba, 233
Australia, 73, 231

Backhouse, Constance, 228
Barak, Azy, 244
Bernstein, Anita, 233, 235
Bernstein, Richard, 229
bisexuality, 183–87, 191, 248
Blackstone, William, 226
Bork, Robert H., 248
Brown, Helen Gurley, 90, 234
Brown, Janice R., 241
Browne, Kingsley R., 132, 136, 138, 150, 227, 231, 237–42
Bryant, Barbara S., 226

Calabresi, Guido, 118, 121, 237
Canada, 59, 235–36
captive audience, 140
Carpenter, Dale, 249
celibacy, 129–30
Chamallas, Martha, 234, 251
children, 15, 45
Christensen, F. M., 230, 249
Clinton, William J., 11, 23
Cohen, Leah, 228
comparative wrongs, 186, 194, 196, 217
confidentaility of sexual harassment proceedings, 161
conflicts of interests, 31–32
consent, 49–55, 228
constructive discharge, 83–84
content neutrality in the regulation of speech, 136–37, 140, 148–49, 220, 241
contracts, 215–17, 221–23, 243
Cooper, Stacy J., 232
Crichton, Michael, 11
Crosthwaite, Jan, 225
Crull, Peggy, 226

Dalmiya, Vrinda, 225, 247, 252
DeBruin, Debra A., 225
DeCosse, Sarah A., 233, 235
discrimination, 14, 20, 132, 138–40, 172–213, 217, 249, 252
disparate impact and disparate treatment distinguished, 188
Dodds, Susan M., 225, 249
Dolkart, Jane L., 233, 235
Donnellan, Austen, 159
Donohue, John J., III, 249
Dooling, Richard, 238
Dragel, Cheryl L., 233, 235
due process, 157–63
Dworkin, Andrea, 161
Dziech, Billie Wright, 226–28, 231

education, sexual harassment in, 15–16, 27–29, 34–36, 45, 144–45, 147, 150, 163–64, 220, 227–28, 241, 243, 246–47
effeminacy, 197

Ellis, Judy Trent, 236
Ellis, Shmuel, 244
Elliston, Frederick, 226
emotional distress, intentional infliction of, 218–20
empirical research, 18–19, 21, 34–35, 77–79, 90–91, 98, 163, 188, 207, 226, 234, 237, 249
employment at will, 216
Epstein, Deborah, 229, 238–39
Epstein, Richard A., 173, 245, 253
Equal Employment Opportunity Commission, 53, 68, 103, 197, 205–7, 229, 247. *See also* Guidelines on Sexual Harassment
equality. *See* discrimination
Estlund, Cynthia L., 239
Estrich, Susan, 227
European Communities, Commission of, 61–62, 229, 230, 247
Evidence, Federal Rules of, 226–27
externalities, 156

Fallon, Richard H., Jr., 238
Farley, Lin, 227–28
favoritism, sexual, 200–207, 216–17
Feminists for Free Expression, 150
fighting words, 134–36,148–50, 241
Finley, Lucinda M., 249
First Amendment, 46, 80–82, 131–53, 221, 239–42
Fitzgerald, Louise F., 225, 236, 244
foreign (non-U.S.) law, 16, 53, 59, 61–62, 73, 101, 159, 235–36, 247
fornication, 226
France, 16
Franke, Katherine M., 249, 252
Franklin, Estelle D., 243
friendship, nonsexual, 64–65

Gadlin, Howard, 242
Gallop, Jane, 237
gambling, 107
Gedrose, David I., 233
gender harassment, 58
Gerard, Jules B., 132, 238–39
Gettle, Jeffrey A., 233
Gohmann, Stephan F., 249
Gomez-Preston, Cheryl, 229, 231, 236
Greve, Michael S., 231, 240, 242, 244
Guidelines on Sexual Harassment (EEOC), 53, 57–64, 66, 72–73, 95–96, 101, 103, 131, 152, 154, 170, 177, 228, 241, 247
Gutek, Barbara A., 90, 226, 234–35, 237

Haiman, Franklyn S., 240
Hand, Learned, 113, 117, 124–25
Hart, H. L. A., 228
hearsay evidence, 159
Hill, Anita F., 12–13, 80
Holmes, Robert L., 248
homosexuality, 176, 185–86, 191, 193, 196–200, 204, 251
Horton, Amy, 238–39
hotels, 159
Hughes, John C., 227, 252

inalienability rules, 121–22
incest, 47–48
inequality. *See* discrimination
informal ways of dealing with sexual harassment, 156, 242–43
insensitivity, 13, 36, 63–64, 193, 221
insults, 74, 97, 102–8, 114, 124, 133, 135, 173, 187, 193, 197, 212
insurance: against liability for sexual harassment, 119–20; as an analogy for the practice of advance-making, 128–29
intrusion (tort), 219–21
Israel, 16

Jaffe, David M., 239
Johnson, Paul B., 233, 235, 237
jokes, 25, 31, 52, 62, 71, 74–76, 90–92, 116–17, 210, 222, 230
Jones, Paula C., 11

Karner, Jessica M., 232, 238–39
Kenealy, Kathleen A., 232, 236
Kors, Alan Charles, 243

Lafontaine, Edward, 244
Laird, Jo Backer, 244
Lamberson, Phillip L., 230
Larison, Dorraine A., 226
LaVite, Christine M., 245
legal counsel for people accused of sexual harassment, 157–58, 162, 164
Lester, Toni, 230
Leventer, Jan C., 228

Levesque, Laurie L., 244, 252
Levitsky, Sandra, 251–52
liability rules, 118–22
Ludwig, Dorene, 228

MacKinnon, Catharine A., 132, 139, 188, 208, 226, 238–39, 248–49, 252
Mappes, Thomas A., 227
Marcosson, Samuel A., 251
May, Larry, 227, 236, 247, 252
Mcauliffe, Shannon, 239
McCann, Nancy Dodd, 90–91, 228, 234
McFarland, Deborah N., 249
McGinn, Thomas A., 90–91, 228, 234
McLain, Lynn, 72, 231, 247, 251
Mead, Margaret, 47–48, 228
mediation. *See* informal ways of dealing with sexual harassment
Melamed, A. Douglas, 118, 121, 237
moralism, 20–23, 61, 93, 114, 230

Narveson, Jan, 227
negligence, 117–20, 124–25, 175–76, 245, 247
New Zealand, 53, 229

obscenity, 80–82
offers, 29–30
Oh, James J., 243, 245
Olk, Mary E., 226
Oswald, Sharon L., 225

Papish, Pamela J., 250–51
Pareto-improvements, 102–3, 110
Patai, Daphne, 244
Paul, Ellen Frankel, 246, 248, 250, 252
Peirce, Ellen R., 242
Peirce, Michelle Ridgeway, 249–50
penumbra, 42, 69, 114, 220
Pinto, Adaya, 244
Playboy, 90, 145–46, 241
Pollack, Wendy, 66, 230
Posner, Joseph, 236
Posner, Richard A., 246
power: informal, 33–34, 37–39, 104–5; institutional, 13, 27–32, 37–40, 175
pregnancy, 179–81
Priest, Graham, 225
privacy, 165, 219–22, 245
productivity, 25–26, 214–15, 227
promiscuity, 13–14, 20–23, 39, 78, 226
proof, standards of, 159–61, 243
property rules, 121–22
prostitution, 217
Pryor, John B., 226, 232, 245
psychology. *See* empirical research
public debate about the law, 11–12, 14–15, 19–21, 41, 93, 158, 161, 167–71
public employees, 141–45, 147
public scrutiny of the law. *See* public debate about the law

quid pro quo, 27–30, 58–59, 91, 95, 114, 175, 193, 212, 214–18

Rabinowitz, Vita C., 227
racial harassment, 84, 103–4, 140, 241
Radford, Mary F., 52–53, 108, 228, 236
rape, 40, 49–51, 67–68, 85, 159, 161, 218, 220
reasonable person standard, 72–80, 83–90, 92, 96–100, 115, 220, 232–33, 236
reasonable victim standard, 86
reasonable woman standard, 83–94, 96–97, 188, 232–34
Remick, Helen, 244
retaliation: for attempts to defend oneself against sexual harassment accusations, 158; for making complaints of sexual harassment, 166
Risser, Rita, 243
Rosen, Jeffrey, 226–27, 253
Rowe, Mary P., 236

same-sex harassment, 196–200
Sandler, Bernice R., 235, 245
Sangree, Suzanne, 235, 238
Scalia, Antonin, 218
Scalia, Eugene, 229
Schneider, Beth E., 226
Schulhofer, Stephen J., 242
Segrave, Kerry, 236
selective enforcement, 46
severe-or-pervasive test, 65–71, 73, 89, 154
"sex plus" criteria, 177–83, 196, 201–2
sexual annoyance, 58
Shahan, Amy, 251
Shepela, Sharon Toffey, 244, 252
Sherer, Jill. L., 226
Silverglate, Harvey A., 243

Smith, J. Clay, Jr., 236
speech, freedom of. *See* First Amendment
Starr, Kenneth W., 248
stereotyoes, 209–12
stigma of being found guilty of sexual harassment, 119, 160–61, 237
Stites, M. Cynara, 227
Stockdale, Margaret S., 244
Stoller, Lynnette M., 245
Stone, Geoffrey R., 239
Strauss, Marcy, 139, 239
strict liability, 63, 117–20, 125
Strossen, Nadine, 132, 238
Superson, Anita M., 225, 252
Swanton, Christine, 225

taboo, 47–48
Terrasa, Gabriel A., 251
Thacker, Rebecca A., 249
third-party harassment, 60, 229
Thomas, Clarence, 11–13, 80, 199
threats, 29–30, 37
Tol, Joan E. Van, 252
Tong, Rosemarie, 228
torts, 75–76, 97, 113, 115, 117–18, 124–25, 175, 217–21
"training" programs about sexual harassment, 13, 21–22, 156–57
Tredeau, Leslie, 244
Treger, Tracy L., 233
Tuana, Nancy, 227
two-level structure of the law, 67–71, 119, 143–44, 152, 154–72, 213, 222–23, 242–43, 245

Unikel, Robert, 233
United Kingdom, 159, 230

Vaux, Alan, 244
Vermeulen, Joan, 236
viewpoint neutrality in the regulation of speech, 136–38, 140–41, 148–49, 239
Volokh, Eugene, 231, 240, 242

Wagner, Ellen J., 245
Wall, Edmund, 228
Wasserstrom, Richard, 226
Weiner, Linda, 226–28, 231
Weiner, Richard L., 233
Weiss, Mary Anne, 232–33
Woerner, William L., 225
Wood, Diane P., 246

Young, Sherry, 227

Index of Cases Cited

Aguilar v. Avis Rent a Car System, Inc., 529 U.S. 1138 (2000), 240

Aguilar v. Avis Rent a Car System, Inc., 21 Cal. 4th 121 (1999), 240–41

American Booksellers Association v. Hudnut, 771 F. 2d 323 (7th Cir. 1985), 141–42

Andrews v. City of Philadelphia, 895 F. 2d 1469 (3d Cir. 1990), 66, 83, 85, 253

Arnold v. City of Seminole, Okl., 614 F. Supp. 853 (E.D. Okl. 1985), 238

Ashworth v. RoundUp Co., 897 F. Supp. 489 (W.D. Wash. 1995), 250

Ayers v. American Telephone & Telegraph Co., 826 F. Supp. 443 (S.D. Fla. 1993), 207

Barnes v. Costle, 561 F. 2d 983 (D.C. Cir. 1977), 246, 248–49, 251

Barnes v. Train, 13 FEP Cases 123 (D.D.C. 1974), 174

Baty v. Willamette Industries, Inc., 172 F. 3d 1232 (10th Cir. 1999), 142

Becerra v. Dalton, 94 F. 3d 145 (4th Cir. 1996), 251

Bennett v. Corroon & Black Corp., 845 F. 2d. 104 (5th Cir. 1988), 86, 233

Berman v. Washington Times Corp., 1994 WL 750274 (D.D.C.), 240

Black v. City of Auburn, Ala., 857 F. Supp. 1540 (M.D. Ala. 1994), 142

Blozis v. Mike Raisor Ford, Inc., 896 F. Supp. 805 (N.D. Ind. 1995), 250

Booher v. Board of Regents, Northern Kentucky University, 1998 U.S.Dist. LEXIS 11404 (E.D. Ky.), 147–48, 241

Bowersox v. P. H. Glatfelter Co., 677 F. Supp. 307 (M.D. Pa. 1988), 238

Bowman v. Heller, 420 Mass. 517 (1995), 146–47

Brassfield v. Jack McLendon Furniture, Inc., 953 F. Supp. 1438 (M.D. Ala. 1996), 229

Bray v. Alexandria Women's Health Clinic, 506 U.S. 263 (1993), 180

Broderick v. Ruder, 685 F. Supp. 1269 (D.D.C. 1988), 229, 251

Bundy v. Jackson, 641 F. 2d 934 (D.C.Cir. 1981), 248, 251

Burilington Industries, Inc. v. Ellerth, 524 U.S. 742 (1998), 176, 229, 247

Burns v. McGregor Electronic Industries, Inc., 955 F. 2d 559 (8th Cir. 1992), 229

Burns v. McGregor Electronic Industries, Inc., 989 F. 2d 959 (8th Cir. 1993), 60, 229, 232

Busby v. Truswal Systems Corp., 551 So. 2d 322 (Ala. 1989), 253

Campbell v. Florida Steel Corporation, 919 S.W. 2d 26 (Tenn. 1996), 238–39

Canada v. Boyd Group, Inc., 809 F. Supp. 771 (D. Nev. 1992), 234

Cardin v. Via Tropical Fruits, Inc., 1993 U.S.Dist. LEXIS 16302 (S.D. Fla), 249

Carreno v. Local Union No. 226, International Brotherhood of Electrical Workers, 54 FEP Cases 81 (D. Kan. 1990), 251

Chamberlin v. 101 Realty, Inc., 915 F. 2d 777 (1st Cir. 1990), 229

Chaplinsky v. New Hampshire, 315 U.S. 568 (1942), 134–35, 239
Chiapuzio v. BLT Operating Corp., 826 F.Supp 1334 (D. Wyo. 1993), 249
Cleveland Board of Education v. Loudermill, 470 U.S. 532 (1985), 243
Coates v. Cincinnati, 402 U.S. 611 (1971), 100, 236
Cohen v. San Bernardino Valley College, 92 F. 3d 968 (9th Cir. 1996), 147
Connick v. Meyers, 461 U.S. 138 (1983), 240
Corne v. Bausch and Lomb Inc., 390 F. Supp. 161 (D. Ariz. 1975), 173–74, 184, 245–46
Cotran v. Rollins Hudig Hall International, Inc., 17 Cal. 4th 93 (1998), 243–44
Crosier v. United Parcel Service, Inc., 150 Cal. App. 3d 1132 (1983), 242
Crowe v. Wiltel Communications Systems, 103 F. 3d 897 (9th Cir. 1996), 84–85, 233

Davis v. Monroe County Board of Education, 526 U.S. 629 (1999), 150, 247
Davis v. Monsanto Chemical Co., 858 F. 2d 345 (6th Cir. 1988), 241
DeAngelis v. El Paso Municipal Police Officers Association, 51 F. 3d 591 (5th Cir. 1995), 63–64, 84, 146, 232, 241
DeCintio v. Westchester County Medical Center, 807 F. 2d 304 (2d Cir. 1986), 202, 205, 251
DeSantis v. Pacific Telephone & Telegraph Co., Inc., 608 F. 2d 327 (9th Cir. 1979), 251
Dillon v. Frank, 1992 WL 5436 (6th Cir.), 251
Dirksen v. City of Springfield, 842 F. Supp. 1117 (C.D. Ill. 1994), 251
Duet v. Martin Marietta Corp., 720 So. 2d 1290 (La. Ct. App. 1998), 252

Easton v. Crossland Mortgage Corp., 905 F. Supp. 1368 (C.D. Cal. 1995), 250
EEOC v. Walden Book Co., Inc., 885 F. Supp. 1100 (M.D. Tenn. 1995), 250
Ellerth v. Burlington Industries, Inc., 102 F. 3d 848 (7th Cir. 1996), 229, 246
Ellison v. Brady, 924 F. 2d 872 (9th Cir. 1991), 83–89, 91–92, 105, 188, 230, 233, 236, 241
Erickson v. Marsh & McLennan Co., Inc., 569 A. 2d 793 (N.J. 1990), 252

Faragher v. City of Boca Raton, 524 U.S. 775 (1998), 176, 229
FCC v. Pacifica Foundation, 438 U.S. 726 (1978), 136, 239
Fleenor v. Hewitt Soap Co., 67 FEP Cases 1625 (S.D. Ohio 1994), 250
Fuller v. City of Oakland, California, 47 F. 3d 1522 (9th Cir. 1995), 84, 233

Garcia v. Elf Atochem North America, 28 F. 3d 446 (5th Cir. 1994), 250
Gary v. Long, 59 F. 3d 1391 (D.C. Cir. 1995), 230
Gebser v. Lago Vista Independent School District, 524 U.S. 274 (1998), 246–47
General Electric Co. v. Gilbert, 429 U.S. 125 (1976), 179, 228
Giddens v. Shell Oil. Co., 67 FEP Cases 576 (5th Cir. 1993), 250
Gillming v. Simmons Industries, 91 F. 3d 1168 (8th Cir. 1996), 84, 232
Goluszek v. Smith, 697 F. Supp. 1452 (N.D. Ill. 1988), 198, 250
Grant v. Lone Star Co., 21 F. 3d 649 (5th Cir. 1994), 230
Greer v. Spock, 424 U.S. 828 (1976), 137, 239
Grissom v. Waterloo Industries, Inc., 902 F. Supp. 867 (E.D. Ark. 1995), 230

Hall v. Gus Construction Co., Inc., 842 F. 2d 1010 (8th Cir. 1988), 60, 229, 236, 246
Harris v. Forklift Systems, Inc., 510 U.S. 17 (1993), 75, 84, 141, 150, 177, 199, 238, 247
Harris v. International Paper Co., 765 F. Supp. 1509 (D. Me. 1991), 84
Harvey v. Chevron U.S.A., Inc., 961 F. Supp. 1017 (S.D. Tex. 1997), 251
Haynes v. Williams, 88 F. 3d 898 (10th Cir. 1996), 230
Henson v. City of Dundee, 682 F. 2d 897 (11th Cir. 1982), 60, 65–66, 228–29, 246, 248–49

Hicks v. Gates Rubber Co., 833 F. 2d 1406 (10th Cir. 1987), 246
Holman v. Indiana, 211 F. 3d 399 (7th Cir. 2000), 248
Hopkins v. Baltimore Gas & Electric Co., 871 F. Supp. 822 (D. Md. 1994), 247, 251
Horn v. Duke Homes, Division of Windsor Mobile Homes, Inc., 755 F. 2d 599 (7th Cir. 1985), 242, 246
Huebschen v. Department of Health and Social Services, 716 F. 2d 1167 (7th Cir. 1983), 181–83
Huff v. County of Butler, 524 F. Supp. 751 (W.D. Pa. 1981), 237
Hurley v. Irish-American Gay, Lesbian and Bisexual Group of Boston, Inc., 515 U.S. 557 (1995), 241

Insitu Cleaning Co. Ltd. v. Heads, [1995] IRLR 4, 230

Jansen v. Packaging Corporation of America, 123 F. 3d 490 (7th Cir. 1997), 246
Janzen v. Platy Enterprises, Ltd., 59 D.L.R. 4th 352 (1989), 229
Johnson v. Community Nursing Services, 932 F. Supp. 269 (D. Utah 1996), 250
Johnson v. County of Los Angeles Fire Department, 865 F. Supp. 1430 (C.D. Cal. 1994), 90, 145–48, 241
Jones v. Flagship International, 793 F. 2d 714 (5th Cir. 1986), 248
Joyner v. AAA Cooper Transportation, 597 F. Supp. 537 (M.D. Ala. 1983), 191, 249–50

Kennedy v. Marion Correctional Institution, 630 N.E. 2d 324 (Ohio 1994), 243
Kersul v. Skulls Angels, Inc., 495 N.Y.S. 2d 886 (Sup. 1985), 252
Keyes v. Keyes, 392 S.E. 2d 693 (W.Va. 1990), 253
King v. Board of Regents of the University of Wisconsin System, 898 F. 2d 533 (7th Cir. 1990), 182, 230
King v. M.R. Brown, Inc., 911 F. Supp. 161 (E.D. Pa. 1995), 250
King v. Palmer, 598 F. Supp. 65 (D.D.C. 1984), 204
King v. Palmer, 778 F. 2d 878 (D.C. Cir. 1985), 204

Lehman v. City of Shaker Heights, 418 U.S. 298 (1974), 137, 239
Lehmann v. Toys 'R' Us, Inc., 626 A.2d 445 (N.J. 1993), 230, 232
Lipsett v. Rive-Mora, 669 F. Supp. 1188 (D.P.R. 1987), 232
Lipsett v. University of Puerto Rico, 864 F. 2d 881 (1st Cir. 1988), 238
Logan v. Bennington College Corp., 72 F. 3d 1017 (2d Cir. 1995), 243
Lucas v. Brown & Root, Inc., 736 F. 2d 1202 (8th Cir. 1984), 217

Martin v. Cavalier Hotel Corp., 48 F. 3d 1343 (4th Cir. 1995), 246
Martin v. Norfolk Southern Railway Co., 926 F. Supp. 1044 (N.D. Ala. 1996), 250
Martone v. State of Rhode Island/Registry of Motor Vehicles, 611 A.2d 384 (R.I. 1992), 246
McCoy v. Johnson Controls World Services Inc., 878 F. Supp. 229 (S.D. Ga. 1995), 250
McDonnell v. Cisneros, 84 F. 3d 256 (7th Cir. 1996), 186, 249
McWilliams v. Fairfax County Board of Supervisors, 72 F. 3d 1191 (4th Cir. 1996), 250
Members of the City Council v. Taxpayers for Vincent, 466 U.S. 789 (1984), 239
Meritor Savings Bank v. Vinson, 477 U.S. 57 (1986), 12, 53, 64–65, 175, 177, 199, 225, 228, 230, 246–47, 250
Mich. Cent. R. Co. v. Hasseneyer, 12 N.W. 155 (Mich. 1882), 86
Miller v. Aluminum Co. of America, 679 F. Supp. 495 (W.D. Pa. 1988), 205, 251
Miller v. Bank of America, 418 F. Supp. 233 (N.D. Cal. 1976), 174
Miller v. Bank of America, 600 F. 2d 211 (9th Cir. 1979), 246
Miller v. California, 413 U.S. 15 (1973), 80, 232, 236
Miller v. Maxwell's International, Inc., 991 F. 2d 583 (9th Cir. 1991), 230
Mogilefsky v. Superior Court, 20 Cal. App. 4th 1409 (1993), 250

Monell v. Department of Social Services of the City of New York, 436 U.S. 658 (1978), 231
Monge v. Beebe Rubber Company, 316 A. 2d 549 (N.H. 1974), 216
Morgan v. Hertz Corp., 542 F. Supp. 123 (W.D. Tenn. 1981), 90
Moylan v. Maries County, 792 F. 2d 746 (8th Cir. 1986), 229
Myers v. City of El Paso, 874 F. Supp. 1546 (W.D. Tex. 1995), 250

NAACP v. Claiborne Hardware Co., 458 U.S. 886 (1982), 136, 239
Neal v. Evitts, 55 FEP Cases 473 (E.D. Ky. 1991), 183, 248
Nichols v. Frank, 42 F. 3d 503 (9th Cir. 1994), 84, 233
Nicolo v. Citibank New York State, N.A., 554 N.Y.S. 2d 795 (Sup. 1990), 252

Oncale v. Sundowner Offshore Services, Inc., 83 F. 3d 118 (5th Cir. 1996), 250
Oncale v. Sundowner Offshore Services, Inc., 523 U.S. 75 (1998), 177, 199
O'Rourke v. City of Providence, 235 F. 3d 713 (1st Cir. 2001), 241

Paroline v. Unisys Corp., 879 F. 2d 100 (4th Cir. 1989), 230
Peric v. Board of Trustees of the University of Illinois, 71 FEP Cases 1760 (N.D. Ill. 1996), 250
Phillips v. Martin Marietta Corp., 400 U.S. 542 (1971), 178–79, 248
Phillips v. Smalley Maintenance Services, 435 So. 2d 705 (Ala. 1983), 253
Pickering v. Board of Education, 391 U.S. 563 (1968), 240
Piech v. Arthur Andersen & Co., S.C., 841 F. Supp. 825 (N.D. Ill. 1994), 251
Prescott v. Independent Life and Accident Insurance Co., 878 F. Supp. 1545 (M.D. Ala. 1995), 248, 250
Price Waterhouse v. Hopkins, 490 U.S. 228, 241 (1989), 180, 248
Priest v. Rotary, 634 F. Supp. 571 (N.D. Cal. 1986), 251

Quick v. Donaldson Co., Inc., 90 F. 3d 1372 (8th Cir. 1996), 250

R. A. V. v. City of St. Paul, Minnesota, 505 U.S. 377 (1992), 148–50, 239, 241
Rabidue v. Osceola Refining Co., 805 F. 2d 611 (6th Cir. 1986), 72, 83–84, 86, 92, 230, 231, 233, 248
Radtke v. Everett, 501 N.W. 2d 155 (Mich. 1993), 84, 230, 233
Rankin v. McPherson, 483 U.S. 378 (1987), 240
Rauh v. Coyne, 744 F. Supp. 1186 (D.D.C. 1990), 246
Roberts v. United States Jaycees, 468 U.S. 609 (1984), 191, 239, 249
Robinson v. Jacksonville Shipyards, Inc., 760 F.Supp. 1486 (M.D. Fla. 1991), 84, 139–42, 234, 240, 242
Rosenberger v. Rector and Visitors of University of Virginia, 515 U.S. 819 (1995), 239
Roth v. United States, 354 U.S. 476 (1957), 80, 232
Rowan v. United States Post Office Department, 397 U.S. 728 (1970), 239
Rubin v. Ikenberry, 933 F. Supp. 1425 (C.D. Ill. 1996), 145
Ryczek v. Guest Services, Inc., 877 F. Supp. 754 (D.D.C. 1995), 248

Sardinia v. Dellwood Foods, 69 FEP Cases 705 (S.D.N.Y. 1995), 250
Sauers v. Salt Lake County, 1 F. 3d 1122 (10th Cir. 1993), 230
Saulpaugh v. Monroe Community Hospital, 4 F. 3d 134 (2d Cir. 1993), 248
Saville v. Houston County Healthcare Authority, 852 F. Supp. 1512 (M.D. Ala 1994), 251
Saxe v. State College Area School District, 240 F. 3d 200 (3d Cir. 2001), 241–42
Schoiber v. Emro Marketing Co., 941 F. Supp. 730 (N.D. Ill. 1996), 250
Silva v. University of New Hampshire, 888 F. Supp. 293 (D.N.H. 1994), 143–45, 147–48, 237
Smith v. Sheahan, 189 F. 3d 529 (7th Cir. 1999), 230
Smolsky v. Consolidated Rail Corp., 780 F. Supp. 283 (E.D. Pa. 1991), 232
Sparks v. Pilot Freight Carriers, Inc., 830 F. 2d 1554 (11th Cir. 1987), 246

Spencer v. General Electric Co., 697 F. Supp. 204 (E.D. Va. 1988), 83, 229, 232, 238
Sprogis v. United Air Lines Inc., 444 F. 2d 1194 (7th Cir. 1971), 178–79, 248
State v. Wal-Mart Stores, Inc., 621 N.Y.S. 2d 158 (A.D. 3 Dept. 1995), 230
Steiner v. Showboat Operating Co., 25 F. 3d 1459 (9th Cir. 1994), 187–89
Stewart v. Cartessa Corp., 771 F. Supp. 876 (S.D. Ohio 1990), 191, 249

Tanner v. Prima Donna Resorts Inc., 919 F. Supp. 351 (D. Nev. 1996), 250
Texas v. Johnson, 491 U.S. 397 (1989), 139, 240
Tietgen v. Brown's Westminster Motors, Inc., 921 F. Supp. 1495 (E.D. Va. 1996), 250
Tindall v. Housing Authority, 762 F. Supp. 259 (W.D. Ark. 1991), 234
Tomka v. Seiler Corp., 66 F. 3d 1295 (2d. Cir. 1995), 230
Torres v. National Precision Blanking, 943 F. Supp. 952 (N.D. Ill. 1996), 250
Toscano v. Nimmo, 570 F. Supp. 1197 (D. Del. 1983), 23, 203–5, 226, 251
Trautvetter v. Quick, 916 F. 2d 1140 (7th Cir. 1990), 182–83, 248
Tunis v. Corning Glass Works, 747 F. Supp. 951 (S.D.N.Y. 1990), 145–46

United States v. Carroll Towing Co., 159 F. 2d 169 (2d Cir. 1947), 237
United States v. Lee, 6 F. 3d 1297 (8th Cir. 1993), 140, 240
United States v. Morrison, 529 U.S. 598 (2000), 244
United States v. Treatman, 524 F. 2d 320 (8th Cir. 1975), 82

Valdez v. Church's Fried Chicken, Inc., 683 F. Supp. 596 (W.D. Tex. 1988), 231
Van Jelgerhuis v. Mercury Finance Co., 940 F. Supp. 1344 (S.D. Ind. 1996), 253
Vandeventer v. Wabash National Corporation, 867 F. Supp. 790 (N.D. Ind. 1994), 250
Vandeventer v. Wabash National Corporation, 887 F. Supp. 1178 (N.D. Ind. 1995), 250
Vermett v. Hough, 627 F. Supp. 587 (W.D. Mich. 1986), 232
Vinson v. Taylor, 753 F. 2d 141 (D.C. Cir. 1985), 229
Vinson v. Taylor, 760 F. 2d 1330 (D.C. Cir. 1985), 184, 228, 248
Volk v. Coler, 845 F. 2d 1422 (7th Cir. 1988), 182, 248

Waltman v. International Paper Co., 875 F. 2d 468 (5th Cir. 1989), 71
Waters v. Churchill, 511 U.S. 661 (1994), 141, 240
West Virginia State Board of Education v. Barnette, 319 U.S. 624 (1943), 241
Williams v. Bannings, 72 F. 3d 552 (7th Cir. 1996), 230
Williams v. Civiletti, 487 F. Supp. 1387 (D.D.C. 1980), 245
Williams v. Saxbe, 413 F. Supp. 654 (D.D.C. 1976), 12, 172, 174, 176–79, 225
Wilson v. Taylor, 733 F. 2d 1539 (11th Cir. 1984), 228
Womack v. Runyon, 147 F. 3d 1298 (11th Cir. 1998), 251
Wooley v. Maynard, 430 U.S. 705 (1977), 241
Wright v. Methodist Youth Services, Inc., 511 F. Supp. 307 (N.D. Ill. 1981), 250
Wrightson v. Pizza Hut of America, 99 F. 3d 138 (4th Cir. 1996), 250

Yates v. Avco Corp., 819 F. 2d 630 (6th Cir. 1987), 83, 84
Young v. American Mini Theatres, Inc., 427 U.S. 50 (1976), 137, 239